THE CHRIST CONNECTION

Roy Abraham Varghese

The
CHRIST
Connection

How the World Religions Prepared
the Way for the Phenomenon of Jesus

Foreword by
Cardinal Oscar Andrés Rodríguez Maradiaga, SDB

PARACLETE PRESS
BREWSTER, MASSACHUSETTS

The Christ Connection: How the World Religions Prepared the Way for the Phenomenon of Jesus

Copyright © 2011 by Roy Abraham Varghese

ISBN 978-1-55725-699-7

Library of Congress Cataloging-in-Publication Data

Varghese, Roy Abraham.
  The Christ connection : how the world religions prepared the way for the
      phenomenon of Jesus / Roy Abraham Varghese.
    p. cm.
  Includes bibliographical references (p.   ) and index.
  ISBN 978-1-55725-699-7 (pbk.)
  1. Jesus Christ—Person and offices. 2. Christianity and other religions. 3. Catholic Church—Doctrines. I. Title.
  BT205.V27 2011
  261.2—dc22   2011003134

10 9 8 7 6 5 4 3 2 1

Published by Paraclete Press
Brewster, Massachusetts
www.paracletepress.com

Printed in the United States of America

FOR MY WIFE
Anila
in thanksgiving

———

All of history is a search for salvation. This is the universal quest. This is the human journey. This is all that matters in the end. And it is this quest, this journey, that is the subject of our meditation. None of the major world religions can be understood except as a search for salvation, for atonement, deliverance, empowerment, union, love. And it is an understanding of this search that leads us to a discovery, the discovery of God as Savior, and of his salvific activity in human history. This is what I call the Christ Connection.

CONTENTS

As Roy Abraham Varghese's new book makes so clear, since the beginning of written history, man has asked of himself, who am I? and, what is the purpose of life? I believe these are the two main questions, the most important questions that every person asks at some point in life. And the same is true in the history of the world. People try to decipher: Who am I? How can I achieve eternity? Vatican II says that the most fundamental enigma of human existence is just that: What happens after death? And that is precisely the enigma that the philosophers have never been able to solve.

Life is the most basic gift that a person can receive, and this is why when life is under threat the most powerful instinct we have is the instinct of conservation of life. In the same way, when facing the problem of death, man questions himself: What is the purpose of life if we are destined to disappear?

In answer to these questions, Christ appears in history as the perfect human being, of course as God himself, giving a transcendent meaning to human existence. After Christ we know that death is not the end, that there is a different life, an eternal life, that human creatures are not made to disappear but to live eternally with God being members of his mystical body. I believe this is the greatest gift we have received from God: the incarnation of his only begotten Son to give meaning to human existence and a purpose even to those things that appear to be contradictions, such as illness and the suffering of the innocent and death. Jesus was the only person, a divine person, who could resolve this enigma and offer a horizon of hope to human life.

Those who were attracted by the wisdom of his words, by his kindness, and by the power of his miracles received the gift of faith and came to be disciples of Jesus. Upon leaving the darkness and the shadow of death (see Lk. 1:79), their lives achieved an extraordinary fullness: that of having been enriched by the gift of the Father. They lived through the history of their people and of their own time and passed through the roads of the Roman Empire without ever forgetting the most important and decisive encounter of their lives, which had filled them with light, with force, and with hope: their encounter with Jesus, their rock, their peace, their life.

The salvation offered by Christ is not easy because we are not the ones who save ourselves. God saves us. But he does not save us automatically; it is a process of collaboration. He wants to save us, but he wants us to accept salvation as a way of living, as a way of dying, as a way of having eternal life. It is a gift that is offered to us, and we are free to accept it or to reject it. But there is the tragedy that the human being is so weak as to be subject to the danger of not accepting salvation. This is tragic.

People always want to save themselves, and, especially in our times, people are looking for any kind of insurance. You have to insure your house; you have to insure even your bank accounts; you have to insure your health; you have to insure against fires, earthquakes, hurricanes. But those are only relative insurances because the only insurance we have is the Word of God, which tells us, "Whoever eats my flesh and drinks my blood has eternal life" (Jn. 6:54). This is what many people do not consider. Not knowing the Word of God, they cannot imagine that great gift. It is the only insurance that does not have little phrases on the back that you can only read with a magnifying lens.

The gift of the Eucharist offered by Jesus is something humanity could never have imagined. When Jesus announced the Eucharist to his followers, many people left him because they thought, "cannibalism is not for us." They were thinking in a human way, and what Christ was offering was something completely beyond anything conceived by the human mind. We could never have imagined that we were going to be able to "consume" our God, our Creator, that he would inhabit us. And this is the marvel of love. We in Spanish have a phrase that is very descriptive. When there is a beautiful baby, we say, "How beautiful he is. I would like to eat him with kisses." With this we are trying to express the greatest love. You love somebody so much that you would like to eat that person if it were possible. And God made it possible by love. He loved us so much that he wanted to be within us, and that is the reason for the Eucharist. Nobody could ever, humanly speaking, have imagined this. Only love and only God could make this possible. It is a gift we could never have dreamed about, and it is the most precious gift we have. It is the gift of God.

We have no other happiness or greater priority than to be instruments of God's Spirit, as a church, in order that Jesus Christ is found, followed, loved, adored, proclaimed, and made known to all, despite all the difficulties and resistance. The word *disciple* refers to linking oneself to another person, not so much on a theoretical level or on the level of what the teacher conveys through ideas, but affectively and vitally, to the point of assuming the teacher's way of life. No one is born a disciple of Jesus.

To be a disciple, conversion is necessary; change of mentality is necessary. This new radical vision is obtained through our encounter with Christ (Jn. 8, 12). It is a matter of meeting him, of entering his world, of being illuminated by his light and, in this way, learning to reason in a different way. This meeting allows us to achieve a mysterious kinship with Christ himself and with our brothers and sisters, to such a point that Christ becomes our father, mother, sister, brother, and so on. To be a disciple involves—as an inevitable consequence—the gift of perseverance. And it is a matter of persevering with him in his tribulations. The disciple is sent like a lamb among wolves. A Christian is a disparity, a prophecy, a shock. The disciple is capable of saying no, of choosing to oppose sin. The disciple assumes more and more every day the logic "of the small numbers"—that is to say, Jesus' logic. Finally, and probably the hardest thing: disciples are those who are willing to give their life for their teacher.

Conversion is not a question of one more word, of a word that we are already tired of hearing. It is not an exterior or partial change but a deep change in the person, a change in identity. It is not us who convert ourselves, but God. It is not by comparing who we are with ourselves that we are converted but by comparing ourselves with God's plan that we discover the direction of the change. Converting is to change your life, to start over with a clean slate. It is to open your heart and allow it to be refreshed by the cleansing rain of God's Word. It is to admit that we were wrong and to be prepared for transformation. It is to be led in the darkness by the hand of someone who loves us. It is to rely fully on the Father: to see with his eyes, to try to love with his heart. It is to sign a blank check. It is to be reborn. It is to ask for forgiveness. It is to be resurrected.

—*Cardinal Oscar Andrés Rodríguez Maradiaga,* SDB

THE CHRIST CONNECTION

This book is a journey through the religious history of humanity. Our fellow travelers are historians and theologians, anthropologists and psychologists, logicians and scientists, saints and mystics, and above all, the man and woman on the street. At another level, our companions fall under one of three categories: religious believers, skeptics, and seekers of ultimate truth. Our journey must traverse the concerns and priorities of all three categories.

Before we embark, let me put my cards on the table. I am a card-carrying Catholic Christian. I was not always thus. At one time I was an atheist. And before and after, I have been talking and listening to people of all persuasions— from atheists and agnostics to Hindus, Jews, Zoroastrians, Muslims, Buddhists, animists, and Christians of various kinds. I was an attendee at the 1993 Parliament of World Religions and the 2000 UN Millennium World Peace Summit of Spiritual and Religious Leaders. At these events and in all my own personal interactions, I was impressed and moved by the depth of the human desire for the divine. Deep within the hearts of those who take their religions seriously (this excludes any for whom religion is an instrument of hatred) there burns a love and yearning for God that is heartbreaking.

As moved as I was by this unbounded openness, I was just as aware that there was one taboo in interreligious dialogue and interfaith celebrations. You can take your religion seriously but not to the point of inviting anyone else to share it. Any attempt to solicit conversion is an unspeakable abomination. Polite society can tolerate piety, but proselytism is entirely out of bounds. As with all our taboos, historical antecedents have surely played a role. Wars over religion, coercive conversion, threats of damnation, harsh enforcement of orthodoxy, insults and acrimonious exchanges, persecution of infidels, terrorist attacks by fanatics—the only antidote against these seemed to be a culture of "live and let live." Tolerance of pluralism called for intolerance of exclusivism. Hence the taboo against discussing the truth claims of religion.

VERTICAL AND HORIZONTAL

But this taboo assumes that we're dealing simply with ourselves. If religion is a matter entirely of the horizontal, then such a taboo might be conducive to harmonious interaction. But most of the world religions assume that we are configuring ourselves with the vertical plane, "connecting" to the source of being. And here we have to assess what, if anything, can be known about or from this source. It is a question that is at once of supreme importance and that requires honest collaborative effort. If we are dealing entirely on the plane of the horizontal, then there's no point going any further.

This book seeks to address the question of what we know from the source of being—God. To do this we should set aside any idea of engaging in a polemical encounter between one or more religions. We do not seek a contest of religions with one group saying the other is deluded or damned. In fact, if it were possible (and admittedly it is not), we should at least initially set aside all preconceptions and presuppositions other than the reality of our mortality.

Let us talk at a human-to-human level, living as we do on the edge of oblivion. We know this: we will die. We want to know if what we do here and now has any bearing on what happens after we die. We want to know if life has meaning. This is not a matter of scoring points in an argument. This is a common search for truth motivated by our common human interest in discovering the map of reality that applies to all human beings. We leave aside our labels of Hindu, Christian, Muslim, Jew, Buddhist, and the like and are guided by one ruling principle: we have to be messengers and vessels of divine love, a love that is self-giving and unconditional.

THE IDEA OF DIVINE INCARNATION

Having said this, I must add that in this book I focus on the idea of divine incarnation as it relates to this common quest. As many would agree, this idea is manifested most clearly in the phenomenon of Jesus, and it is an assessment of this phenomenon that will be the core concern of this book. Some might say that, given this focus on divine incarnation with particular reference to the phenomenon of Jesus, my talk of avoiding preconceptions and presuppositions is both hollow and hypocritical. What I am doing, they will say, is building my whole story around a particular view of the world while imploring all others not to do the same around their world-visions.

In my own defense, let me say the following:

First, my main request is that this discussion should be carried on in the specific context of our imminent demise and the urgency of the quest of our salvation. Second, this context of death and salvation highlights the urgency of definitive answers, and *the* definitive answer, it would seem, can only come from the Creator of us all (if there is a Creator). Any claim of such a divine answer must be judged on the basis of whether the answerer has the authority of God. Hence the relevance of the idea of God incarnate. Third, I consider this idea in the light of the message that has come to us from various religions and philosophies. Fourth, I review what historians and other scholars have said of the idea of divine incarnation and in particular of the claims relating to the life, teaching, death, and resurrection of Jesus. Finally, I try to spell out the full implications of the claim of divine incarnation and in particular its significance for our vision of reality. All this is carried out in the spirit of drawing all of humanity to the discussion since death affects us all and salvation—if there is such a thing—is equally relevant to every human person.

But more important than all of these considerations is the nature of the approach. I begin by first flashing an image of a completed jigsaw puzzle, after which I take the pieces apart and then try to show how they all fit together.

NEITHER POLEMICS NOR PLATITUDES

It hardly needs to be said that discussions on this topic tend to be controversial, charged as they are with polemical overtones and capable even of sparking interreligious disharmony. Alternatively, they can sometimes become attempts to find the lowest common denominator, which hide the elephants in the room behind veils of platitudes.

The strategy here is different. This is not an exercise in polemics or platitudes. Instead, we will be looking at the pieces of the puzzle that make up the religious history of humanity to see if we can connect them; we will be looking at religions as pieces in a jigsaw puzzle that might possibly yield a coherent picture if placed in the right order. And we will do all this in the light of divine incarnation and revelation as these relate to salvation. We start with one picture in which the claims of incarnation, revelation, and salvation are seamlessly integrated, namely, Jesus perceived as a phenomenon. Thus, I start with a big picture before honing in on the fine print. The devil is often in the details, but there are times when you cannot see the forest for the trees.

Now it could be said that my perspective on Jesus might cloud or at least bias my judgment when it comes to my presentation of religious history. There is no question that my evaluation of the Jesus phenomenon will influence my thinking when it comes to other matters. But it by no means follows that I will necessarily put together the pieces of the puzzle so as to support my prior view of Jesus. Someone can just as easily believe that Jesus is God and man and also hold that all other religions are false or diabolic—thus concluding that the pieces do not add up to a picture. Alternatively, some might adhere to no religion at all while asserting that the pieces can be put together to form a picture that tells us something not about God but about the human psyche.

So there are no predetermined inferences built into this exercise. We survey the panorama of what is known, propose a hypothesis, and let the chips fall where they may.

As can be gathered from its title, this book argues for a particular paradigm whereby certain religions are seen to form a pattern. The paradigm may be likened to the anthropic principle in cosmology, according to which the fundamental laws and constants of nature seem to be finely tuned to permit the appearance of life; the slightest change to these values and ratios would have eliminated any possibility of life. The principle seeks to find an explanation for this fine-tuning: the options are either a multiplicity of universes that has various sets of parameters or a supreme mind who deliberately prepared the universe for life.

Applying this paradigm to the present situation, we find certain common themes in the great pre-Christian world religions that appear to reach a climax in not just the teachings but also the very life of Jesus. Just as the explosions of certain stars were required for the production of precise proportions of the chemicals that were essential for life, it could be argued that the human movement toward the divine across the world and across history had to be "guided" along certain paths before the divine could directly manifest itself in recorded human history. This, in fact, is the hypothesis proposed here.

The hypothesis moves away from the ideas of competition and toward an exciting journey of exploration into the mind of God, for if the hypothesis is right, what we have is a window into the workings of providence in the midst of primeval tribes and ancient societies, great civilizations and intricate religious systems. Thus, the story of Jesus becomes in a sense the climax and consummation of movements across the landscape of the human psyche and the dynamism of history.

RELIGION DETERMINED BY BIRTH?

Now it is true that, for the most part, we "believe" in the religion into which we are born. (This includes the religion of skepticism.) But no matter what we believe, in principle, it is possible to compare the themes and teachings of various religions and even to study each religion as a phenomenon. In the following chapters, we will study the Jesus phenomenon in relation to the religions that preceded the coming of Jesus. In so doing, we wish to lay out the hard facts about certain of their teachings. These are the pieces of the puzzle. How and whether we then put together these pieces to form a picture is, of course, an individual decision.

What I am trying to achieve here is to talk as one human person to another. We want to know the truth about why we are here. Consequently, it is of the utmost urgency that we search for clues about the purpose of it all. In the most real sense, our lives depend on it! If we think of ourselves as climbers hanging by our fingernails from a ten-thousand-foot cliff with only a few seconds left before we plunge down, shouldn't we at least consider the possibility that there might be some way to break our fall—whether it be by examining potential parachutes within our reach or reaching out to what seems to be a helicopter rope ladder? We have nothing to lose and everything to gain!

That is the spirit in which the hypotheses of this book are developed—as potential solutions to the mystery of the meaning of life, as explanations of the myriad forms of religious expression that have shaped human history. We proceed, above all, with the understanding that we are all creations of the one Creator, children of the same God, seeking the truth that comes from the source of our being.

And so, on our brief journey from womb to tomb, we cannot act like politicians hammering out compromises in a back room to produce a commonly agreed-on bill that pleases the majority. We just do not have this luxury.

One final point: I said I am a Christian, and it is now incumbent on me to eliminate a few common misconceptions about the Christian vision before we get started. The underlying perspective of this book is that God is infinite-eternal love, and God is Savior:

- God's nature, God's very being, is love—a love that expresses itself in an eternal and never-ending act of self-giving.

- All of God's actions as they relate to humanity are salvific—intended to draw humans into eternal union with him. Very few grasp the astounding nature of what is offered as the end state of salvation: a life of unending joy. We will live *forever*. The magnitude of the gift is simply incredible and, of course, overwhelming. It is the greatest possible gift, one in the light of which we see all else. And it is a gift offered to every person.

- God the salvific lover speaks to us from the dawn of history.

It is in the context of this vision that we will consider the world religions.

PART ONE

THE CHRIST CONNECTION

Phenomenon

We have spoken of Jesus as phenomenon. Let us now unpack this thought and commence our journey. Some might find it is precisely Jesus-as-phenomenon who will serve as a map for the journey, a beacon lighting the way. Others who have no interest or particular belief in Jesus may find this approach helpful in understanding his effect on humanity. At any rate, the perspective presented here will serve as a point of entry into the history of humankind's search for salvation. So let us begin.

A SHOCKING CLAIM

The appearance of Jesus of Nazareth on the horizon of human history was an event utterly without precedent, a phenomenon that was not simply unique but also transformative of all that came in its wake, from the world and its future to the very fabric of human existence. Even for those who reject it, the fundamental claim embodied in the phenomenon was as shocking as it was intriguing: in this person, it is affirmed, the very Creator of the world has "landed" in his creation; the Other has decisively "touched" us.

Now, by "history" we usually mean a writer transmitting records of memories of persons and events to a reader. But in the present instance we have a person transmitting his writers to us who are the readers: the senders themselves are sent to us. They come as his proclaimers, not as mere recorders of memories. Consequently, what we have here is not the recording of a phenomenon but a proclamation that is itself an integral part of the phenomenon. It is not as if we read the writings to discover the phenomenon: it is more true to say that the phenomenon discovers us through these writings.

WHY THIS PHENOMENON?

Why, it may be asked, should we single out this particular phenomenon when there are thousands of religions and faith structures, each triggered by some phenomenon or another? The answer is simply in the shocking, even outrageous nature of the claims made regarding Jesus—claims that are not even remotely contemplated in any of the other belief systems.

This claim is of the kind that demands stringent scrutiny, if only because it is so outrageous that it should be condemned in the strongest terms if shown to be untrue. For what is at stake is unthinkably potent in its magnitude: we are told that this Jesus was the infinite-eternal itself united with a finite nature, that his acts at a particular time and place have reversed the verdict of damnation hanging over the human race, that total commitment to him will enable one to partake of his divine nature, that he is inaugurating a new world order that unites heaven and earth, and that he is himself the gateway to eternity.

Whether you scoff at the claims, whether you reject them wholeheartedly, whether you find the whole story well intentioned but untenable, the fact remains that nothing quite so astounding has been conceived or proclaimed by the progenitors of any of the world's major religions.

The question, of course, is whether or not the claims about Jesus are true. How do we determine if it was all a pious pipe dream, a local event that was completely blown out of proportion—that is, if it took place at all?

VEHICLES OF THE PHENOMENON

Now one thing should be clarified at the outset. If we want to assess the phenomenon, we have to grasp it in its entirety. But to grasp it we have to study the vehicles that manifest it. And, contrary to what many think, these vehicles are not strictly and simply the books that constitute the New Testament. In point of fact, the phenomenon that is Jesus of Nazareth reveals itself through a plethora of platforms:

- The religious history of humanity
- The unique experience of the people of Israel
- The witness of the church said to have been founded by Jesus and ruling with his authority
- The startling claim that he rose from the dead
- The writings of his apostles and Evangelists that were "certified" by his church

- The worldwide missionary journeys of his apostles and their followers
- The ancient liturgies of the church that were said to make him present here and now
- The "laying on" of hands by the apostles, by which they passed on their authority to their successors, who were called bishops
- The councils of the church that defined the organic body of doctrine that constitutes Christianity
- The martyrs, mystics, and saints whose lives in some mysterious way mirrored, and pointed to, the life of their Lord

And at the heart of the phenomenon there was the explicit understanding that Jesus was not simply the divine in human flesh but that his mission was one of divinizing us: removing the curse that afflicts humanity, exorcizing us of evil, filling us with the divine life. Not only was he God-with-us; but he also brought all creation to a climax with a divinizing mission that transforms the world as a whole: in and through him history is drawn to a new and everlasting destiny, and the space-time continuum is charged with a supernal momentum culminating in a new heaven and a new earth.

THE SKEPTICAL CHALLENGE

While the preceding exposition summarizes the full nature and extent of the claim I am making, it does not in itself address the question of why we should believe the claim to be true. And here we have to understand and assess the challenges posed by the skeptics. Challenges come from different directions, ranging from atheists to adherents of other belief systems. They also emerge from Christians who profess different degrees of belief in the tenets of historic Christianity. Clearly the skeptical challenge has not been wholly successful because the assault on the Christian understanding of Christ keeps morphing day by day. For instance, a rash of recent books seeks to radically reconfigure our understanding of Jesus. These range from *The Five Gospels* of the Jesus Seminar to *The Da Vinci Code* and *The Gospel of Judas*.

But such books add nothing new to the kinds of assaults launched by the second- and third-century Gnostics, the nineteenth-century New Testament critics, and the *Myth of God Incarnate* debate of the 1970s—in fact, they are simply variations on the ancient heresies denounced by the first councils of the church. If nothing else, these assaults testify to the inherent dynamism of the story of Jesus. They are, in fact, testimonies to the power of a phenomenon that resurrects itself after every burial by would-be undertakers.

For both skeptics and seekers, the only thing that counts is evidence. So what would constitute evidence in the present quest? Even if every living historian acknowledged that the historical records about Jesus are reliable accounts of things that took place, this would by no means show that Jesus was indeed who his followers say he was. In other words, no event at all could show that a given human being is a divine person.

It is not possible to understand or assess Christianity without recognizing it as a manifestation of the supernatural. It is supernatural through and through, right from the start. But it is not supernatural in the sense we normally think of the supernatural. Christianity is not supernatural in the sense of magic, sorcery, or paranormal phenomena of any kind. It is not supernatural in the sense in which some Pentecostals think of it: speaking in tongues and the like (although there are legitimate manifestations of such phenomena). The specifically supernatural dimension of the phenomenon we are considering here is unique, unlike anything before or since.

On one level, everything about it is supernatural in the sense of transcending the natural: from Jesus being God and man to his resurrection from the dead; from the sacraments and their incandescent effect on recipients to the celebration of the Eucharist and the celestial-temporal magnitude of this performance; from the ongoing interaction with those who have left this life to the quantum leap of the human person made possible by "the gifts of the Spirit." On another level, everything that is supernatural is "natural": we see nothing out of the "ordinary" when we see Jesus, when we receive the sacraments, when we witness the celebration of the Eucharist or ask for the intercession of the holy ones of God in heaven. But despite this "naturalness," there is a supernatural underpinning that shows itself in miracles of the Eucharist, apparitions and visions, healing miracles, and other kinds of ethereal events.

In reviewing the dimensions of proclamation and action, the natural and the supernatural, we begin to see that the evidence is not this or that item or even the entire amalgam of items. In point of fact, the evidence is identical to the phenomenon itself; for if we truly and fully understand the phenomenon in its entirety, then we face not a weighing of evidence or an ongoing cycle of debate and discussion but a choice between accepting Jesus as who his church says he is—or not.

COMPELLING BUT NOT COERCIVE

It is a choice because the evidence is compelling but not coercive. It is just enough to say yes but not enough to exclude a no. For instance, we have just enough historically reliable information to grasp Jesus' life and teachings; we know just enough about the lives of the apostles to know that something transformed them and that they affirmed this to be the resurrection of their leader; we know just enough about the early church to know that they taught with the authority of their Lord and that they held that their liturgies and sacraments made him present. The web as a whole is a chain that is stronger than any of the individual links.

Given these intricate interconnections, we must weigh, explore, and assimilate the totality of the evidence. Historians and New Testament scholars play a valuable role because their work helps us to realize that Jesus was a flesh-and-blood person who actually trod this earth at a particular point in its history. The radical transformation of the original witnesses and their resulting globe-spanning journeys tell us that certain primordial, this-world events lie at the root of this new movement. The councils and liturgies and the letters of popes, bishops, and church fathers give us tangible data bearing on the actual beliefs of the ancient followers of Jesus.

The existence of a body, the church, which has taught and applied the same truths over two thousand years, is a living contemporary testimony to the phenomenon. Pre-Christian religious history in general and Judaism in particular help us to "locate" the Jesus story in the context of the overall interaction of human and divine. The mystics and saints and the claims of miracles and apparitions show us the chess pieces coming to life. All of this collectively constitutes the evidence to be assessed.

But above all: the phenomenon is the evidence.

CHAPTER 1

Popular Models of the Growth of Religion

Any further exploration of the phenomenon that is Jesus of Nazareth requires first a consideration of the global religions that preceded the coming of Jesus. If Jesus was indeed who his church claims he was, if he was the climax of God's revelation of himself to humankind, then the coming of Jesus must have bearing on the religious history of humanity. If the Christian message that God seeks the salvation of all humans is true, then we are led to ask if this salvific vision is reflected in the religious life of Homo sapiens. And by salvation, it should be said, we mean not simply ultimate destiny but the transformation of the human person here and now and liberation from evil.

Let me start with a quiz. Which religion or people:

1. says that only a divine sacrifice will suffice for the atonement of the sins of humanity?
2. adds that an efficacious sacrifice will require that: the victim be placed on a wooden pole; his hands and legs be pierced but no bones broken; a vine with thorns be placed on his head; a drink of sour liquid be given to him; his clothes be divided among the offerers?
3. claims that the savior of humanity will dispense final judgment, bring about the resurrection of the dead, and inaugurate a new world?
4. believes that a "scapegoat" will take on the sins of the people?
5. reports a solar eclipse at the time of the death of the savior and says, "The man from heaven just died"?

The answers may surprise you. Numbers 1 and 2 are found in the holiest books of Hinduism. Number 3 is from the religion of Persia that once dominated the world. Number 4 is from ancient Greece. Number 5 is from China. The history of the religions that preceded Christ has many other surprises pertaining to the phenomenon of Jesus.

The idea of a rendezvous of religions, of a convergence of beliefs and practices, is by no means novel in the scholarly world. We will consider two popular models that suggest just such a movement in religious history before presenting the model adopted in this book. The first of the two models is the Axial Age idea propounded by Karl Jaspers and popularized by Karen Armstrong and others; the second is a more precise and systematic formulation proposed by an interdisciplinary team of researchers. But before considering the different "convergence" theories, we first turn to the Victorian era and early-twentieth-century theories of the origin of religion.

THE REDUCTIONISTS — Seeing a Poem as Print Marks on Paper

To be credible, any theory of the origin of religion must derive from two streams of data: (a) physical remains—including texts—from premodern times and (b) field studies of those primeval societies that have survived with minimal assimilation into modern times. But, often enough, influential theories were constructed without any hard evidence; they were by-products of the theorist's own philosophy and associated speculation.

Interestingly, most of the best-known theories were constructed in the same general time frame: the late nineteenth through the early twentieth century. This was a period when Charles Darwin's theory of evolution was being applied to domains outside biology. The assumption was that the evolutionary model used for explaining the origin of species was just as valid in every other sphere—psychology, sociology, anthropology, and religion.

In both theory and practice, this meant two things: first, everything was a matter of the simple gradually progressing to the complex and, second, in the case of religion, what seemed to be a phenomenon in its own right was nothing more than an external expression of underlying psychological, sociological, or even biological forces. Nothing is what it seems to be. Everything can be "reduced" to something else.

Thus, there was a profusion of reductionist theories purporting to explain the "real" roots of religion. The most prominent of these were:

- Sir James Frazer's theory of magic, religion, and science and of myth and ritual;
- Edward Tylor's animist account of religion;
- Emile Durkheim's collectivity theory of totemism; and
- Sigmund Freud's wish-fulfillment theory.

Without exception, these theories have died without a trace. But a post-mortem will be helpful so that we can avoid the pitfalls peculiar to the frame of mind that produced them and so that we can understand how their ideas gave birth to similar theories in recent years: Karl Jaspers's and Karen Armstrong's Axial Age theory.

SIR JAMES FRAZER

The godfather of the reductionists was Sir James Frazer (1854–1941), author of *The Golden Bough* (1890), a celebrated twelve-volume work on anthropology and comparative religion that popularized the universal dying-and-rising-god myth. Although Frazer was a pioneer in social anthropology, his principal theses are today almost entirely rejected by modern anthropologists. Like Ptolemy and his cosmology, Frazer may be thought of as a genius whose works today are primarily of historical interest. Coincidentally, his work on ancient nature and goddess worship and the like has led to a rebirth of paganism in Western society, and his (factually flawed) work has served as the source material for a variety of esoteric groups and alternative accounts of history.

Frazer's hypotheses were based on his study of a few ancient texts and responses to questionnaires about the customs and beliefs of natives sent to missionaries, doctors, and civil servants living across the British Empire. Using such information, he created a massive work on myths, religions, rituals, and customs. He generated his own theory of the origin of religion while producing a study of parallels between ancient cults, rites, and myths. Drawing attention to the relation between myth and ritual, he held that religion was grounded in a myth enacted in the rituals of a god-king who incarnated fertility, was killed every year, and then rose like the grain. He cited the myths of Attis, Adonis, and Osiris and suggested that these were paralleled by the Christian story. But his hypotheses have been rejected by today's anthropologists for various reasons:

- The data he used came not from field researchers but from white colonialists who lacked specialized training and often did not understand the subtleties of information provided by the natives.

- Archaeologists and historians have invalidated his assumptions and conclusions. For instance, there is no annual killing of the "king" in ancient cultures.

- His guiding paradigm that all societies progressed from magic to religion to science has been decisively refuted through the study of primitive societies.

- His attempt to show parallels between pagan beliefs and rituals and early forms of Christianity is now known to be radically misguided.

The most celebrated feature of Frazer's model was his idea of the dying-and-rising god, and it is this idea that has been decisively discarded. Walter Burkert points out that there is very little evidence of resurrection in the case of Adonis and Attis; Osiris comes back to life not in this world but the next. J. Z. Smith, one of today's leaders in this domain of study, writes in *The Encyclopedia of Religion* that "the category of dying and rising Gods, once a major topic of scholarly investigation, must now be understood to have been largely a misnomer based on imaginative reconstructions and exceedingly late or highly ambiguous texts." What then do we find from a study of the myths? "Some of these divine figures simply disappear, some disappear only to return again in the near or distant future; some disappear and reappear with monotonous frequency. All the deities that have been identified as belonging to the class of dying and rising deities can be subsumed under the two larger classes of disappearing deities or dying deities. In the first case, the deities return but have not died; in the second case, the gods die but do not return. There is no unambiguous instance in the history of religions of a dying and rising deity."[1]

In *The Riddle of Resurrection: "Dying and Rising Gods" in the Ancient Near East*, T.N.D. Mettinger, another noted researcher, says of the idea of dying-and-rising gods that "there is now what amounts to a scholarly consensus against the appropriateness of the concept. Those who still think differently are looked upon as residual members of an almost extinct species."[2]

EDWARD TYLOR'S PRIMITIVE CULTURE

After Frazer, the most influential theorist of his day was probably Edward Tylor (1832–1917). In his *Primitive Culture*, Tylor, who had very little field data and no formal training, defined religion as a "belief in spiritual beings." His explanation for the origin of religion was fairly straightforward:

- Dreams of dead relatives led primitive humans to believe in a spirit world because they could not distinguish between dream and waking states.

- They also assumed that all physical beings, including inanimate objects, had some form of life, soul, or spirit.

- Moreover, trees and streams and stars and the various forces of nature, they came to believe, were possessed by spirits.

- By a process of evolutionary consolidation, human society moved from this world of spirits to a pantheon of gods and then finally to a supreme god who was higher than all the rest.

Tylor had one problem: he not only had no evidence for his theory; but also, all the evidence that became available flew in the face of the primary thesis.

In his own day, one of his former disciples, Andrew Lang, showed the mismatch between Tylor's theory and facts from the field. Field studies of primitive cultures such as those found in Tierra del Fuego (off the southernmost tip of South America), aboriginal Australia, and elsewhere showed that these societies fervently believed in a supreme all-knowing and all-good being who transcended nature divinities and ancestral spirits; in these cultures, it was the supreme being that came first and the subsidiary spirits that came later. Also, there was no evidence that primitive people were any less intelligent than the average European colonialist or that they could not tell the difference between animate and inanimate objects. For this and other reasons, the animist theory of the origin of religion is now regarded simply as a Victorian curiosity.

Lang was followed by other scholars whose painstaking and original work changed the entire landscape of the study of early religions. These include the distinguished anthropologist and ethnographer Wilhelm Schmidt, the phenomenologist of religion Rudolf Otto, and the great historian of religion Mircea Eliade. We will review their work as we consider the debate over animism, polytheism, and monotheism.

DURKHEIM AND FREUD

Two other reductionist approaches should be mentioned in passing. The sociologist Emile Durkheim developed the theory of totemism in his *The Elementary Forms of the Religious Life*. The totem was an animal, plant, or other object considered to have certain special powers because it had a resident deity or ancestor; the totem god was considered the sacred protector of the tribe or clan. Durkheim suggested that the totem was simply an exercise of the imagination in which the tribe or group personified itself through a symbol; totem worship was thus the group's projection and worship of itself through this symbol. Here again the problems facing the thesis were insurmountable. To begin with, the idea that the totem is a projection of the group is implausible on the face of it. Moreover, there was no society in which totemism was the central form of religion, and there were many societies in which there was no totemism at all. Most important, even those who had beliefs in a totem god had a prior belief in a supreme deity.

Yet another popular reductionist ploy is that of rejecting religion as wish-fulfillment. The most famous proponent of this approach was, of course, Sigmund Freud. But what is little known is that Freud's own personal and family problems were the template in which he saw all human religious experience, whether historical or contemporary. Freud had written that "young people lose their religious beliefs as soon as their father's authority breaks down." In *Sigmund Freud's Christian Unconscious*, the psychologist Paul Vitz points out what is well established: for various reasons, Freud had rejected his father and, in fact, detested him. This led him to reject God: Vitz notes, "There is conclusive evidence throughout Freud's writings that he reliably associated the concepts of father and God." It has been argued that Freud's Oedipus theory, ironically, explained not just his own atheism but atheism as a whole. "One striking thing about Oedipal motivation," writes Vitz, "is that, in postulating it, Freud was inadvertently proposing a powerful, unconscious, universal, childish and neurotic wish for the death not only of the father but also of his symbolic surrogate, God. As a consequence, Freud himself has given us the conceptual basis for understanding atheism as Oedipal wish-fulfillment. By Freud's own definition, atheism is an illusion like any other—a belief where 'wish-fulfillment is a prominent factor in its motivation.' Freud's life is a rich testimony to his theory." But Freud is not the only instance of atheism as neurosis. Vitz has done case studies of many of the famous atheists and arrived at a similar diagnosis. He thinks too that at least some contemporary atheists are driven by "shame, disappointment, or rage directed at the father. For many people, disbelief in 'God the Father' is the closest to revenge they can get."[3]

In any case, Freud's wish-fulfillment argument cuts both ways. It could just as easily be argued that atheism is a wish-fulfillment of the desire to be free of moral laws and obligations and of the fear of divine retribution here and hereafter. Alternatively, it could be said that atheism is a fear-fulfillment; after all, we are motivated by both fears and wishes. It should be remembered that if God exists, and if God is protective and compassionate, it is only to be expected that his creatures (including human fathers) will reflect his attributes.

THE AXIAL AGE PARADIGM — The Axis on Which Organized Religions Revolve

A relatively recent theory of the evolution of religious beliefs and practices is that of the so-called Axial Age. One of today's popular religion writers, Karen Armstrong, has reenergized this paradigm, which was originated by the philosopher Karl Jaspers in his 1949 work *The Origin and Goal of History*. The German existentialist proposed that the period between 800 and 200 BC might be thought of as the "axis" or pivot of history given the parallel emergence of similar transformative trains of thought in different parts of the world.

Cultural-religious revolutions in Israel, Persia, Greece, India, and China resulted in social, economic, and political changes that continue to affect us today. Several new religions, such as Buddhism, Confucianism, Taoism, and Zoroastrianism were created, while older religions like Hinduism and Judaism were internally transformed. Similarities between the new and transformed religions included an emphasis on moral precepts (often held in common by all of them), the generation of written scriptures, a focus on the internal as opposed to the external, and the key role played by leaders. Some have theorized that nature deities gave way to a universal deity.

"Let us designate this period as the 'axial age,'" wrote Jaspers.

> Extraordinary events are crowded into this period. In China lived Confucius and Lao Tse, all the trends in Chinese philosophy arose. . . . In India it was the age of the Upanishads and of Buddha; as in China, all philosophical trends, including skepticism and materialism, sophistry and nihilism, were developed. In Iran Zarathustra put forward his challenging conception of the cosmic process as a struggle between good and evil; in Palestine prophets arose: Elijah, Isaiah, Jeremiah, Deutero-Isaiah; Greece produced Homer, the philosophers Parmenides, Heraclitus, Plato, the tragic poets, Thucydides and Archimedes. All the vast development of which these names are a mere intimation took place in those few centuries, independently and almost simultaneously in China, India and the West.[4]

The idea of the Axial Age continues to interest some academics and was the subject of a July 2008 conference in Germany titled, "The Axial Age and Its Consequences for Subsequent History and the Present." Speakers noted that the era was prominent for its "renouncers" and social critics like the Buddha and Confucius. It was also the age of great utopian visions and in some respects gave birth to the notion of "theory."

Although many historians today dismiss correlations between "axial" beliefs and world events, it has to be admitted that the advent of increasingly urban civilization in various parts of the world was accompanied by changes in spiritual practice such as a turn to the inner self. Moreover, the emergence of empires fostered common ecosystems of culture and law. It might be said that there was a new relationship between humans and society that went beyond hunter-gatherer, nomadic, and tribal models. The Golden Rule, love your neighbor as yourself, was certainly common to all the Axial religions. Did these changes come about because of urban civilization and a greater use of technology, or were there other factors at work?

First, there is little question that the developments of the "Axial" Age were monumental in their impact, but if you take a sufficiently long time frame as your point of reference then you can easily identify "breakthroughs." Take the Middle Ages or the modern age for instance. In fact, the dimensions of the Axial "Age" are quite elastic and some have suggested that it might be extended to AD 600!

Second, one might say to the axialist: let's assume you are right: so what? Are you saying that the hand of providence is at work? Or is it just a coincidence? Or are you suggesting that there is some inescapable evolutionary trend at work? Clearly, proponents do not favor either providence or coincidence. Their strategy is to draw correlations between the beliefs and the sociopolitical changes, but this, of course, invites disputes with historians. And the critics have rightly said that the kinds of revolutionary belief in each of the regions under study are different.

Finally, the Axial Age theory ignores or brushes aside key data points that do not jell with the preferred conclusion. These include pre–Axial Age beliefs and practices that exerted an enormous influence in all subsequent periods. It is these we consider here:

- belief in a supreme deity,
- the universality of sacrifice,
- the premonitions of a coming savior, and
- the belief in an afterlife, which has been a constant from primordial times to the present.

It is the provenance and prevalence of these beliefs that have to be explained.

The Axial Age does present a plausible perspective when it comes to certain phenomena: the parallel trends relating to written scriptures, systems of morality, and dynamic leaders. But it leaves out the great pillars laid down in pre-Axial times:

- the Vedas (which cannot simply be dismissed as nature worship);
- Abraham, Moses, and the Jewish tradition of a God acting in history (as will be seen, the attempts to portray Yahweh as a tribal deity do not work);

- the protomonotheism of Babylon and Egypt;
- the primordial focus on sacrifice and incarnation;
- the universal belief in the afterlife; and
- the high God of primeval peoples.

Clearly a "bigger" picture than the Axial theory is required.

THE NEURAL-TEXTUAL PARADIGM — How the Evolution of Religion Mirrors the Evolution of the Brain and the Development of Written Communication

Recently, Michael Witzel, professor of Sanskrit at Harvard University, along with Steve Farmer and John B. Henderson, has created a model that attempts to ingeniously explain the genesis of "premodern" religious beliefs in terms of both neurobiology and the evolution of texts and concepts. They point out that structurally similar religious and philosophical ideas evolved in different world civilizations. This happened, they argue, because of certain cross-cultural factors. Brain research indicates that abstract thinking is carried out by the prefrontal cortex. It is the last area to develop in children and was also the last to develop in evolutionary history. The history of religion, they assert, reflects this evolutionary path toward the prefrontal cortex because initial religious beliefs tended to be animistic—seeing deities in everything—and anthropomorphic—God as superman—thus not requiring abstract thought.

They realize that this theory cannot easily account for the available data and try to address the challenge with innovative proposals. They admit that later developments in religious history cannot be explained simply in terms of brain development but believe the solution lies in studying the role of texts. What has to be explained is the accelerated development of abstract systems "that occurred in all advanced Old World societies in the second half of the first millennium BCE." [5] In their view, the generation of texts and the interaction of neural and textual processes gave rise to increasingly complex systems.

As they see it, the sequence is fairly clear. The primordial texts were supposed to have come from certain prophets or seers. But contradictions in these texts had to be ironed out. Later commentators tried to reconcile conflicts by exegetical methods. These attempts to harmonize conflicts in early texts, they argue, gave rise to monotheistic deities and ethical principles. Dualistic or Trinitarian paradoxes were subsequent "exegetical by-products."

For the purposes of our study of universal themes, some of the features they highlight are significant. Interestingly, they point out that exegetical methods were invariant across cultures, although the degree of use varied in each setting. Moreover, although there was some degree of long-distance transmission, this was not sufficient to explain the "sudden appearance" of parallel developments across cultures. Rather, they note the "near simultaneity" of the appearance "throughout the Old World" of abstract principles like heaven, Brahman/Atman, and Logos "in the last half of the first millennium BCE."

Now, traditional religious believers might see all this as evidence of the same God revealing himself gradually across continents and cultures. But this, of course, is not where Witzel and his colleagues are headed. Rather, they explain the emergence of monotheism as the product of fusing different gods to create a transcendent deity. When references to divine beings or cosmic principles conflicted, exegetes identified these in paradoxical ways to show the unity of the body of texts; this strategy gave rise to simultaneously transcendent and immanent gods. Similarities in abstract ideas professed by peoples of different ages and societies, they claim, simply spring from exegetical exercises.

So how plausible is this theory? Without question, the Witzel model is innovative and well thought out. But it fails for various reasons, including one acknowledged by the authors.

To begin with, it is clear that this theory is ultimately another variation of the simple-to-complex progression so beloved of certain experts. (The authors even draw an analogy of their perspective to evolutionary discussions of cumulative mutations leading to new life-forms.) Just as a child, as it grows older, moves from simpler kinds of thought to more abstract forms, so also Homo sapiens progresses from primitive ideas of divinity to more sophisticated versions. And when you add texts and their exegesis, this evolutionary process incorporates another variable that follows predictable patterns.

The first problem with this model is its uncritical acceptance of physicalism, the notion that thinking is purely and simply a function of the brain and that concepts are nothing but derivatives of neuronal processes. Leading logicians and philosophers of language such as Peter Geach, James F. Ross, and David Braine have shown that conceptual thinking and the use of language cannot be described or explained in terms of physical processes.[6]

Our senses make us aware of the physical world. We then process what we perceive—the percepts, if you will—to produce a concept, something that does not refer to a specific physical thing or being. (From dogs we encounter, for example, we can understand the concept of a dog, something that does not refer to a specific animal.) There is no organ that performs "understanding." Thus, concept generation or the use of symbols to convey meaning cannot be explained in terms of brain states, although the brain, along with blood circulation, oxygen, and the like, is required for thought to take place in Homo sapiens, at least in the present world.

Second, while primitive animism and nature deities can be easily explained as attempts to personalize forces of nature, the same cannot be said of the concept of a supreme being. It is entirely abstract, with no physical or imaginative correlate; and yet it came naturally to humans throughout history.

What is even worse, the simple-to-complex model fails if the complex is found at the very beginning of premodern history. The creators of this new twist on an old model readily admit that it would all be "falsified by the discovery of 'primitive monotheism' or abstract cosmological principles that did *not* emerge from integrations of primitive animistic traditions." Here they face formidable obstacles in the work of such distinguished researchers as William Schmidt and Mircea Eliade. The authors point out that "few academics today would publicly endorse Schmidt's ideas," but they acknowledge Eliade's continued influence in religious studies.[7]

Another problem is their failure to address the cross-cultural prevalence of certain key beliefs and practices: expiatory sacrifice (this is found in both early and later Judaism and Hinduism as well as across religious history), a god who becomes man to save humanity, the relation between life here and now and an afterlife. How did such notions take root? And, of course, the model begs the questions of whether or not there actually is a God and whether this God reveals himself.

Despite these shortcomings, their neural-textual model is important because it unifies seemingly isolated trends and highlights the emergence of virtually concurrent common themes. Their quest for patterns that remain invariant across cultures is commendable and legitimate, but their conclusions are fundamentally flawed. This is because of the gratuitous limitations they enforce on admissible data and their reliance on a fallacious neurobiological paradigm.

FROM POLYTHEISM TO MONOTHEISM OR VICE VERSA?

Three things are apparent in the Axial Age and neural-textual models. First, they adopt the simple-to-complex, animism-to-polytheism-to-monotheism picture. Second, they dogmatically rule out the possibility that a complex idea such as monotheism could have appeared in early religion. Third, they deny any possibility of religious experience being a contact with the real. All three of these problematic positions are adopted without argument, and consequently these models function as contemporary versions of the older reductionism.

But such an approach is no longer defensible without addressing the issues raised by, among others, the three great contributors to the history and phenomenology of religion mentioned earlier: Rudolph Otto, Wilhelm Schmidt, and Mircea Eliade. Is the religious impulse explicable simply in naturalist and Darwinian terms? Do we know for a fact that primeval humanity began with polytheism before evolving to monotheism? At the very least, it is safe to say that no scholar can today credibly answer yes to these questions without a plausible analysis of the data and interpretations made available by these authors and their like-minded successors.

When they first appeared, Otto's *The Idea of the Holy* (1917) and Schmidt's *The Origin of the Idea of God* (1912) effectively dismantled the Victorian-era model of the genesis and nature of religious belief.

Otto took aim at all attempts to "reduce" religion to biology, psychology, or sociology. Authentic religion, as Otto saw it, is an encounter with the holy, which he called "the numinous." The numinous, as he put it, is a "non-rational, non-sensory experience or feeling whose primary and immediate object is outside the self." "Numinous" derives from the Latin term *numen*, which means "presence." The numinous is simultaneously terrifying and fascinating and cannot be reduced to anything other than itself. It is the numinous, in Otto's account, "that has presided over the origins and development of religion."[8]

At around the same time that Otto was charting the architecture of religion as an encounter with the Other, William Schmidt was trying to create a comprehensive map of the facts on the ground, the religious beliefs and practices of peoples who remained in the setting of our primeval forebears. Schmidt was a linguist, ethnographer, and anthropologist who began publishing his twelve-volume work over a period of decades, starting in 1912. He cataloged the religious beliefs of primitive tribes in remote corners of the world using the data from his own fieldwork among them as well as that of others.

According to Schmidt, and several other researchers who came after him, primordial cultures across the world—from Native Americans to Australian aborigines to African tribes to the Eskimos—have believed in a supreme being. This being, sometimes called the Sky-God, Father, Creator, or simply "Eternal," was worshiped as the source of all things, beyond all images, eternal, all-knowing, all-powerful, and the ground of all goodness and the moral law. Schmidt himself did not insist that it was monotheism pure and simple across the board. He maintained, however, that the idea of a "high" God extended to the earliest times.

Both Otto and Schmidt have been criticized on various grounds. Otto periodically comes back into fashion, fades away, then returns to start another cycle. Schmidt is usually dismissed as a Catholic priest driven by the agenda of "proving" a primeval revelation of monotheism. Our concern here is not with defending the conclusions of these individual thinkers but understanding the dynamic programs of research they inaugurated.

Otto's work is oriented toward the subjective. It asks us to pay attention to our own experience without preconceptions and preconditions. It takes religious experience on its own terms. Here Otto adopts the approach of the phenomenologists, who seek to understand and explain the structures of experience in terms of how they manifest themselves rather than in terms of a preexisting theory or assumption. Reductionists from various schools have sought to "explain" religious experience in extraneous terms. The question is, which approach is right? It seems to me that, as in any instance of matters involving our personal experience, the burden of proof lies with those who want to deny what seems obvious. If we sense the presence of the Other, the biologist or the psychologist may assure us that this apparent "presence" is simply a product of genetic or psychological factors. But there is no way, of course, that they can definitively demonstrate the truth of their theories. Nevertheless, they can try to assemble various pieces of data and speculation to present a plausible theory. This is what reductionists from various disciplines have been trying to do with regard to religious experience for some three centuries. Interestingly, their theories have had to change on a regular basis precisely because they were found to be wanting in some crucial area or another. The approach taken by Otto was simply to explore our apparent experience of the Other on its own terms. Since the reductionists have, to date, failed to give a plausible and consistent account of religious experience, Otto's account continues to be of interest because it studies the experience as it presents itself. And, in the final analysis, it is we who have to decide whether or not we have a sense of the numinous by examining our own experience. If our experience reveals to us the presence of the numinous, we are in a better position to assess the religious experience of humanity than the reductionist to whom the numinous is an alien idea.

Schmidt's contribution was different. Although many scholars question his thesis of primitive monotheism, very few dispute the scope and reach of his data. Witzel and company acknowledge that most contemporary scholars are unlikely to have "waded" through his "twelve thick volumes of proofs."[9] From our standpoint, Schmidt's thesis is less important than the virtually indisputable fact he established: at least some primeval peoples believed in a high God.

Schmidt's significance can be better understood when compared with that of Darwin. It should be remembered that Darwin's influence did not originate in his theory of evolution, which predated him by several generations. Rather, it was his meticulous assembly of a wide range of data that won him a hearing in the arena of ideas. And although his thesis predated modern genetics and numerous other developments, he established a program of research that continues to set the agenda for critics, defenders, and contemporary studies.

Much the same can be said about Schmidt and his work. Schmidt was no armchair researcher. He and his colleagues were out in the field collecting a prodigious body of data on the beliefs of primeval peoples around the world. His assumption was that the hunter-gatherer communities around the world that survived into the early twentieth century held to essentially the same beliefs as their forebears. At the very least, as Schmidt put it, they practiced "the oldest forms of religion we can hope to find."[10] Tribes like these that used Stone Age tools and methods to eke out their existence were concerned primarily with their survival. They made no technological breakthroughs and lived essentially like their ancestors thousands of years before. There is no evidence that they made any novel shift either in their intellectual frame of reference, and it is reasonable to assume that here too they adopted the attitudes and practices of their ancestors. What Schmidt found was a fundamentally similar pattern of belief in most of these tribes scattered across the globe: a belief in a supreme deity as opposed to nature spirits and multiple gods.

In one respect, unlike Darwin, Schmidt was mining a comprehensive range of data now no longer available. It might be said that Schmidt's research was done just in time. David Rooney, a contemporary commentator, writes,

> As twentieth century civilization has made further encroachments around the globe, the outposts of primitive peoples have correspondingly shrunk. Indeed anthropologists may be said to have discovered the importance of studying primitives just barely in time to salvage any knowledge of them. A great amount of fieldwork was carried out during the 1920s that would be impossible to replicate today, because many of the primitive tribes have since disappeared from the face of the earth due to a combination of disease, dispersion and intermarriage with other tribes. Typically, the most primitive races had occupied the fringes of the continents, slowly pushed thither by the pressure of advancing more civilized peoples. Their habitations were in places like Tierra del Fuego, the dense forests of Central Africa, the Philippines and Malaysia, the frozen reaches of Siberia, and the extreme southeast of Australia. Some, such as the Tasmanians, were completely exterminated before they could be studied.[11]

Schmidt is not the only notable scholar to have held the view that the primevals were not simply animists or polytheists. Other field researchers have independently come to similar conclusions. Moreover, just as Darwin's theory of evolution was customized and upgraded with the onset of molecular biology (and called "the Modern Synthesis"), Schmidt's basic thesis was modified and given a new "look" in the work of Mircea Eliade, the preeminent twentieth-century interpreter of historical and comparative religious experience.

With appropriate qualifications, Eliade draws pointed attention to Schmidt's relevance:

> The most popular prayer in the world is addressed to "Our Father who art in heaven." It is possible that man's earliest prayers were addressed to the same heavenly father. The Vienna school of ethnology (particularly in the person of Fr. W. Schmidt, the author of the fullest monograph yet on the subject of the origins of the idea of divinity) even claims to have established the existence of primitive monotheism, basing the proof chiefly on the belief in sky gods among the most primitive human societies.
>
> For the moment we will leave to one side the problem of primeval monotheism. What is quite beyond doubt is that there is an almost universal belief in a celestial divine being, who created the universe and guarantees the fecundity of the earth (by pouring rain upon it). These beings are endowed with infinite foreknowledge and wisdom; moral laws and often tribal ritual as well are established by them during their brief visit to the earth; they watch to see that their laws are obeyed, and lightning strikes all who infringe them.[12]

According to Eliade, then, without doubt there was "an almost universal belief in a celestial divine being." Ninian Smart, a prominent anthropologist of religion who died in 2001, takes a similar approach.

> Ruling over the world which teems with divinities and sacred forces, there is—high above in the sky, but not *of* the sky—some kind of supreme Being. Among many primitive peoples outside Africa a similar belief is attested. . . . In any event it is a striking fact that many primitive cultures have a belief in some sort of High God, even though there very often is no specific ritual directed toward such a Being. . . . The existence of such conceptions among folk as far apart as the inhabitants of Tierra del Fuego and the Arctic is a significant indication that primitive religion . . . possesses sophisticated ideas about the beginning and creation of the world, and about a supreme architect of the world.[13]

So we are left with this question: did religion evolve from animism to polytheism to monotheism? Or was monotheism the primordial belief system, which then devolved into polytheism, animism, fetishism, idolatry, and the like? The Victorian view that religious beliefs evolved from animism to monotheism can no longer be taken as a default position, although this is precisely what happens in Karen Armstrong's revival of Axial Age thinking.

Certainly the animism-to-monotheism thesis accords well with evolutionary theory and its idea of the simple evolving into the complex. But as with any thesis, what matters in the end is how the facts stack up. And here we have nothing definitive.

On the one side there are theories based on limited or no field research. This includes Tylor and Durkheim, who had access only to a relatively narrow range of sources. Frazer had more data, but much of it was colored by the sources, much was inaccurate, and he himself was only an armchair expert. The Axial Age and neural-textual theorists, for their part, do not take seriously the beliefs of primeval peoples. Nor do they take into account the universal and perennial themes of sacrifice and salvation. On the other side we have researchers who start with a comprehensive range of data rather than preconceived theories and who seek to understand religious experience on its own terms. Here we have scholars ranging from Lang and Schmidt to Otto and Eliade.

What emerges from a review of the different positions is that we cannot definitively affirm either purebred animism or monotheism at the start of humanity's religious history. But the field research done over the last century and around the world points indisputably to one conclusion: primeval peoples and cultures that had no contact with the outside world believed in a high God and manifested an inexplicable awareness of the numinous.

CHAPTER 2

A New Model—the Rendezvous of the Religions

As we have seen, there are two basic ways of understanding the religious history of humanity. There is the reductionist perspective, which implicitly assumes or explicitly states that there is no reality beyond the physical world and portrays primitive humans as progressing from simpler to more complex delusions, from animism to polytheism to monotheism. And then there is the thoughtful and expansive approach, which takes the available data on its own terms and, on that basis, argues that religious experience from the primeval to the sophisticated manifests an awareness of a transcendent source of all being.

Quite apart from the question of high gods in primeval cultures, the reductionists have claimed that Indian, Persian, and Chinese religions—as well as others—started with animism and polytheism and then moved to henotheism, where one god is higher than the others and, in rare cases, came to rest in monotheism. Even Jewish monotheism, they have said, is a later development that appeared only in the time of King Josiah. We will consider these critiques in more detail shortly, but a few things should be said at this stage:

- Primeval people had a high God that went beyond all other gods. Studies of those peoples that have clearly primeval roots—the natives of Tierra del Fuego, the pygmies, aborigines, Mongols, Native Americans—have made it clear that the high God is a central belief.

- Polytheism and idolatry were all-pervasive in the secondary cultures of the ancient world.

- Although there was polytheism in Hinduism, there was nevertheless a clear sense of a supreme Godhead behind the various deities; likewise in China, polytheism and later Taoism and Confucianism coexisted with the belief in a supreme being, Shang Di; the same thing is true of the Persians. So the major organized religions held to the idea of a supreme God that grounded the profusion of secondary deities.

- The idea that monotheism came late to Judaism is a scholarly myth built on the fanciful idea of collective amnesia. Certainly the polytheistic temptation remained a constant threat to the Jews for several hundred years, but by Jesus' time monotheism reigned supreme.

- Polytheism was still prevalent among Romans and other religions by the time of Jesus, but Christianity made monotheism preeminent.

- None of the nineteenth-century explanations of religious belief (or their more-recent counterparts) have even considered these factors, and so their pictures of the world religions are impoverished. Even those who do not subscribe to the idea of a primitive monotheism today have to concede that the idea of the high God was universal. The flaw in ideas like animism is this: someone might see spirits in material objects or in nature, but how could they come by the idea of a supreme spirit and of this supreme spirit being a Father (which is how many of the primevals saw God)?

It seems clear then that the evidence for belief in a high God in primeval societies, coupled with the sense of a supreme Godhead in the most ancient

TABLE 2.1

Religion	God	Sacrifice
Primeval Peoples	Father in Heaven, Creator, Eternal	"Sacrificial rituals . . . are impressive evidence for a continuity spanning thousands of years" (Walter Burkert). "The feelings of guilt expressed in the old rituals of atonement are stated at their extremes by myths telling about killing and eating a god" (Burkert).
Africa	Supreme being in all African religion. God is good, merciful, holy, all-powerful, all-knowing, present everywhere, limitless, self-existent, spirit. He never changes and is unknowable.	"The practice of making sacrifices and offerings is found all over Africa." The difference between sacrifice and offering is that in sacrifice blood is shed. Since blood is associated with life, it means giving back life to God. Sacrifice "marks the point where the visible and invisible worlds meet" (John Mbiti).

religions, refutes the simple-to-complex thesis. We see a living awareness of a supreme Godhead not just in primeval peoples but also in the religious life of ancient India, China, Persia, and Mesopotamia. Granted, there was polytheism and henotheism as well, but the sense of a transcendent Other was the dominant theme. The awareness of the absolute came to a climax in the history of the Jews. These are some of the dimensions of pre-Christian religious history that we will be exploring.

Part of the thesis I advance here is that there are several key commonalities of theme in the major pre-Christian religious systems. The ancient religious world visions do not simply speak of a supreme spirit or creator. They also share an awareness of a life after death where one's destiny is determined by one's deeds in this life. Then there is a universal focus on offering up sacrifices to the divine in expiation and petition. In many cases there is talk of a divine initiative taken in the blueprint of salvation. There is even the suggestion of the divine becoming human and being sacrificed for the redemption of humanity.

Table 2.1 is comparative, laying out the beliefs and concepts relating to God, sacrifice, savior, afterlife, and the inner being of God in the major world religions prior to the coming of Christ.

Savior	Afterlife	Pre-Trinitarian ideas of the nature of God
"With remarkable consistency, myths tell of the origins of man in a fall, a crime that is often a bloody act of violence" (Burkert). Many ancient peoples have preserved legends and intuitions of a divine figure walking the earth.	Yes, tied to actions in this world	
"All these many myths about the creation of men say . . . they lived in a paradise at the beginning, God was close to them and gave them all that they needed. They were meant to live forever. . . . But this state did not last very long. For various reasons the original paradise was lost: men's direct link with God was severed or eclipsed, the closeness between the heavens and the earth was replaced by a vast gap without a bridge, the gifts of immortality and resurrection melted away, and death, disease and disharmony came and have reigned ever since. In short, paradise became a thing of the distant past, and African Religion has never been able to show men how to regain paradise" (Mbiti).	Yes, tied to actions in this world	

TABLE 2.1 cont.

Religion	God	Sacrifice
Greeks, Romans	The two greatest Greek thinkers were monotheists (Plato, with his idea of the Good, and Aristotle, with his idea of the Prime Mover), although polytheism was prevalent in popular culture.	"Animal sacrifice was an all-pervasive reality in the ancient world. . . . Whatever complexities, layers, and changes in cultural tradition underlie the individual peculiarities, it is astounding, details aside, to observe the similarity of action and experience from Athens to Jerusalem and on to Babylon" (Burkert).
Judaism	I AM WHO AM (Jewish exegete Nahum M. Sarna observes that "the true etymology of the Tetragrammaton" passage in Exodus 3:14 "remains an enigma" to this day. But "Whether it means 'I Am that I Am,' or 'I Am Who I Am,' or 'I Will Be What I Will Be'—and it can mean any of these—God's pronouncement of His own Name indicates that the Divine Personality can be known only in terms of itself, and not by analogy with something else."*)	Sacrifices of Abel, Noah, Abraham, Melchizedek; Passover sacrifice
India-Hinduism	Nirguna Brahman—the supreme Godhead) "I AM" (Upanishads)	Sacrifices of the Vedas; sacrifice of Prajapathi
Persian-Zoroaster	Ahura Mazda I AM (Zoroaster)	Sacrifice of hoama
China	Shang Di (the one true God)	Sacrifice to Heaven performed annually by the emperor

* Nahum M. Sarna, *Exploring Exodus: The Origin of Biblical Israel* (New York: Schocken, 1986), 52.

Savior	Afterlife	Pre-Trinitarian ideas of the nature of God
The pharmakos is the animal that is the scapegoat, which takes on the sins of the people and is put to death. Writing in 40 BC, the Roman poet Virgil reported the prophecy of the coming of a divine-human ruler born of a virgin: "Now the virgin is returning. . . . A new human race is descending from the heights of heaven. . . . The birth of a child, with whom the iron age of humanity will end and the golden age begin" (Fourth Ecologue).	Elysian Fields for the good, Tartarus for the wicked	
Moses offering life for his people; Suffering Servant of Isaiah	Resurrection at the end of history	Yahweh Logos/Wisdom Shekinah/Spirit of God
Prajapathi	Vedas showed the righteous living in the World of the Fathers or the World of the Gods while the wicked were consigned to the House of Clay. Reincarnation is not in the Vedas.	Saccidananda (being, consciousness, bliss)
The three Saoshyants. The last of them, Saoshyans, was prophesied by Zoroaster.	Our actions in this life determine our destiny after death. The good will be resurrected at the end of time.	
Blood covenant idea; astral phenomena at the birth and death of Jesus; Dao = Logos.	Life with God after death	The Three Pure Ones of religious Taoism

All of these beliefs and practices indicate fundamentally shared beliefs in the reality of:

- a God who is supreme
- the soul
- the human thirst for God
- the need for expiation and propitiation, with this obligation being met through sacrifice
- the need for a system of salvation
- a destiny after death that is determined by the kind of life we lead on earth
- interaction between God and humanity, including prophecies and stories of the divine taking on a human nature to help save humanity.

Researchers have found that when human societies developed across the globe, even in such relatively isolated areas as Australia and the Americas, they manifested certain common structures such as farming, which is a sophisticated activity; language, which often included scripts and writing; culture and art; and city-states and kingship. Our preliminary overview here draws attention to certain other kinds of structures that have been common to societies across the world: from worship of one God to sacrifice in reparation for sin.

Now, if we assume that there is a God and that God created the world with the express purpose of bringing about finite beings with the attributes of intellect and will so that they could enter into eternal loving union with him, these beings could be of two kinds—either pure spirits or spiritual beings united with matter, angels, and humans respectively. Since loving union is possible only if it can be freely chosen, these beings would have to be offered the choice of accepting or rejecting such a union in such a manner as to preserve their freedom of will. The choice could not be one involving God in all his infinite glory since this would eliminate the possibility of freedom. The choice as offered would be consonant with the preservation of freedom and also with the nature of the kind of being involved. In the case of the pure spirits, the superiority of their intellect and will meant that the choice they made would be immediate and final. In the case of the ensouled embodied beings, the final choice would come only from learning, development, and a series of mediated proximate choices. And the environment in which these choices are made is one that has been formed by the choices of all who went before. Thus, we have the solidarity of the human family.

This is the vision of the human condition that is presented here. This is the vision that makes sense of evil and suffering in a world created by a good and loving God. It is a vision, above all, of love. No reductionist, no skeptic can explain the mystery of the message of love that lies at the center of this vision. We are told that the infinite Creator of trillions of galaxies is an infinite lover, that he can be known most fully in the poor and the lowly, that he asks nothing of us but our love. Who could have thought up such an idea?

In the following chapters of part 1, we will examine each of the major religious thought-worlds and try to determine whether or not the model proposed here is plausible. There is, of course, nothing illegitimate about constructing models that purport to show common patterns in the world religions. This is what the Axial Age and neural-textual models and their nineteenth-century predecessors sought to do. But there is a crucial difference between those models and the present project. We approach religious experience as an interaction with the real and do not seek to "reduce" it to something else. We also allow the possibility of there being some kind of revelatory activity from the divine. In the final analysis, it is the evidence, and not presuppositions from either side, that will determine whether or not the model works.

CHAPTER 3

The Primevals

With our new model of common patterns among the world's religions in mind, we continue our journey through the religious life of humanity, starting with the idea of the high God in the hunter-gatherers who lived in primeval times. We focus on the primeval peoples of Africa, America, Australia, and Asia.

THE SUPREME GOD IN PRIMEVAL PEOPLES

As Andrew Lang, Wilhelm Schmidt, and numerous other field researchers have shown, belief in a high God can be found in the primeval cultures of all the inhabited continents. Whether or not this amounted to belief in the infinite-eternal God of classical monotheism is debatable. But it cannot be denied that a good many of the hunter-gatherers thought of their deity as supreme.

No one has chronicled the belief of these primeval peoples in as much detail as Schmidt in his twelve-volume *The Origin of the Idea of God*. Schmidt points out that the African and Asiatic Pygmies believed in a supreme being. The same is true of the Bushmen in South Africa; the inhabitants of Tierra del Fuego in South America; the Aborigines of Australia; the Samoyeds, Koryaks, and Eskimos of the Arctic; and major Native American tribes. The notion of a supreme being is truly global.

The names most commonly given to the supreme being, says Schmidt, denote his "fatherhood, creative power and residence in the sky." The primeval peoples also highlight key attributes of the supreme being:

1. Eternity
2. Omniscience
3. Beneficence
4. Morality
5. Omnipotence
6. Creative power

7. Giver of the moral code

8. Author of moral rewards and punishments

Schmidt notes that "all primitive peoples without exception believe in another life." Although there are differing views on what happens after death, the majority recognize "a distinction of good and bad in a future life."[14]

HUNTER-GATHERERS AND SACRIFICE

Religion is not simply a matter of belief; action is just as integral to its being. If belief in a high God was a consistent theme across history and prehistory, its counterpart in the realm of action was sacrifice. Understanding this is crucial to gaining an understanding of the primeval age religions.

Walter Burkert, an authority on the ancient world, takes it as an "indisputable fact" that "the age of the hunter, the Paleolithic, comprises by far the largest part of human history. No matter that estimates range between 95 and 99 percent. . . . By comparison, the period since the invention of agriculture—10,000 years, at most—is a drop in the bucket."[15] Sacrifice is found from the time of the Paleolithic hunter:

> In animal sacrifice we find a Paleolithic, basically human action pattern, hunting for food, evolving more and more from pragmatic to symbolic level, while preserving characteristic features in striking detail, and preserving, too, a message and a function. It established cooperation and solidarity by some kind of shared guilt, by traumatic repetition of bloodshed and killing; it tells and visibly demonstrates that Life is unique, but not autonomous; it must accept death in order to perpetuate itself.[16]

Burkert points out that

> the rituals of purification and atonement surrounding the slaughter could persist nearly unchanged; they could be stressed to mark the passage to and from a sacred center. . . .
>
> A further step of ritualization was to substitute other kinds of food for the animal: bread for meat, and wine for blood. This probably goes back at least to the Bronze Age. The symbolic value is raised once more; the

feelings of guilt expressed in the old rituals of atonement are stated at their extremes by myths telling about killing and eating a god. Its latest and most sublime form appears in Christian ritual.[17]

Sacrifice is intrinsic to religion: "We cannot grasp religion as a fixed form if it is merely personal; it becomes a formative construct only over the course of generations. Sacrificial rituals, in any case, are impressive evidence for a continuity spanning thousands of years."[18]

All of this points to the depth and breadth of belief in a high God and the ubiquity of sacrifice among the hunter-gatherers who lived on every continent in primeval times. While names and other details varied, the fundamental concepts were remarkably similar. From the primeval period we move now to the major organized societies of the ancient world: Africa, India, Persia, China, Greece, the Near Eastern societies, and the people of Israel.

CHAPTER 4

Africa

It is commonly held that Africa is the cradle of the human race. Remarkably, the people of Africa have affirmed a supreme being throughout their known history. Kenyan scholar John Mbiti, one of the leading authorities on African religion, said of the three hundred main traditional religions, "In all these societies, without a single exception, people have a notion of God as the Supreme Being."[19] And according to Aloysius Lugira, "Most African oral traditions have pointed to the existence of a power above which there is no other power, a Supreme Being, creator, and originator of the world. People who follow traditional African religion understand the Supreme Being to be one and only one, God with a capital 'G.'"[20]

Africa is home to an astounding variety of ethnic groups. Says Lugira, "It is estimated that there are more than 6,000 different peoples in Africa today. Many of these people continue to live by the spiritual influence of their ancestral way of life."[21] The religion indigenous to Africa is conventionally called African religion, a term that describes the native religions that, per Lugira, over 100 million Africans continue to practice. "African religion is not the only religion found in Africa today," he continues. "However, it is the only religion that can claim to have originated in Africa. Other religions found in Africa have their origins in other parts of the world."[22]

African religion is oral through and through. According to Lugira, "Traditional African lore has always been passed down orally. There is no written set of beliefs, no 'holy book' such as the Bible or the Koran. Cultural beliefs and rules for living are passed down from generation to generation by word of mouth. Most African peoples have no written language."[23]

BELIEF IN GOD
As Mbiti and other scholars have pointed out, the history of religion in Africa is replete with belief in God. It forms the foundation for everything else. All

the peoples have a specific word for God as well as thousands of other names given to him. These names just mean "God" or describe his various characteristics. It is striking that "some of the names like Chiuta, Jok, Leza, Mulungu, Nyame, Nzambi and others, are commonly used in several African languages. This suggests that a long time ago, before these languages became separate, the names of God were already being used, and the belief in God had already become a major feature of African thinking and life."[24]

The African understanding of the nature of God touches universal themes. God is good, merciful, holy, all-powerful, all-knowing, present everywhere, limitless, self-existent, spirit, changeless, and unknowable. As for his actions, God is the Creator of all things. He sustains his creation, provides for what he has created, and rules over the universe. As in many other cultures, God is often seen as Father: "A number of African people look at God as Father and themselves as his children. This image gives the idea of a family. It shows a close relationship between people and God. It implies that God has not only 'begotten' or made the people, but is also their protector, provider and keeper."[25]

As for matters of personal piety, all African societies practice prayer. As in nearly every religious tradition that the world has ever seen, prayer is the most common way that the African people, since ancient days, have taken their emotions and petitions to God. Prayer is both individual and communal.

Mbiti emphasizes that African religion is not animism. Although spirits are believed to exist, it is in the context of "the African view of the world in which God is considered to be supreme, and He has under him spirits and men."[26] Lugira describes African belief in God as monotheism while noting certain variations:

> The African concept of monotheism is one of a hierarchy, with the Supreme Being at its head. . . . African understanding of the structure of the heavenly kingdom might be compared to the Christian concept of God ruling over the saints and angels.[27]

It is important to understand that the African vision of God sees the supreme being as distinct from all physical representations. Henryk Zimo observes that "the Supreme Being is not presented in the material form, either, for example as statues, figures, masks or pictures."[28]

DIVINE ORDER, SACRIFICE, MEDIATORS, AND THE AFTERLIFE

African religion includes several other dimensions that are prominent in ancient religions. What are of particular interest are the roles played by the divine order of the universe, sacrifice, mediators, and the afterlife. God's order in African religion is found in the laws of nature, the moral order among people, the religious order in the universe, and the mystical order in the universe. All African societies believe that there is a mystical hidden "power in the universe and that it comes from God." African religion also has a specific understanding of the original state of humanity.

> All these many myths about the creation of men say that even they were largely in a state of ignorance, they lived in a paradise at the beginning, God was close to them and gave them all that they needed. They were meant to live forever. The heavenly and earthly worlds were joined or close together, this being the symbol of harmony and tranquility. For various reasons the original paradise was lost: men's direct link with God was severed or eclipsed, the closeness between the heavens and the earth was replaced by a vast gap without a bridge, the gifts of immortality and resurrection melted away, and death, disease and disharmony came and have reigned ever since. In short, paradise became a thing of the distant past, and African Religion has never been able to show men how to regain paradise.
>
> This was a severe loss and blow to mankind. But life did not become altogether hopeless. There are many myths which go on to tell us how God made other provisions for men to live and cope with their new situations.

Sacrifice is also fundamental to African religion. "The practice of making sacrifices and offerings is found all over Africa," says Mbiti. "By this practice material or physical things are given to God and other spiritual beings." Sacrifice is distinct from offerings because all sacrifice involves the shedding of blood, whereas offering concerns the giving of anything else. "In

African societies, life is closely associated with blood. When blood is shed in making a sacrifice, it means that human or animal life is being given back to God who is in fact the ultimate source of all life. The life of one person or animal, or of a few of either, is destroyed in the belief that this will save the life of many people. Thus, the destruction of one becomes the protection of many."

In African religion, the average person often approaches God through intermediaries, who could be either a human or a spiritual being. Human intermediaries "include priests, kings, medicine men, seers, oracles, diviners, rain-makers and ritual elders."

And finally, the belief in the afterlife is all but universal in Africa. The dead continue to exist in the hereafter. "This continuation of life beyond death is recognized through a very widespread practice of remembering the departed, which is found throughout Africa."[29] Mbiti argues that these acts of respect for the departed cannot be construed to be ancestor worship. Ancestor worship as such has been regarded as a primitive form of religious belief stemming from an attempt to placate departed souls. But Mbiti's point here is that in Africa the attitude toward deceased friends and family reflects a prior belief in both life after death and the actuality of continuing communion with those who have passed on. This brief study of African religion points to themes and patterns that are echoed in the major world religions. Collectively they form a global mosaic of commonality and continuity.

CHAPTER 5

India

It is a matter of history that theories about the history of the ancient world tend to be transient. Hence, we will primarily rely on currently available written sources of data. A key question in this context is the relationship between the inhabitants of India and Persia, a factor that is of critical importance in understanding the texts that underpinned their religious beliefs and practices. Thus, before considering the religions of these ancient peoples, we have to consider the role played by the so-called Aryans, who were the ancestors of many Persians and Indians. The standard view is that these Aryans split into two groups somewhere in central Asia, one going to India and the other to what is today Iran. There is much evidence supporting this view: language, religious texts, customs, and the like. In recent years, some have said that there was no real Aryan invasion of India, that the Aryans were originally based in India and then moved out to other regions. For various reasons, the vast majority of scholars have rejected this "out of India" hypothesis, although they also reject the Aryan invasion idea and suggest there was a gradual migration of the Aryans into India.

But no resolution of this dispute is required in studying the religions of India and Persia since we are dealing with the actual texts we have today. The linguistic and conceptual evidence available in these texts makes one thing clear: the Indian Vedas and the Persian Zend Avesta had a common point of origin, wherever or whenever that might be. Harvard professor Michael Witzel, an authority on ancient Indian and Persian texts, notes that both the ancient Iranians and the inhabitants of India who spoke Vedic Sanksrit called themselves and their language *Ārya*. About the relationship between the Vedic Indo-Aryans and the Iranians, Witzel writes that

> not only are their languages so closely related that their oldest attested forms might often be taken as dialects of the same language, but their society, their rituals, their religion and their traditional poetry resemble each other so closely that it has always been regarded as certain that the

Vedic Indo-Aryans, the Iranians and the Kafiri (Nuristani) are but offshoots of one group speaking IIr. [Indo-Iranian], a few hundred years before the RV [*Rig-Veda*] and the Old Avestan texts.[30]

HINDUISM

The complex system of religious beliefs and practices that sprang up on the Indian subcontinent some three to four thousand years ago is commonly called Hinduism. Our concern is with the themes that are dominant in the primary Hindu scriptures: the Vedas and their ancillaries, the Upanishads and the epics and Puranas. The Vedas offer a religious vision, the Upanishads a philosophical perspective, and the epics and Puranas a devotional paradigm. We will examine the idea of God in the Vedas, the focus on sacrifice and the cosmic order, and the ancient notion of a semidivine savior who will offer his life for the redemption of humanity. We will also briefly consider the Hindu understanding of the inner being of God (*saccidananda*).

The antecedents of Hinduism are lost in antiquity. The word "Hindu" is derived from the Sanskrit word for the River Indus and was used by invaders of the first millennium AD to designate the religion of the peoples of the region. What we know about Hinduism begins with the Vedas (although there were different stages of development going back to the Indus Valley civilization and before). Witzel notes that the Vedas are made up of "hymns addressed to the gods, other mantras in verse or prose which are used in the solemn Vedic (*śrauta*) ritual and the 'theological' explanations, composed in the expository prose of the ritual, and the Mantras used therein."[31] There are four Vedas: *Rig-Veda*, *Yajur-Veda*, *Sama-Veda*, and *Atharva-Veda*. The most important, the *Rig-Veda*, is made up of 1,028 hymns divided into ten mandalas, or chapters. These hymns "were sung in praise of those deities who were worshipped and to whom sacrifices were addressed," writes P. T. Raju. Much later came the Upanishads, "treatises which contain the teachings of sages about the nature of the soul, the spirit, the world, and the Supreme Being."[32] The Vedas go back to at least 1200 BC, while the Upanishads were composed around 500–400 BC.

FIRST THEME: GOD

The Vedas speak of many gods of whom the principal were the sky god Dyaus Pitra; Indra, god of war and storms; Agni, god of fire; Soma, god of sacrifice;

Yama, god of the dead; Apas, god of the waters; Vayu, god of the wind; Surya, god of the sun; and Varuna, god who observes behavior, punishes, and forgives. Despite this profusion of deities, there is an indication that the underlying divine reality is one. The first book of the *Rig-Veda* states clearly: "They [men of wisdom] call him Indra, Mitra, Varuna, Agni, and he is the heavenly, noble-winged Garutman. The Reality is one, but sages call it by many names; they call it Agni, Yama, Matarishvan," and so on.[33] In like vein, the tenth book of the *Rig-Veda* says, "The One Being is contemplated by the sages in many forms: Ekam santam bahudha kalpayanti."[34]

The *Yajur-Veda* says: "We meditate on the energy of the supreme godhead. . . . The supreme godhead is the receptacle of all good qualities. . . . When one meditates on the supreme godhead, it is on these qualities that one meditates. One meditates on infinite strength, infinite power, infinite energy, infinite bliss and infinite purification, and is accordingly blessed with these qualities."[35]

What we have here is not full-blown monotheism, but neither is it mere polytheism. It is not even henotheism, the idea that there is one supreme god but also other gods, as simplistically postulated by Max Muller. Nor is it a question of calling different gods supreme in different contexts (of sacrifices or hymns). There is a clear awareness of one transcendent reality, which is the ground of all being—an awareness that is calibrated with greater clarity in such later texts as the Upanishads with the notion of Nirguna Brahman. Why did the Vedic sages use the language of gods (and sometimes) goddesses? Here we enter the realm of speculation.

Do we find here some intrusion of nature worship (fire, air, sky)? Some have said the pantheon of gods and demons (devas and asuras) plays the role of the hierarchy of angels and demons (fallen angels) in the Judeo-Christian world. Others say that these gods and goddesses are presented as different manifestations of one and the same reality. No definitive judgment is possible on these lines of speculation, but one thing is clear: there is an awareness of a single underlying divine reality.

Eventually, the Vedic gods, for the most part, faded from the minds of the populace. But what remained alive was the sense of the supreme Godhead.

The tendency of the Vedic gods to merge into one another and to interchange their attributes, combined with the theistic tendency of the worshipper to treat one God as if he were the Supreme God, made the gods appear merely as so many forms and names of the All-God, the All-Power, which became the Absolute. It was called *brahman*. The older meanings of *brahman* as the Vedic mantras or as the power of the sacrifice, were replaced by a more comprehensive understanding of *brahman* as the ultimate or absolute reality of the universe.[36]

So central is this idea of the One that Hinduism—which is often equated with polytheism—is paradoxically also thought of as monism, a belief that only the divine exists and nothing else! On the one hand it is said to call for the worship of many gods and goddesses, and on the other it is deemed to deny the existence of all beings other than the one divine being.

So is Hinduism monism (there exists one divine reality and nothing else) or theism (there is a God and everything else is his creation)? The Vedas and the Upanishads have been collectively interpreted in both of these ways by later commentators, one offering a monist (*advaita*) and the other a theist (*dvaita*) view of God.

The *advaita* interpretation of Sankaracharya (AD 788–820) holds that the absolute, Nirguna Brahman, is wholly impersonal and without attributes; it is the one and only existent that is real; everything other than Brahman is an appearance; the idea that we exist separate from Brahman is an illusion.

Some have said that *advaita* is not actually monism but simply emphasizes the dependence of the finite on the infinite. Madhvacharya (ca. AD 1238–1317) rejected *advaita* and, contrasting human limitations with the perfection of God, said it is simply blasphemous to suggest that we are identical with God. We are aware of ourselves as limited and dependent, he noted, and our experience of our imperfection is not an illusion, because our inmost self sees it to be real and true; but God is totally independent and without any limitation, and there could not be any identity between two such entirely different realities.

Although the *advaita* view is currently more influential, the preponderance of texts in the Vedas and the Upanishads support Madhvacharya's theistic vision. In fact, his whole mission carried on by later generations of followers was to reclaim the original theism of the Hindu scriptures that had been obscured by many centuries of Buddhist influence. At the level of popular piety, most Hindus tend to be theistic.

The emphasis on the formlessness of God in the Upanishads might raise questions about idols in Hindu practice. It should be noted that the Vedic Hindus did not have idols or temples, and idol worship was, in fact, prohibited. Idols are thought to have been introduced between the seventh and third centuries BC, perhaps in imitation of Buddhist practices. Hindu reform groups like the Brahmo Samaj and the Arya Samaj have sought to return Hindus to Vedic religion. The Arya Samaj "rejects [idolatry] entirely, not only as a harmless error, but as a positive sin."[37] Swami Dayananda, a prominent nineteenth-century exponent of the Vedas, said, "There is not a single verse in the Vedas to sanction the invocation of the Deity, and likewise there is nothing to indicate that it is right to invoke idols." He also said, "Idol worship is a sin." Different verses from the Vedas have been cited in this regard: "The Formless Supreme Spirit that pervades the universe can have no material representation, likeness or image."[38] "Those who worship visible things born of the prakriti, such as the earth, trees, bodies (human and the like) in place of God are enveloped in still greater darkness, fall into an awful hell of pain and sorrow, and suffer terribly for a long time."[39]

One final note on the Hindu understanding of God's nature. Amazingly, the name used to describe God in the self-sufficiency of his eternal Now without past or future is the same in Hinduism as it is in Zoroaster and the Hebrew Bible. We find this in Verse 17 of the *Isavaya Upanishad Basya*, "SO AHAM ASMI." As Madhvacharya points out: "This is the great ineffable name of God, 'I am that I AM' 'That Supreme Being (asau) which indwells in Asu is the I AM.'"[40]

SECOND THEME: SACRIFICE

As in all the most-ancient religions, and in Judeo-Christianity in particular, another central theme in Hinduism is sacrifice. Sacrifice was tied to the belief in *rtá*, the sacred order of the universe that includes both the workings of nature and the dictates of justice and righteousness: "O Indra, lead us on the path of Rtá, on the right path over all evils."[41] It is also related to the idea of a divine incarnation.

The significance of sacrifice in ancient Hinduism cannot be stressed enough. As a matter of fact, Vedic Hinduism has been described as a religion of sacrifice. The Vedas themselves have been characterized as the prayer book (*Rig-Veda*), songbook (*Sama-Veda*), and ritual text (*Yajur-Veda*) for sacrifice.

The act of creation itself was the product of a divine sacrifice, and all other sacrifices mirror this primal one. Rightly performed sacrifice was essential for sustaining the cosmos and preserving its order.

THIRD THEME: DIVINE INCARNATION

The original sacrifice in the Vedas is that of a divine person called Purusha Prajapathi, who sacrificed himself so as to bring into being the cosmos and all the different classes of human beings (priests, warriors, and others). He is both sacrificial victim and the one to whom the sacrifice is offered.

The theme of divine incarnation combines with sacrifice and comes to a climax with this revelation of Prajapathi. *Prajapathi* has been translated both as "one who generates" and "Savior of Man" (*praja*, "man," and *pathi*, "savior"). A number of recent writers, Hindu and Christian, have written on the subject of Prajapathi. They have seen remarkable resemblances to the life and death of Christ, and some have said that the Prajapathi idea

TABLE 5.1

Rig-Veda	Commentator
"Hiranyagarbha Samavarthathagre Bhoothasya jaatha pathireka aasid Sadaadhara pridhivim dyamuthemam Kasmai devaya havisha vidhema." (*Rig-Veda* 10:121:1)	Sayanacharya
Same as above	Menon
"Purusha evedam Sarvam yad bhootham yachcha bhavyam uthamrutha-thwasya Isaana yadannena athirohati." (*Rig-Veda* 10:90:2)	Sayanacharya
Same as above	Menon
Same passages	Bibek Debroy and Dipavali Debroy

is nothing less than a primordial prophecy of the life of Christ—much like the Suffering Servant prophecy in Isaiah 53. As far back as 1875, the prominent Indian thinker Krishna Mohan Banerjea remarked that "the meaning of *Prajapati* . . . coincides with the meaning of the historical reality of Jesus Christ; and that no other person than Jesus of Nazareth has ever appeared in the world claiming the character and position of the self-sacrificing *Prajapati*, half mortal and half immortal."[42] In *The Aryan Witness* he said that "if the writers of Rigveda could visit India today, then in comparison to all the faiths that prevail here today they would identify Christians as closest to their own religion."[43] This claim is no doubt controversial. The problem is magnified by the diversity of teaching in the Vedas and the lack of any definitive English translation of the Vedas.

Nonetheless, there is no doubt that the Vedas speak of a personage named Prajapathi and provide details of his attributes and sacrifice. (The Prajapathi sacrifice is also described in the Upanishads and the Brahmanas.) Prajapathi is

Translation/Commentary

From Paramatma,the Great Glorious Self, Prajapathi is born in the same glorious form as firstborn (self-made) before all the creatures of the universe. On his birth itself he is ordained as the only protector and sustainer of all the creatures he created in the universe. He is the protector of all the visible and invisible on earth and in the rest of the universe. That is to say, he is appointed as heir to all things.

In the beginning, God and his supreme spirit alone existed. From the supreme Spirit of God proceeded Hiranya Garbha, alias Prajapathi, the firstborn of God in the form of light. As soon as born, he became the savior of all the worlds.

Prajapathi is the protector of the present world. He was the Creator of the world in the Past, and he will be the savior of the world in the future also. He Is the Lord of everlasting life in his eternal state. Even though he is such a supreme authority, he crosses over to the visible state of man that grows by the earthly nourishment (eating and drinking son of man). It indicates his birth on earth as wonderful or mysterious.

As Sayanacharya sees it, this is the message conveyed by the text: "Prajapathi is the Lord or Distributor of immortality because he becomes [present in] the visible world in order that living beings may obtain the fruits of their actions and gain moksha or final liberation from their bonds." Purusha is identified with Prajapathi.

This man, the first born of the God is all that was, all that is and all that has to be. And he comes to this world to give recompense to everybody as per his deeds.

Some English versions of the *Rig-Veda* translate *Hiranyagarbha* as Golden Embryo or Womb or "one embodying a golden core." However you translate it, there is no question that *Hiranyagarbha* refers to Prajapathi. In other texts, for instance the Upanishads, *Hiranyagarbha* is identified with Prajapathi. A Sanskrit glossary defines *Hiranyagarbha* as "Golden egg; cosmic womb; cosmic intelligence; the Supreme Lord of the universe; also called Brahman."*

* "A Brief Sanskrit Glossary," Atma Jyoti Ashram, http://www.atmajyoti.org/sw_glossary.asp, accessed December 21, 2010..

introduced for the first time in the tenth book of the *Rig-Veda*. Table 5.1 provides translations and commentaries from two authors. The first commentary comes from the fourteenth-century Vedic scholar Sayanacharya,[44] and the second is from Aravindaksha Menon (who uses a translation certified by the national literary society of India).[45]

FOURTH THEME: DIVINE SELF-SACRIFICE

It has been said that this divine self-sacrifice of the Purusha Prajapathi, outlined in the *Rig-Veda* and then elaborated in the other Vedas and Brahmanas (annotations on the four Vedas), is the most important event in the Hindu scriptures: "Since the Purusha Suktam is seen in all Vedas, it is cited as the essence of all Srutis by Veda Vyasa in the Mahabharata."[46]

The Purusha who is sacrificed is Prajapathi: "The creative power of the Brahman (Devathma sakthi) is saluted by Svethasvatara Upanishad. Lord is recognized as the source of the Universe (Bhuthayoni) by Mundaka Upanishad. This Purusha propounded in Upanishads is celebrated as the creator of the Universe (Prajapathi, Hiranyagarbha) with the names and forms (Naama roopa Prapancham)."[47]

As laid out in the Vedic texts, the sacrifice of the God-man Prajapathi was performed by the kings and the priests. It is a sacrifice that is required for the redemption of humanity, and only those who accept Prajapathi will be redeemed. The original is given first, with different translations below.

> Tham yajnam barhishi proukshan
>
> Purusham jaathamagratha
>
> Thena deva ayajantha
>
> Saadhya rushayaschaye. "Purushasookta," *Rig-Veda* 10:90:7

This man, the first born of the God, was tied to a wooden sacrificial post and the gods and the Kings along with the seers performed the sacrifice. "Devas of heaven and the earthly fraternity along with the hermits offered the first-born male in sacrifice by consecrating him as the animal of offering by tying him on a wooden sacrificial post."[48]

Seven Devas were the sticks that enclose the place of Yajña [sacrificial fire rituals], thrice seven [twenty-one] philosophical principles were made the fuel sticks; the Devas performed the Yajña and they bound the Purusha as the cow at the Yajña.[49]

As the sacrifice on the Yajña they besprinkled the Purusha, born in the beginning. With him the Devas performed the Yajña along with Saadhyas [other Devas] and the Sages.[50]

Thamevam Vidwanamruthaiha bhavathy
Nanya pandha ayanaya vidyathe. *Rig-Veda* 10:90:16

This [sacrifice] is the only way for redemption and liberation of mankind. Those who meditate and attain this man, believe in heart and chant with the lips, get liberated in this world itself and there is no other way for salvation too.[51]

The Devas who worshipped this Purusha, by this Yajña and by all the Dharma, attained high levels in Svarga [heaven]. All persons performing this Yajña [sacrifice] shall reach similar status.[52]

The preconditions for the Prajapathi sacrifice bear an eerie resemblance to the crucifixion of Christ. The *Yajur-Veda* and the Shatapatha Brahmana lay out the rules for the sacrifice of a man, and Prajapathi is, of course, Purusha, a man. Each of the Vedas includes a Brahmana that lays out the formulas and rules for performing its rituals, and the Shatapatha Brahmana plays this role for the *Yajur-Veda*. "After the Rig-Veda, this text [*Yajur-Veda*] is considered the most important work in the entire range of Vedic literature."[53] Below are the verses setting out the procedures for the sacrifice.

"His hands and legs are to be bound to a yoopa [a wooden pole] causing blood shed" (Brihadaranyakaopanishad 3.9.28; Aitareya Brahmana 2:6).

"The sacrificial victim is to be crowned with a crown made of thorny vines" (*Rig-Veda* 10:90:7, 15; Brihadaranyakaopanishad 3:9:28).

"None of His bones must be broken" (*Yajur-Veda* 31; Aitareya Brahmana 2:6).

"The skin/garment of the sacrificial victim must not be torn" (Aitareya Brahmana 2:6).

"Before death he should be given a drink of somarasa [sour wine made of an herb called somalatha]" (*Yajur-Veda* 31).

Christian commentators, for instance Adhyaksha Anubhavananda Kesava Raya Sarma Mandapaka,[54] have cited several other verses in making the case that the Vedas and Upanishads seem to prefigure the life and mission of Jesus. By far the most comprehensive and profound work on the great mystery of divine self-sacrifice in the Hindu scriptures is *Prajapathiyagam*, by Dr. Koshy Abraham. Below are some of the relevant citations referenced in the writings of these commentators.

"The Supreme Creator took a perfect human body (Nishkalanka Purusha) and offered it up as a self-sacrifice (Brihad Aranyak Upanishad 1:2:8). The symbol of the Purusha, says the Maddyandiniya Sathpathbrahmana III, was the lamb, the animal most often used in sacrificial offerings. The Sathpatha Brahmanam also says, 'Prajapathi yagnayaga' and 'Yagnova avati tasya cchaya kriyate,' which means all animal sacrifices are shadows of the perfect sacrifice."

"If you want to be delivered from the sin, which you commit through eyes, mouth, ears and mind, bloodshed is necessary. Without shedding the blood, there is no remission for sin. That must be the blood of the Holy one. God is our creator. He is our King. When we were perishing, He came to save us by offering even his own body on our behalf" (Tandya Mahabrahmana 4.15).

"The redemption is through shedding of blood only and that blood has to be through the sacrifice of God himself" (Taittiriya Aranyaka, verse 3).

"God, the Purusha is the sacrifice" (Chandokyopanishad 3:16:1).

"God will offer himself as a sacrifice for the redemption of mankind" (*Sama-Veda*, Tandya Mahabrahmana).

"The Purusha was above sin, and only in knowing Him does one obtain immortality" (Chandogyopanishad 1:6:6–7).

"Acknowledging the Purush-sacrifice imparts eternal life" (Kathopanishad 1, 3:8, 11).

"There is none superior to this Purusha and He is the paragathi [Only way to Moksha]" (Kathopanishad 3:11).

"After giving Himself as the supreme sacrifice, this Purush resurrected himself" (Brihadaranyakaupanishad 3.9.28.4 5; Kathopanishad 3:15).

"The purpose of this sacrifice is to provide the only way to Heaven and the only way of escape from Hell" (*Rig-Veda* 9:113:7–11; 4:5:5; 7:104:3).

But even those who see a prefiguration of Jesus in the texts of ancient religions and mythologies admit that such parallels cannot be literal, flawless, or comprehensive. On the level of history, theology, and moral principles, there are definite points of difference. Two common misconceptions must be addressed. *Rig-Veda* 10:61:5–7 states that, in the process of creation,

Prajapathi cohabits with his daughter Ushas, the dawn, who gives birth to Vasthoshpathi, the sun. About this the Vedic scholar O.M.C. Namboothiripad writes, "The birth of a child, SUN, by Ushas from Prajapathi is only a figure of speech which actually indicates the creation of a bright day light, namely SUN. Prajapathi is the Creator. USHAS, Dawn or the first light or daybreak, is his creation. The powerful SUN (Surya) is created after the first light only. This is the actual meaning of the vedic hymn."[55] It should also be noted that later legendary writings like the Puranas talk of twenty-one prajapathis. Prajapathi is understood in these writings as one who generates or establishes a family. These prajapathis have nothing to do with the Vedic Prajapathi. In any event, the parallels between the Vedic Prajapathi and the Jesus of Christianity can at best be seen only as prefigurations.

Nonetheless, the remarkable resemblance between the sacrifice of the Purusha Prajapathi and the life, death, and resurrection of Jesus Christ cannot be denied. This parallel was poignantly explored in a recent popular article titled "The Rigveda's Revelation" in India's leading national newspaper, the *Hindu*:

> It should be a matter of joy that Jesus was revealed not only through the Jewish prophets but also through our Indian rishis. The rishis recorded their intuitions in the Vedas.
>
> According to Thandiya Maha Bramana in Sama Veda, for the forgiveness of all sins blood is necessary. That blood is realized by the Paramatma offering himself as sacrifice. Prajapathi (God) himself must become the "Yagna" or sacrifice. Offering himself as Yagna, Prajapathi atoned for the sins of man. This has been fulfilled and accomplished in Christ's sacrifice on the Cross on Calvary.
>
> According to the Rigveda, the "yagna pasu" (animal) should be a pure and spotless lamb. Thorns must be tightly tied around its head and the lamb must be tied to a pillar. The cloth covering the lamb must be shared by the people and not a bone of the lamb must be broken. To the fainting lamb, *Soma* should be given. At the end of the sacrifice, there should be *prana prathista* to the lamb. The meat of this sanctified sacrificial lamb should be eaten.

All these stipulations are fulfilled in Jesus. Jesus is a pure spotless lamb. He is scourged. He is crowned with a coronet of thorns. The soldiers divided his garments though they had to cast lots for his seamless robe.

Scriptures say that not a bone of Jesus was broken though the legs of the two thieves beside him were broken. Christ has conquered death and has become victorious. Jesus has instituted the sacrament of his body and blood, the Holy Eucharist for people to receive forever-lasting life.[56]

HINDUISM AND THE HOLY TRINITY

Some Hindu thinkers have even extended their identifying of religious parallels to Christian thought, seeing the echoes of a doctrine of the Trinity in Vedic Hinduism. The conception of God as *satchitananda*, said Mahadev Govind Ranade (1842–1906), is "an analogy of these component parts of the Sanskrit name of God to the Christian Trinity: Sat corresponding to the absolute existence of the Father, Chit to the Logos, and Ananda to the Holy Comforter."[57]

According to Pratap Chander Mozoomdar (1838–1884), being, reason, and joy in God have the names Brahman, Paramatman, and Bhagavan in Hinduism: "Three forces of the Divine nature have, according to Hindu wisdom, entered into the formation of all things. The first is the force whereby God holds his own being and gives being to others; the second is the force by which he has intelligence and gives intelligence to others; and the third is the force whereby he has love and joy and confers love and joy upon others." He then compares this conception to the Christian doctrine of the Trinity: "Now, no possible conception of the Divine nature, ancient or modern, Eastern or Western, is possible beyond the threefold principle. The closest parallel between the Christian faith and Hindu conceptions of the threefold nature of God is here observable."[58]

The twentieth-century Benedictine monk and Christian thinker Dom Bede Griffiths embraced these parallels, arguing that the Hindu idea of God as *saccidananda*—being, knowledge, and bliss—has important connotations with respect to the doctrine of the Trinity: *sat*, the ground of being, can be thought of as the Father; *cid*, the self-consciousness of eternal being as the

Son; and *ananda*, the outpouring of the superabundant being and conscious-ness of the eternal, as the Spirit.[59] By no means can we take these as anything but analogies.

But Jose Pereira, an eminent authority on comparative religion, highlights the clear differences between the Christian Trinity and the Hindu triad: "In the Christian Trinity the Persons are irreducibly distinct in reality; a 'relational opposition' of origin exists between them. But Being-Consciousness-Bliss are no more than different aspects of the same reality, distinguished from one another only in concept. With no question of any of them originating from either or both the others."[60] They are better described in terms of the traditional attributes of being—unity, truth, and goodness. Nevertheless, they can legitimately be regarded as analogies to certain dimensions of the Trinity if not prefigurations. Pereira's concluding comments show the significance of the Hindu thought world for Christianity as a whole.

> It was in Hinduism that there were first enunciated some of the mysteries that Christian theology believes are wholly supernatural, and hence unknowable to the human mind except through revelation. Ideas such as the mysterious plurality of beings in the unique and transcendent being of God (whether it be dyadic or triadic); the assumption of this being of creaturely form (the Incarnation); the intimate personal union with this being as constituting man's supreme happiness (the Beatific Vision); and the unattainability of that except through His favor (grace).[61]

Given the scope of the present study, this overview of pervasive themes in Hinduism is unavoidably brief and selective. Nevertheless it cannot be denied that these themes play a foundational role in the Hindu scriptures.

CHAPTER 6

Persia

At one time, Zoroastrianism was the most influential religion in the world because it was the state religion of the Persian Empire under the Achaemenid kings (560–330 BC), who ruled the civilized world before the Greeks and Romans.

In many of its fundamental beliefs it was so close to Judaism and Christianity that some writers have even tried to portray it as the source of the Judeo-Christian worldview. This latter thesis is an exaggeration because of the historically separate origins of Judaism and Zoroastrianism as well as certain fundamental differences. Nevertheless, there are common themes present in these three religions that also appear in other geographically and culturally distinct ancient religions. This is significant to a key question being explored in this book: Are the commonalities of belief and practice across the globe some two to four thousand years ago simply a coincidence? Or are the primordial religions variations on a central theme that was to be actualized at "the appointed time"?

There were three phases in the growth of the religion of pre-Islamic Persia. Initially, the pre-Aryan inhabitants of the land practiced their own religion. Then came the Aryan immigrants with their new religious system (which we reviewed in chapter 5). Finally Zoroaster reformed the Aryan religion, developing what we now know as Zoroastrianism.

The linguistic and theological similarities between the Aryans of India and Persia become evident from a study of their scriptures. The holy books of India are called the Vedas, those of Persia Zend Avesta (very few of the latter have survived) and the Gathas of Zoroaster. Michael Witzel points out, "The Iranians have a set-up of texts quite similar to that of the Vedas (though this is little observed). However, only about a quarter of the original Avesta has been preserved after Iran became an Islamic country in the 7th c. CE."[62] Vedic deities are found in the Avesta. But in both religious texts, there was an awareness of a supreme Godhead. There was no idol worship among the Persians. "Indo-Iranians honored personifications of the sun, moon, earth, heaven, and all other natural forces. Despite this, Aryan religion forbade the use of statues or images. Nonetheless, they worshipped and propitiated their deities with sacrificial meals to which they were invited as guests of honor."[63] The central idea of a cosmic and moral order, *rtá*, in the Vedas has a counterpart in the Avesta called *Asha*. Also, both Indians and Persians worshiped as divine the Haoma plant in Persia, which was the same as the Soma plant of India, and the offering of the juice of this plant played a key part in religious rituals.

THE ZOROASTRIAN REVOLUTION

The religion of the Aryans of Persia was radically transformed with the appearance of Zoroaster, or Zarathustra, the great prophet of monotheism. There is no consensus as to when Zoroaster was born and where he lived, as the libraries of Persia were burned down by later invaders (including Alexander the Great). Witzel places him even before 1000 BC.[64] He is believed to have received a divine revelation that led him to propose a reform of the existing Persian religion. He was able to convert a local ruler and, in time, the entire empire of Persia became Zoroastrian. Zoroaster himself is believed to have been murdered, his teachings preserved in seventeen hymns called the Gathas.

The central tenet of Zoroaster's religious reform was his assertion that there is only one God, Ahura Mazda. All other beings are to be seen as creatures, although some, such as the Six Immortals, were thought of as higher in the hierarchy of creation, much like angels and archangels. Departing from the beliefs and practices of the past, Zoroaster had no goddesses.

Although a monotheist, Zoroaster introduced an ethical dualism. He taught that there was an evil spirit, Ahriman or the devil, who is responsible for all evil, including disease and death. There are also numerous good and evil spirits. Nevertheless, Ahura Mazda was the supreme God. (Years after Zoroaster, however, dualism and polytheism crept back into popular religion.) Zoroaster's God has the same self-description as Yahweh to Moses: "Thus spake Zarathustra—'Tell them, O Pure Ahuramazda, the name which is the greatest, best, fairest and which is the most efficacious for prayer.' Thus answered Ahuramazda . . . 'Ahmi yad Ahmi Mazdo: I am that I AM.'"[65] As we have seen, this is also the name of God that we find in the Hindu scriptures.

Another key Zoroastrian theme was the afterlife. Mary Boyce, one of the leading authorities on the Zoroastrian religion, notes, "From the evidence of both the *Vedas* and the most archaic *Avestan* texts, the continuance of life after death was something taken for granted as self-evident and not open to question."[66] Zoroaster's Gathas, in fact, constantly talks of the afterlife and the relation between every thought, word, and deed in this life and one's destiny after death. Every human being

> is free and must choose either the Wise Lord and his rule or Ahriman, the Lie. The same is true of the spiritual beings, who are good or bad according to their choices. From man's freedom of decision it follows that he is finally responsible for his fate. Through his good deeds, the righteous person (*ashavan*) earns an everlasting reward, namely integrity and immortality. He who opts for the lie is condemned by his own conscience as well as by the judgment of the Wise Lord and must expect to continue in the most miserable form of existence, one more or less corresponding to the Christian concept of hell. According to Avestan belief, there is no reversal and no deviation possible once a man has made his decision.[67]

Just as in other ancient religions, sacrifice played a significant role in the Zoroastrian faith: "*Haoma* is a plant, but more than that, it is the god Haoma on earth," writes Geoffrey Parrinder. "In the *haoma* ritual, the god is pounded and from the juice comes the drink of immortality. In this bloodless sacrifice the offering is at once god, priest and victim, and the faithful consume the divine sacrifice in anticipation of the sacrifice at the end of the world which will make all humans immortal."[68]

Especially interesting is Zoroaster's concept of "savior." The conflict between truth and falsehood will not go on forever. "There will come 'the last turning point of the world,' when the 'two great hostile armies come together,'" observes Parrinder. "Men and women will have to submit to 'the great test' by fire, and 'justice shall be realized.'" It is in this context that Zoroaster introduces a savior. The world "will be 'renovated' by the 'benefactors' or saviors of the good religion, who will suppress passion by just deeds and the spread of the wise teaching."[69] Among Zoroaster's "most revolutionary concepts," writes Peter Clark, is "that of the savior. It is this savior figure—also referred to in the plural—who will bring about the renovation of the world."[70]

Of the three saviors Zoroaster predicted, the last plays a role that is reminiscent of the eschatological Christ proclaimed in the New Testament. "On the day of resurrection," says Parrinder, everyone will "be raised by the savior to face the final judgment."[71] The Avesta prophecy is clear: "He shall be the victorious Benefactor [Saoshyant] by name and World-renovator [Astavat-ereta] by name. He is Benefactor because he will benefit the entire physical world; he is World-renovator because he will establish the physical living existence indestructible."[72] "The last Saoshyant will bring about the final judgment of humanity and will secure the harmony of the world."[73]

CHAPTER 7

China

Our journey around the world and down the centuries brings us now to the ancient civilization of China. Of particular interest to our present project are certain deep-rooted religious beliefs and practices in ancient China that parallel those of Hebrew culture and religion.

Confucianism, Taoism, and Buddhism, along with a few other belief systems, have been very influential in China. But standard works of comparative religion have ignored foundational beliefs and practices that precede and were subsumed by Confucian and later systems. It is these that we will treat here.

PARALLELS WITH THE OLD AND NEW TESTAMENTS

There are fascinating parallels between the Judeo-Christian worldview and ancient Chinese religion. This is clear in considering just these broad themes:

- From at least 2600 BC the Chinese people and their rulers have believed in and worshiped a supreme God and Creator they called Shang Di, Di, or Tian, whom they believed was active in their lives and in the affairs of the world. The emperors ruled at the pleasure of Shang Di with what was called "the Mandate of Heaven," and if they or the people fell into evil then they would be punished by Shang Di. Even with the advent of Buddhism, Confucianism, and Taoism, there was no change in the understanding of Shang Di as supreme. Shang Di shared many of the attributes of Yahweh of the Old Testament. He was all-holy, all-knowing, all-forgiving.

- For four thousand years, until AD 1911 (when China ceased to have a monarchy), the emperor of China would offer an annual sacrifice of an unblemished calf to Shang Di in the Temple of Heaven. This annual sacrifice was performed in atonement for the nation's sins. The sacrificial animal was believed to take on the penalty that should have been borne by the worshipers, and the emperor represented the nation.

- The idea of covenant was as prominent in China as it was with the Hebrews. This included China's self-awareness of being "God's country." The affairs of state and the fortunes of the nation were understood to be dependent on the will of heaven.

- The idea of the Tao/Dao, it has been argued, in some way mirrors that of the Hebrew idea of the Word that in the Gospel of John is described as the divine Logos.

- Perhaps most astonishing of all is the fact that imperial records dating back to the approximate years when Christ was born and when he was crucified show that the Chinese were aware, from their study of celestial phenomena, that something momentous had taken place.

- The ancient Chinese believed in eternal life. They said of an emperor, "May the Son of Heaven live forever." About one of their kings they said, "King Wen's soul is active and he lives in the presence of Shang Di."[74] Respect for ancestors, and sometimes worship of ancestors, was common, and "reverence for the powerful dead and the invoking of their manna for the sustenance of the clan became part of Chinese social mores, and filial piety a central Confucian teaching."[75]

Standard histories of religion in China confirm the ancient belief in Shang Di, the annual sacrifice at the Altar of Heaven and the importance of the Mandate from Heaven.

SHANG DI

Confucianism, Taoism, and Buddhism are generally considered the main religions in China, but the worship of Shang Di and the annual sacrifice preceded them. "Even before the rise of Confucianism and Taoism," says Geoffrey Parrinder, "an earlier religion (from which Confucianism and Taoism each in its own way grew) had held sway in China for nearly a thousand years." And these systems "had both been in existence for some five hundred years before Buddhism was introduced from India."[76]

Confucianism and Taoism were initially philosophies rather than religions. Parrinder points out that "in speaking of Confucianism and Taoism as religions it is important to remind the Western reader that, in the Chinese mind, they are *chiao* (teachings), and teachings which are not exclusively or specifically religious though they are concerned with much that we should think of as religion."[77] Buddhism in China took on a specifically Chinese character. In addition to these three religious systems, at the popular level there was worship of idols, spirits, and ancestors; the prevalence of shamans; and the fear of dragons—although such practices coexisted with the belief that Shang Di was supreme.

In *Faith of Our Fathers: God in Ancient China*, Chan Kei Thong points out that many beliefs at odds with classic monotheism have crept into Chinese popular religion. These include the prevalence of idols and the idea of dragons. He draws attention to the ascendancy of the dragon—an object of fear and power among the Chinese and an image of the devil among Christians—as the symbol of the emperor starting with the reign of Qin Shi Huang Di (259–209 BC): "When the Chinese stopped worshipping Shang Di and started to revere and worship the dragon, they fell into the practice of idolatry and became worshippers of a totem."[78]

Nevertheless, the prayers "from the Border Sacrifice, the marked absence of idols or icons at the Altar of Heaven, and the presence at the Altar of only a tablet inscribed with nothing but the name of Shang Di to indicate the object of worship all constitute substantive evidence that the ancient Chinese, like the Hebrews, were solidly aniconic and monotheistic—until the dragon crept in. By the time of Confucius in the 5th century B.C., the state of affairs had so degenerated that the sage longed for a return to the days of the virtuous rulers."[79]

It should be noted that in deviating from monotheism, the Chinese seem to have followed a pattern that was pervasive in ancient religion.

COVENANTS IN CHINESE HISTORY

The Chinese understanding of covenants, a notion so fundamental in the history of Western religion, is also similar to that of Jews and Christians.

After a long drought and famine, the emperor Tang of the Shang Dynasty (1766–1753 BC) offered himself up as a sacrifice to Shang Di and prayed,

"I myself have sinned; the ten thousand people [i.e., all my subjects] have no part [in my sins]. If, however, the ten thousand people have sinned, the offenses must also rest upon me. So, pray, Shang Di, and pray, you spirits, do not let the fact that I am without virtue be a cause for the destruction of so many lives!"[80] Shortly after this prayer, there was (according to historical records) a heavy rain, and the drought ended.

Thong comments that "this remarkable prayer reveals an understanding that the sins of an entire people can be imputed or placed on a single person. Emperor Tang sought to spare his people further tragedy by taking upon himself the full brunt of the consequences of their sins: he was willing to die for his people because he loved them so much."

As Thong observes, Hebrew and Chinese historical records indicate that both nations believed that only a death that was a perfect sacrifice could atone for their sins. In fact, the Chinese idea of covenant is intimately associated with blood. The Chinese word translated as "covenant" is *xue meng*, which literally means, "blood covenant." Thong notes other similarities between the Chinese and the Hebrew ideas of covenant,[81] including imprecatory prayers and oaths, an exchange of gifts, and the indissolubility of the covenant and its renewal.

Ancient China extended its understanding of covenant with God, seeing itself as belonging to God and its emperors ruling with the Mandate of Heaven. "*The Chinese Classics* repeatedly teach that God judges rulers and kingdoms by their morals. His standard of right and wrong is absolute and unquestioned."[82]

The idea of the Mandate of Heaven is still influential in the popular Chinese imagination. An article on the 2008 Sichuan earthquakes titled "Earthquakes and the Mandate of Heaven" noted that the Tangshan earthquake of 1976 came just before the death of Mao Zedong—and the populace had linked the two events "according to the long-held belief that natural catastrophes always foreshadow the death of the reigning emperor."[83]

THE GREAT ANNUAL SACRIFICE

The annual sacrifice to Shang Di performed by the emperors of China for over four millennia was remarkably similar to the sacrificial system found in ancient Judaism. There were three sacrifices offered annually at the Altar of

Heaven. The Border Sacrifice, called such because it took place on the south-
ern border of the empire, was performed on the winter solstice (December)
and was the most important of them all. The emperor had to personally
perform it since it confirmed that he enjoyed the Mandate of Heaven. "The
History of the Han Dynasty," writes Thong, "one of the 26 volumes of the
official dynastic histories dating back to approximately 1100 BC, under-
scores the profound importance of this ceremony: *To an emperor, the most
important thing is to follow the principles of Tian* [heaven]. *In following
Tian, nothing is more important than the sacrifice at the border*."[84]

The rubrics of the ritual were precise. Unblemished firstborn animals
were selected three months before. Closer to the event, the emperor himself
announced it at the altar mound. On the day of the sacrifice, the emperor and
other officials gathered near the altar. The ceremony began with musicians
singing praises about God's creative power, which parallel the verses of
Genesis; the emperor knelt and prostrated himself before Shang Di; officials
offered gems and silks at the altar; the emperor then offered the flesh of
the sacrificial animal to Shang Di on a wooden platter. Other offerings,
prayers, and deeply meaningful musical and dance performances followed.
Finally, there were ceremonies bidding farewell to Shang Di, after which
the sacrificial animal and other offerings were consigned to the flames of a
nearby furnace.

THE TAO

The idea of the Tao or Dao, which has been widely popularized in the West,
is often thought of as mysterious and unfathomable. *Dao* can mean "road,"
"way," "method," and "to speak." According to Thong, the role of Dao in
Chinese belief is that of the Logos—the Word—in Christian thought. While
there have been controversies about the correct translations for "God" in
Chinese, there has been no such dispute over "Logos." "There is no better
translation in Chinese than *Dao*," writes Thong.

> In fact, the word *Dao* is so full of profound meaning that the impact on
> a Chinese reader upon reading the opening words of the Gospel of John
> (tai chu you dao) is far greater than an English reader reading, "In the
> beginning was the Word." . . . A Chinese reader immediately and almost

intuitively grasps the deep and profound meaning captured and contained in *Dao*, which the English word "Word" lacks.

The best-known ancient document on Dao is Lao Zi's *Dao De Jin*. As Thong sees it, Lao Zi refers to Dao as the Creator of heaven and earth much as the Gospel of John speaks of God as Logos. *Dao De Jin* speaks of a reality that is "formless yet complete, existing before heaven and earth without sound, without substance, yet independent and unchanging, ever existing, never failing." While saying he does not know its name, the author says, "If I must give a name, I will say Dao" (*Dao De Jin* 25:1–5).[85] Thong is skeptical about those who find the texts to be obscure or ambiguous. Since Lao Zi uses Dao in the senses of *dao bai* and *dao ming*, which mean to expound and elucidate, Thong argues that the author's intent is to show that Dao wishes to communicate without confusion. Hence the most obvious understanding of the word should be the preferred one.

THE BIRTH AND DEATH OF JESUS IN CHINESE HISTORY

Perhaps the most intriguing connection between Chinese religion and the Judeo-Christian tradition is the apparent correlation between certain significant astral events reported by both. This correlation, highlighted by Chan Kai Thong, emerges from a study of the ancient Chinese astronomical records and their interpretation dating back to the approximate times of the birth and death of Christ.

Like the Hebrews, the Chinese believed that God used the stars to send messages about his interventions in history. Thus, unusual celestial phenomena functioned as divine signs pointing to certain historical events. (They were not believed to cause earthly events, as in astrology.) So important was the study of the heavens that Chinese emperors used to maintain numerous imperial astronomers, fourteen for the night sky and three for the day in one case.

Let's first consider how all this pertains to the birth of Jesus.

- The Gospel of Matthew reports an astral event heralding the birth of Jesus that drew the three Magi.

- According to Thong, historians now say that Jesus was born between 5 and 4 BC. Chinese records show that a major astral event was reported in March–April of 5 BC, which was the second year of the reign of Emperor Xia Ai, who reigned from 7–1 BC:

> In the second month of the second year, the comet was out of Altair for more than 70 days. It is said, "Comets appear to signify the old being replaced by the new." Altair, the sun, the moon and the five stars are in movement to signify the beginning of a new epoch; the beginning of a new year, a new month and a new day. The appearance of this comet undoubtedly symbolizes change. The extended appearance of this comet indicates that this is of great importance.

- This occurrence was considered so significant that the name for that period, the "Second Year of Jian Ping" was briefly changed to the "First Year of Tai Chu," which meant "grand beginning."
- The appearance of the comet was interpreted in terms of the Border Sacrifice. This was because Altair and all phenomena related to it were traditionally associated with the Border Sacrifice.[86]

The other great astral event in the Gospels took place at the crucifixion of Christ, when darkness fell on the land from the sixth to the ninth hour. This would mean an eclipse from noon to about 3:00 PM. Again there is a major tie-in with contemporary Chinese records and interpretations.

- Thong points out that a solar eclipse in Jerusalem would be witnessed as a solar and lunar eclipse in China's imperial capital, which was five hours east: noon to 3:00 PM in Jerusalem would be 5:00 PM to 8:00 PM in China.
- In AD 31, thirty-four years after the appearance of the comet out of Altair, a solar and lunar eclipse was reported during the reign of Emperor Guang Wu (AD 25–57).
- The contemporary Chinese astronomical records state that "in the day of Gui Hai, the last day of the month, there was a solar eclipse. [The emperor] avoided the Throne Room, suspended all military activities, and did not handle official business for five days. And he proclaimed,

'My poor character has caused this calamity, that the sun and the moon were veiled. I am fearful and trembling. What can I say? . . . Anyone who presents a memorial is not allowed to mention the word 'holy.'"[87]

- Another document related to the same event proclaimed: "Summer, fourth month [of the year], on the day of Ren Wu, the imperial edict reads, 'Yin and Yang have mistakenly switched, and the sun and moon were eclipsed. The sins of all the people are now on one man. [The emperor] proclaims pardon to all under heaven."[88]

- The most extraordinary of all the contemporary interpretations of that two-thousand-year-old event was this commentary in the record of the Latter Han Dynasty, "Eclipse on the day of Gui Hai, Man from heaven died."[89]

Thong points out that the emperor's acknowledgment of his sinfulness and acceptance of responsibility for the grave event was unprecedented in Chinese history. Yet more extraordinary was his insight that this event meant that "the sins of all the people [including the emperor's] are now on one man."[90] The man from heaven.

CHAPTER 8

Greece and the Near Eastern Societies

From a religious standpoint, the diverse societies that flourished in ancient Egypt, Mesopotamia, Greece, and Rome are best known for their gods and goddesses and associated idols and rituals. This, of course, fits in with the general pattern of a descent from the sense of the transcendent characteristic of the hunter-gatherers to a predictable polytheism in pastoral and urban settings. It is almost as if God is brought "down to earth" and turned into a thousand terrestrial gods. There were occasional revolts against polytheism—Akhneton, who briefly introduced monotheism in Egypt, and Aristotle and Plato, the greatest thinkers of Greece, who gave the first philosophical articulation of monotheism (although both believed that matter was eternal along with God).

But there is another side to this story, which is of particular relevance to our journey of exploration. It is the persistent idea of incarnate gods who died and the all-pervasive role of sacrifice in these societies (in common with virtually every other ancient society). Sir James Frazer and his followers mistakenly assumed that these gods rose from the dead. What later research showed, as J. Z. Smith remarks, is "that the majority of the gods so denoted appear to have died but not returned; there is death but no rebirth or resurrection."[91] Melquart (Syria), Adonis (Greece and Near East), Osiris (Egypt), and Dumuzi-Tammuz (Mesopotamia) were all gods who came to earth and died.

In addition to this notion of a dying god, sacrifice played an all-pervasive role in ancient societies. Concerning the nature and significance of these sacrifices, we have the monumental works of Walter Burkert, the great modern authority on Greek mythology.

Burkert makes the striking point that there was a fundamental similitude about the understanding of sacrifice in the Near Eastern and Mediterranean world: "Animal sacrifice was an all-pervasive reality in the ancient world," he writes.

The Greeks did not perceive much difference between the substance of their customs, and those of the Egyptians and Phoenicians, Babylonians and Persians, Etruscans and Romans, though ritual details varied greatly among the Greeks themselves. One peculiarity of Greek sacrifice presents a problem for the modern historian: the combination of a fire-altar and a blood-rite, of burning and eating, corresponds only with the burnt offerings of the Old Testament. . . . And yet whatever complexities, layers, and changes in cultural tradition underlie the individual peculiarities, it is astounding, details aside, to observe the similarity of action and experience from Athens to Jerusalem and on to Babylon.[92]

Burkert notes that in all of these societies "sacrifice is a way to deal with gods."[93] The god was believed to be present where the sacrifice was performed. Another dimension of sacrifice, found in the rituals and myths of the Hittites, Greeks, and Romans, was that of the scapegoat. In the Old Testament this is associated with a ritual performed on the Day of Atonement (Yom Kippur). Lots are thrown over two goats in the sanctuary, one being for Yahweh (the Lord) and the other for Azazel (sometimes described as the leader of the rebellious angels). The first (for Yahweh) is sacrificed with a purifying blood ceremony. The second is led to the high priest, who places his hands on its head and by vocal proclamation transfers the sins of Israel onto the goat. It is then taken to the desert and thrown down a ravine. The evil of the people of Israel is transferred to the goat. "The evil transferred is 'sin' in Leviticus."[94] The same scapegoat tradition is found in the Greeks under the name of *pharmakos*. In Greek religion, a common response to catastrophe was to expel and sometimes stone or execute selected persons as a means of purification. The human scapegoat was called a pharmakos.

So, having surveyed many of the world's ancient religions up to this point, what is the significance of sacrifice in the religious history of humanity? Burkert sees sacrifice as tied somehow to evolutionary history. But this is speculation, and implausible speculation at best. The concepts of atonement and protection that are intrinsic to sacrifice throughout the world belong to a plane that transcends the biological. The very word "sacrifice" is derived from Latin *sacrificium*, which means "making sacred," and the consecration of an offering in sacrifice is the window through which the secular enters the sacred. Even Burkert admits that sacrifice "is the basic experience of the 'sacred.'"[95] Interestingly, all contracts and alliances in Israel, Greece, and Rome required sacrifice in order to be ratified.

The fact of the matter is this: we are sacrificers. We seek atonement and protection through sacrifice. Sacrifice is offered in atonement, and to atone means essentially to be at one with the divine and thus to receive all attendant blessings. It is made in reparation for violating the sacred order. It is the ultimate act of worship. If indeed there is a divine direction to human history, then the universal urge to sacrifice as well as the idea of a dying incarnate god can be seen as preparations for an event that affects all of history and all of humanity.

This case has been made by numerous Christian apologists who have argued that God prepared the minds and psyches of those who lived in pre-Christian times for the coming of Christ. In different rituals they shared intuitions, as Odo Casel put it, of "participation in the lives of the gods, who in some way or other had appeared in human form, and taken part in the pain and happiness of mortal men."[96]

CHAPTER 9

The Israelites

Our journey brings us now to a people with a religion that was unique to ancient times, the Jews. It was unique not simply with respect to the content of what they believed. This was distinctive to be sure, although many prominent themes in ancient Judaism were echoed in other religions. But it was the platform on which the divine-human interaction took place that was unique. All other religions had an ahistorical understanding of God's actions relative to humanity: the "sacred time" in which their gods and goddesses operated was not continuous with the temporal history of humankind. In these religions there were sages and teachers who spoke divinely inspired words of wisdom and sacrifices that "connected" the human to the divine, but the supreme Godhead was transcendent and hidden. When it came to Israel, the mind of the Most High directly shared its thoughts, and the will of the Almighty acted visibly in the course of everyday events in the life of a people.

It is precisely on this point that ancient Judaism went beyond all previous conceptions of religion. The Israelites saw themselves as humanity's point of contact with the Holy of Holies, the divinely chosen channel of celestial communication and redemptive action. Of all the world's nations and races, none had claimed direct interaction with God as did the people of Israel—and this not on the scale of decades or centuries but over thousands of years. No other racial and religious group has managed to stay together and survive for as long as the Jewish nation while holding fast to the same beliefs, values, and practices.

The empires of Babylonians and Persians, Greeks and Romans had come and gone. The Israelites who lived under them without a habitat of their own, on the other hand, continued to maintain their theocentric identity.

Theirs was a reign not of force but of ideas. From the prophets, with their moral leadership, and the lawgivers, with their humanitarian principles, to Marx, Freud, Einstein, Wittgenstein, and hundreds of other thinkers, the ideas of Israel's children have had a remarkable impact on history, be it good or bad.

The greatest of these ideas was the conviction that their God was spiritual, not material, and that they were bound in an irrevocable partnership with this unseen deity. Sigmund Freud, no friend of theism or religion, noted that it was the intellectual abstraction required to sustain belief in an invisible God that enabled the Jews to achieve distinction in domains where abstract models of experience were essential—from mathematics and science to literature. In any case, unlike any other people, the Jewish people built both their own communal identity and individual lives around direct divine instructions. By its very existence, the Israelite family is a testimony to a power and a presence that transcends time and space.

Israel's history was a story of supernatural covenants and archetypal leaders, sacrifice and sacrilege, exodus and exile. Above all, as the Israelites saw the matter, it was the tale of God's own family.

The historical and theological patrimony of the Jewish people is laid out in the Hebrew Bible, what Christians call the Old Testament. The first and obvious question we should ask in the context of our voyage of discovery is whether or not the events recorded in the text took place. Here we have to say that believers and critics have made equal and opposite mistakes. Believers seek to "prove" the historicity of the biblical records by referring to archaeological discoveries of artifacts and inscriptions, while critics attempt to "disprove" its claims to veracity by launching speculative free-for-alls when archaeological evidence is absent.

Both forget that we are talking of events that are said to have taken place to an obscure group of people living in inhospitable regions in the shadow of great empires over three to four thousand years ago. We might find a few stray inscriptions or the remnant of a pillar or wall, but that cannot possibly prove anything, just as their absence proves nothing one way or another. Certainly, to the extent that evidence turns up for cities and empires mentioned in the Hebrew Bible, we can credibly draw a correlation. But if we do not find any such evidence, this does not prove their nonexistence. As the saying goes, absence of evidence is not evidence of absence.

Ultimately our basis for accepting these records as on the whole factual is our appraisal of their relation to the lived experience of the Jewish people. The Passover Festival, the Day of Atonement (Yom Kippur), and the Feast of Tabernacles (Sukkoth) are not simply ceremonial observances but dynamic "reconnections" with specific divine actions in history, actions that, in fact, constitute the identity of the people of Israel.

As such, these reconnections testify to the meeting points of the eternal and the temporal; they are not simply affirmations of timeless myths or the teachings of a great prophet. Their point of departure is a God acting in history—their history! The identity of the Jewish people as "chosen" comes from the obedience of Abraham, the mediation of Moses, the passion of David, and the travails and tribulations of a nation in exile.

The history of Israel as a people begins around 1900 BC, with a covenant, a partnership agreement, between Abraham and God: "I will maintain my covenant with you and your descendants after you throughout the ages as an everlasting pact, to be your God and the God of your descendants after you" (Gen. 17:7).

Covenants call forth blessings and curses. To break a covenant is to invite its curses; to uphold it means blessings. Even before Abraham, God had made covenants with Adam and Noah. To Adam he promised that one of his seed would someday win victory over the serpent. To Noah he promised that he would never again wipe out the world, a promise sealed by the sign of the rainbow. The covenant with Abraham, however, was with a specific family, which became a tribe and then a nation. The covenant was further codified, with Moses as mediator, first on Mount Sinai, around 1210 BC, and then again before the people of Israel entered the Promised Land: "These are the words of the covenant which the LORD ordered Moses to make with the Israelites in the land of Moab, in addition to the covenant which he made with them at Horeb" (Deut. 28:69).

The experience of the Jewish people is inextricably connected to these covenantal events. The themes of God's creation and providence, of obedience and the consequence of disobedience, that we find in Genesis 1–3 resonate through the rest of the Hebrew Bible. The archetype of obedience here is Abraham, who is blessed above all precisely because he obeyed God without counting the cost: "I swear by myself, declares the LORD . . . in your descendants all the nations of the earth shall find blessing—all this because you obeyed my command" (Gen. 22:16, 18). The varying fates of the people of Israel at different stages in their history were directly correlated to their obedience to God.

All this makes it evident that theology cannot avoid history when it comes to the story of the Jews. The historical basis of this story determines its theological relevance. But our present journey is concerned with a comparative study of the ancient world religions, and any detailed historical analysis would be a detour from the straight path to our destination.

IS IT HISTORY?

So is the Jewish story, as told in the Old Testament, really history? It can hardly be denied that those who want to explain the historical reality and identity of Israel have to at least consider her self-understanding. We must ultimately say that the claims of the Jewish people as they relate to the acts of God in their history cannot be verified or disconfirmed by the studies of exegetes, historians, or archaeologists. Simply put, we are dealing with the testimony of a people as it relates to their genesis, history, and identity. It is a testimony not simply of battles, journeys, and leaders but of specific interactions with an unseen master, involving directives, agreements, and promises. The testimony, in fact, was not simply a matter of a written text but included a temple, which was the locus of divine action, and a priesthood, which "acted" on behalf of the nation of Israel. Today we have neither the temple nor the priesthood—only the text and the living tradition. At the very least, the text bears witness to the glory that was Israel and offers a potent explanation for the mysterious subsistence of a people that saw itself as chosen.

UNIQUE FEATURES OF THE JEWISH STORY

We should note also that there are three dimensions of the history of the Jews in the Hebrew Bible that are without previous parallel in the history of religions. Two of these have been superbly explicated by the philosopher and historian of science Stanley Jaki.

Jaki points out that the judges and prophets of Israel were "a curious feature of Jewish history and also a unique feature within the framework of the history of religions." We are dealing with a succession of "men who appeared out of nowhere again and again with the same stern message from God." This is baffling because the message of the prophets "was so contrary to the preferences of human nature," and so the repeated appearance of such message-bearers is inexplicable on a purely human level.[97]

The second dimension was the command to love God. "For the first time in the history of religions," writes Jaki, "God was spoken of as a being not merely to be feared or revered, but to be loved and immensely more than any other being." The supreme commandment to "love the LORD, your God, with all your heart, and with all your soul, and with all your strength" (Deut. 6:5) is a persistent theme in Hebrew history. "From Moses to the last prophet this commandment stood in the center of all religious instruction and warning given to Jews."[98]

Third, we have the hard fact of Jewish monotheism. Recent critics have pointed to polytheistic inscriptions dating back to Old Testament times. But given the Old Testament accounts of the Israelites' frequent flirtations with idolatry and polytheism, pagan and polytheistic inscriptions should be the rule rather than the exception. It is astounding that critics would profess bewilderment over finding a few instances of precisely those deviations that we are warned about in the texts. What is truly shocking is how monotheism not only survived the constant onslaught of polytheism but also emerged finally as the universal and normative teaching.

Some have tried to explain away the clear evidence for Jewish monotheism with implausible theories of collective amnesia. But as Richard Bauckham points out, "The essential element in what I have called Jewish monotheism, the element that makes it a kind of monotheism, is not the denial of the existence of other 'gods,' but an understanding of the uniqueness of YHWH that puts him in a class of his own, a wholly different class from any other heavenly or supernatural beings, even if these are called 'gods.' I call this YHWH's transcendent uniqueness."[99]

THE STARTLING NATURE OF JEWISH MONOTHEISM

Both critics who claim that Israel tolerated polytheism and even some defenders of her monotheism forget one crucial fact. It is the simply unprecedented character of the monotheism that is native to the Jewish people. To be sure, polytheism and idol worship had a hypnotic hold on the human psyche. It was a hold that, per the biblical record, only God could remove.

And herein lies the unprecedented nature of Jewish monotheism: the Hebrew Bible is an account of the interaction between the divine mind and a specific race of people over a period of thousands of years. And the crux of this interaction is the deity's insistence on monotheism. ("Thou shalt have no other gods before me.") This insistence is absolute, so much so that idolatry and polytheism are punishable by death. The fate of the nation of Israel depends on their faithfulness to this command—and the history of Israel is just as much a history of punishment for deviation from monotheism as it is anything else.

Nowhere in ancient history do we find anything remotely similar. God is telling a people that they shall have no other god. The Shema is to be recited daily: "Hear, O Israel: the LORD our God, the LORD is one!" (Deut. 6:4). Monotheism had to be drummed into the human mind because of the constant temptation to wander away. And clearly the "treatment" worked, for the Jews by the time of Jesus were as staunchly monotheist as it is possible for a people to be. In point of fact, at the end of the day, the Jewish people became the world's greatest heralds of monotheism. This fact alone is extraordinary enough to call for a transcendent explanation.

A STORY IN SEARCH OF AN ENDING?

By the second millennium of the history of Israel, an intriguing new theme began to appear in the preaching of the prophets. In Isaiah, Jeremiah, and Ezekiel, as also in Micah, Zechariah, Hosea, Daniel, and Malachi, we see prophecies of a new and universal covenant, a new mediator for all human-ity and a never-ending and perfect sacrifice. Chapters seven through eleven of Isaiah were in fact referred to as the Book of Emmanuel because of its message of a divine visitation, "God with us."

Of particular importance was the role of the new mediator, who was also known as the Messiah. The Jewish writer Rabbi Shmuley Boteach has observed that "belief in the coming of the Messiah is more central to Judaism than even the observance of the Sabbath or Yom Kippur." Belief in his coming is "the cardinal principle of Jewish faith."[100]

The promise of a new covenant is laid out by the prophet Jeremiah:

> The days are coming, says the LORD, when I will make a new covenant with the house of Israel and the house of Judah. It will not be like the covenant I made with their fathers the day I took them by the hand to lead them forth from the land of Egypt; for they broke my covenant and I had to show myself their master, says the LORD. But this is the covenant which I will make with the house of Israel after those days, says the LORD. I will place my law within them, and write it upon their hearts; I will be their God, and they shall be my people. (Jer. 31:31–33)

In parallel, starting in Genesis, we see the numerous prophecies of a new mediator, the Messiah:

- "The scepter shall never depart from Judah, or the mace from between his legs, While tribute is brought to him, and he receives the people's homage" (Gen. 49:10).

- "And when your time comes and you rest with your ancestors, I will raise up your heir after you, sprung from your loins, and I will make his kingdom firm. It is he who shall build a house for my name. And I will make his royal throne firm forever" (2 Sam. 7:12–13).

- "For you said, 'My love is established forever; my loyalty will stand as long as the heavens. I have made a covenant with my chosen one; I have sworn to David my servant: I will make your dynasty stand forever and establish your throne through all ages'" (Ps. 89:3–5).

- "Behold, the days are coming, says the LORD, when I will raise up a righteous shoot to David; As king he shall reign and govern wisely, he shall do what is just and right in the land. In his days Judah shall be saved, Israel shall dwell in security. This is the name they give him: 'The LORD our justice'" (Jer. 23:5–6).

- "Lo, I am sending my messenger to prepare the way before me. And suddenly there will come to the temple the LORD whom you seek. And the messenger of the covenant whom you desire. Yes, he is coming, says the LORD of hosts. But who will endure the day of his coming? And who can stand when he appears?" (Mal. 3:1–2).

- "As the visions during the night continued, I saw One like a son of man coming, on the clouds of heaven; when he reached the Ancient One and was presented before him, he received dominion, glory, and kingship; nations and peoples of every language serve him. His dominion is an everlasting dominion that shall not be taken away, his kingship shall not be destroyed" (Dan. 7:13–14).

- "For a child is born to us, a son is given us; upon his shoulder dominion rests. They name him Wonder-Counselor, God-Hero, Father-Forever, Prince of Peace. His dominion is vast and forever peaceful, From David's throne, and over his kingdom, which he confirms and sustains By judgment and justice, both now and forever" (Isa. 9:5–6).

- "But you, Bethlehem-Ephrathah too small to be among the clans of Judah, From you shall come forth for me one who is to be ruler in Israel; Whose origin is from of old, from ancient times" (Mic. 5:1).

- "Therefore the Lord himself will give you this sign: the virgin shall be with child, and bear a son, and shall name him Immanuel" (Isa. 7:14).

- "Rejoice heartily, O daughter Zion, shout for joy, O daughter Jerusalem! See, your king shall come to you; a just savior is he, Meek, and riding on an ass, on a colt, the foal of an ass" (Zech. 9:9).

- "But a shoot shall sprout from the stump of Jesse, and from his roots a bud shall blossom. The spirit of the LORD shall rest upon him: a spirit of wisdom and of understanding, A spirit of counsel and of strength, a spirit of knowledge and of fear of the LORD, and his delight shall be the fear of the LORD" (Isa. 11:1–3).

These prophecies of the Messiah are accompanied by premonitions of a mysterious death. It is a death suffered on our behalf by "a lamb led to the slaughter," who is "the only son." And yet he will be revived after two days and raised up on the third:

"He was pierced for our offenses, crushed for our sins, Upon him was the chastisement that makes us whole, by his stripes we were healed. . . . Like a lamb led to the slaughter or a sheep before the shearers, he was silent and opened not his mouth" (Isa. 53:5, 7).

"Many bulls surround me; fierce bulls of Bashan encircle me. They open their mouths against me, lions that rend and roar. Like water my life drains away; all my bones grow soft. My heart has become like wax, it melts away within me. . . . They divide my garments among them; for my clothing they cast lots" (Ps. 22:13–15, 19).

"Insult has broken my heart, and I am weak; I looked for compassion, but there was none, for comforters, but found none. Instead they put gall in my food; for my thirst they gave me vinegar" (Ps. 69:21–22).

"I will pour out on the house of David and on the inhabitants of Jerusalem a spirit of grace and petition; and they shall look on him whom they have thrust through, and they shall mourn for him as one mourns for an only son, and they shall grieve over him as one grieves over a first-born" (Zech. 12:10).

"Come, let us return to the LORD, For it is he who has rent, but he will heal us; he has struck us, but he will bind our wounds. He will revive us after two days; on the third day he will raise us up, to live in his presence" (Hos. 6:1–2).

A UNIVERSAL OFFERING

"'For from the rising of the sun even to its setting, my name will be great among the nations, and in every place incense is going to be offered to My name, and a grain offering that is pure; for My name will be great among the nations,' says the LORD of hosts" (Mal. 1:11 NASB).

By its very nature as a narrative of promise and prophecy, the Jewish story seems to point to an ending. Moreover, as the plot thickens, the spectators themselves become protagonists.

CHAPTER 10

The Christ Connection

Our brief journey through the ancient world religions shows how a case can be made for seeing in the religious history of humanity a pattern that comes to a climax in the life of Jesus of Nazareth. Our next task, of course, is to study the life of Jesus and see what we can say with any certainty about its historical basis and theological implications. But prior to that, it seems clear that on the level of thought and structure, trajectory and configuration, there is congruence and correspondence between the story of Jesus and the thematic thrust of the primary pre-Christian religions. The primordial peoples who preceded all the organized religions and belief systems believed in a supreme God, a Father, to whom they turned for all their needs. They were also driven by the need to perform sacrifice in expiation and propitiation.

When we come to the first systematically organized religions, those of the Indians, Chinese, and Persians, every one of them, in their own distinctive ways, were alerted to an impending event of great import centered on sacrifice and atonement and salvation: the sacrifice of Prajapathi and the redemption of humanity; the Border Sacrifice to Shang Di and the astral occurrences that seem to have accompanied a birth and death in a remote land; the sacrifice of Haoma and the prophecy of the Saoshyant. The Mediterranean mystery religions were all about sacrifice and the incarnation of deity. And, finally, we have the Jewish nation, who embodied in their own history the reality of sin and salvation, sacrifice and atonement, divine visitation and the promise of resurrection.

All of this leads to the extraordinary possibility that Jesus ("Savior") is the fulfillment not simply of the Jewish "idea" but of the beliefs and aspirations of the Indians, Chinese, and Persians, of the primordial tribes and the Mediterranean mystery religions. Salvation, as universally understood, is liberation from sin and its consequences. Such liberation can come only from atonement. Atonement in turn is possible only through sacrifice and ultimately a perfect sacrifice. This is the thought pattern of humanity, and it also happens to be the life pattern of Jesus. Moreover, it was not simply his life and teaching that is directly relevant to the religious history before him but also the salvific structure he taught and instituted: the divinizing sacraments and the Eucharistic sacrifice.

This would mean that nothing in religious history is a coincidence, nothing is an isolated atomic fact, nothing is unrelated to the phenomenon that is Jesus. The ideas that emerged in the heart of *Homo religiosus*, the ideas of the need for sacrifice and a savior, of a nameless tragedy where a god perished, of salvation and expiation and redemption, of some kind of afterlife that is related to one's deeds, were neither random events nor illusions of the imagination.

This is not to say that God "planned" the evil that men do or the savagery and perversion of many of the religious beliefs and practices of Homo sapiens across millennia. Rather, we are given a story of human choice on the one side and the divine response on the other. It is also a story of a God who plants seeds of light even in the darkest hearts. It is a story of sin and its consequences—punishment and destruction, but also reparation. It is a story of God, who wishes to save—and of a humanity that desperately desires salvation in the midst of darkness and despair.

These workings of providence in history prepare us for the next leg of the journey—the study of the divine humanized.

PART TWO

THE JESUS PHENOMENON

Introduction

The upshot of our journey thus far is this: in one way or another, the great pre-Christian world religions converge on a common set of themes. But does this convergence mean anything? The Christian claim is that these themes come to a head in the life and teachings of Jesus of Nazareth. It is this claim we will consider in the next leg of our journey. We will study what historians, theologians, and skeptics have said about him; what his followers proclaimed; and what we can know from texts and other relevant sources.

BEGINNINGS

Aside from a marginal mention in the works of the historians Tacitus and Josephus, the earliest textual sources of information on Jesus are the Letters of Paul and the Gospels. The life of Jesus as narrated in the Gospels is spare. It is basically as follows.

An angel announced to his mother that she would have a son conceived of the Holy Spirit whose kingdom is to be everlasting. The child was to be born into humble surroundings.

When he was presented in the temple, a great sage announced that "my eyes have seen your salvation, which you [God] prepared in sight of all the peoples" (Lk. 2:30–31). His parents had to flee with the child to Egypt to escape the murderous wrath of Herod. They returned to Nazareth upon the death of Herod, and we see him next at the age of twelve when he is "lost" in the temple, where he astonishes the elders with his wisdom.

The next appearance of Jesus shows him choosing his twelve apostles, being tested by the devil, and performing his first miracle at a wedding, where he turns water into wine. To the crowds that follow him, he proclaims the coming of the kingdom of God, the path to the blessings of God, and the need for being born again.

He does not mince words in rebuking even the powerful Pharisees while also exposing the evil embedded in the human heart. He often teaches through parables. When requested he enables the blind to see and the paralyzed to walk and even restores the dead to life. He exorcises evil spirits.

He institutes Peter as head of his church after the latter's famous profession of faith in Jesus as the Son of the living God. He tells the apostles that he will have to lay down his life but that he will rise again. On the final night of his life, he dines with the apostles and announces that the bread of which they partake is his body and the wine his blood; they are instructed to continue this meal in remembrance of him. After agonizing hours of prayer in the Garden of Gethsemane, he is seized by the soldiers of the high priest and hauled to a trial before the Pharisees and then before Pilate, the Roman prefect. He is sentenced to death by crucifixion.

He is made to carry his cross to the top of Calvary, where he is crucified between two thieves. On the third day, the women who followed him and then the apostles discover that his tomb is empty. Shortly after, they encounter him. He enjoins them to baptize all nations and after forty days ascends to heaven.

Now, hundreds of millions of people form their ideas of Jesus entirely from this portrayal in the Gospels. But historians and New Testament scholars have their own ways of studying the story of Jesus. Unlike the hard sciences, however, this kind of study inevitably relies on subjective preferences and perspectives. So the resultant conclusions range far and wide. Consequently, the history of New Testament studies often becomes like a game of musical chairs in which each chair, including the last one, is progressively removed, after which a new game starts.

FACT, FABRICATION, OR FAITH?

In reviewing the Gospel accounts of the life of Jesus, we are obviously led to ask: To what extent are these sources reliable? Are they statements of fact, fabrication, or faith? These are the questions that have driven the three-century-old discipline of New Testament criticism.

Now, these options are clearly not mutually exclusive. For instance, one could say that the Gospels are a mixture of faith, fact, and fabrication. Indeed, there are some who affirm this even while holding that the New Testament is divinely inspired.

It must be admitted first that no methodology is going to tell us what is historic fact, what pious belief, and what simply an invention serving a theological purpose. All that we have at our disposal from a critical standpoint are a handful of a priori methods (i.e., subjective presumptions) and criteria and an ever-ready stock of speculation.

Neither the skeptic who says it's all a fabrication nor the literalist who says it's all historical and theological fact can be proven wrong if all we have is arbitrary a priori speculation. This is not to say that we should ignore the work of the New Testament critics. It is simply a warning that we should manage our expectations and, in a sense, hedge our bets. Those who put all their eggs in the latest critical theory or speculative reconstruction will soon have to start from scratch, as today's daring idea inevitably becomes yesterday's cliché.

A fundamental question is whether or not our only avenue of accurate information about Jesus is the New Testament as interpreted by the critics. Our answer here is no, although we will give the New Testament the right kind of "reading" in the sense that we will treat it as neither a textbook of history nor a textbook of doctrine. It is a collection of messages from witnesses that should be studied within the context of a wide variety of testimonies and testifiers relating to Jesus. It is the integrated whole of all these varied communications that is to be evaluated for its veracity. Clearly the New Testament narratives are a central element, but historically and theologically they must be situated in the context of the whole.

So we deconstruct and reconstruct and ask: Who was the author of each New Testament document? When was it written? What was the author's intent? What sources did he use? Can books outside the New Testament canon such as the Gnostic "gospels" shed any historical light?

It should be said that an exclusive focus on the text assumes mistakenly that texts themselves can demonstrate truths. Let us say Jesus wrote about his mission and message and his apostles kept daily records of his actions including his death and resurrection—and that the documents with these writings could be authenticated as originating from the authors. Would this "prove" that Jesus existed or that he actually performed miracles? By no means. Self-professed claims and eyewitness accounts can be created out of thin air. Just because someone gives a first-person account of events, individuals, and teachings, we have no reason to believe the account is true—either today or two thousand years ago.

Likewise, let's imagine that the imperial historians of the time had written extensively about Jesus and included it in their official accounts of the era. Would this give us airtight proof? Clearly not, considering that there have been raging controversies about dramatically variant historical accounts of the same event or person that were written at the time of the event or while the person was alive. Many works are written to disparage enemies or praise leaders rather than chronicle facts. Even in the present we have historians producing radically different biographies of prominent personalities of our day. The point of all this is that we have to be realistic about what historical studies can deliver: even what is considered ideal from the historian's standpoint cannot tell us theological truth or establish worldviews.

BEGINNING WITH THE PHENOMENON

This takes us back to the earlier consideration of Jesus as phenomenon. What we have is a proclamation that includes not just written documents but also the transformation of lives and, crucially, the existence of a society that seeks to make Jesus present here and now. Embedded in its very being— in liturgies and sacraments, doctrines and devotions, lifestyles and life-directions—is the Jesus we read about in chapter and verse.

We would do well to consider the behavior of the first followers of Jesus. We see proclamation to the point of martyrdom, liturgies that lie at the center of everyday life, baptisms, synods, councils, a going forth to the world, and a constant sense of the world of departed souls and supernatural realities. Behavior and action incarnated what Christians believed and proclaimed.

The New Testament as Scripture came much later: it was in a sense complementary. There was no question in anyone's mind as to what happened, what had to be believed. The modus operandi was not one of reading a particular biblical text and then deciding, "Okay, we're going to believe this and do this from now on." It was the other way around. They already believed, and their belief was embedded in all they did. The Bible as we know it today came later.

We are not dealing with a court trial where the prosecution is made up of skeptics and the defense attorneys of apologists while the witnesses are the Gospels and epistles and the reader is judge and jury. This manifestly is not how the first Christians saw things. Rather, we have people whose lives were transformed, who introduced a new way of living, who saw all things through the lens of Eucharist and liturgy, sacrament and proclamation.

All this means that we have to move from being text-centered to being act-centered. Jesus was not just Word but also Act: he claimed not simply to be Truth but also Way and Life. His actions were as significant as his words in telling us who he was and what his mission was.

By the same token, we have to consider what his followers did. Agents, not texts, have to be at the center. If we ask, did he exist? did it happen? and then try to find an answer by reference to texts, our line of thought is artificial and futile. We cannot determine what really happened from mining texts alone. The texts of course transmit accounts of acts, but the texts, in this case, have to be illuminated through acts that continue into the present; and the transmission itself is an act. We know the acts of Jesus through the acts of his apostles and the acts of his church—this is the dynamic reality that confronts us through the centuries.

Everything centers on these acts:

- Jesus is born.
- Jesus announces the kingdom of God.
- Jesus is acclaimed as Messiah.
- Jesus is put to death, and his death is presented by the Gospel writers as a salvific sacrifice.
- Jesus rises from the dead.
- Jesus asks his followers to act through the Eucharist, baptism, and proclamation.

The disciples did not seek to prove that Jesus was historical or that the Gospels say this or that. They baptized and administered the sacraments, they worshiped and preached.

It is only when we understand the followers of Jesus as agents that we can grasp the origin and nature of Christianity. In this context, Daniel Schowalter, in an essay in *The Oxford History of the Biblical World*, presents us with a startling fact: "The combination of intentional proselytizing by individuals like Paul and the natural movement of believers meant that by the middle of the first century churches had been established in most of the major cities of the empire, including Rome."[101]

This piece of information is startling because the debates about the existence of Jesus and the historicity of the Gospels pale in significance before the fact that—within two decades of Jesus' reported death—his teaching was proclaimed at the very heart of the Roman Empire. Those pondering and debating whether or not Jesus existed seem almost like philosophers expounding the idea that motion is an illusion while ignoring the automobiles racing all around them.

CHAPTER 11

From Explanation to Encounter

Once we recognize that our journey concerns not simply a series of texts but a phenomenon, we have to tune our thought processes in tandem. It was the failure to apply such tuning that produced much of the chaos today associated with New Testament criticism. The moral of this particular story is that we have to structure our methodologies appropriately to the subject under study. It should be said here that, paradoxically, many modern Jewish thinkers, ranging from Albert Einstein to Sholem Asch, have led the way (as we shall see) in looking at Jesus not simply as a series of texts but as a phenomenon!

We should adopt an approach that is tailored to the nature of the phenomenon before us. Ideally this calls for a tracking system that remains true to the need for both independent intellectual investigation and openness to all relevant data. We begin by assembling all the available data, then proceed to explanations and counterexplanations for the data, and end by seeking a greater understanding of the most plausible explanation. This greater understanding is followed by the discovery of the truth suggested by understanding and, finally, an encounter with the reality that underlies the truth. So, as we can see in figure 11.1, we have *assembly*, *explanation*, *understanding*, *discovery*, and *encounter*.

GUARDRAILS

Our tracking system has five guardrails that will keep us from straying from the straight and narrow path. First, let us remember that theologians and other professional academics are disinclined to admit anything "different" about the subject of their study, anything that transcends what is natural and ordinary.

Second, as we have noted, historical records on their own, no matter how reliable and accurate, cannot "prove" anything about the identity of Jesus. A record is nothing more than a memory. We need something more as a witness.

FIGURE 11.1

Assembly

Relevant data on the phenomenon:

- New Testament records
- Contemporaneous historical writings
- Jewish beliefs and practices of the day
- Lives of the apostles
- Beliefs and practices of the early church: texts of early liturgies and prayers; publications of popes, synods, councils, and church fathers; accounts of miracles, visions, and other mystical experiences
- Belief structures of major pre-Christian religions

Explanation

Proposed explanatory claims and counter-claims for the phenomenon. Criteria:

- Claims that consider phenomenon in its wholeness and integrity, going beyond canonical and Gnostic Gospels, since a hypothesis cannot ignore or suppress facts it purports to explain.
- Textual sources and the witness to the phenomenon in its wholeness: claim as embodied in texts, councils, liturgies, the teaching church.
- Skeptical and traditional accounts.

If explanation is plausible, you move to understanding.

Understanding

An entire universe of ideas, events, and facts have to hang together for the standard explanation to "work." The postulation of an explanation is simply the first step in a journey of connecting the dots and uncovering underlying patterns. If the best explanation of all the events and realities under consideration is x, then we have to understand what x implies and how x can make sense. If it is claimed that Jesus is divine and human, consider how this ties in with our idea of God. How can such a "combination" even be possible? How does this tie in with the religious experience of humanity and the history of the Jewish people?

Discovery

Data, explanation, and understanding set the stage for discovery and encounter. These are free choices. They involve the will as much as they do the intellect. To discover is to take a leap; to encounter is to open one's heart. Neither can be compelled or magically produced. You have to open your eyes to see the hand of God, and you have to reach out to touch him if you want to feel his presence.

Once you understand the big picture, you have to decide what this implies for you and the world. It is a matter of seeing the divine mind active in history and especially in the life and mission of Jesus and his followers.

If the explanation "checks out," you face the very real possibility that Jesus was indeed who he said he was.

This means *everything* is seen differently—your world, your priorities, your life. *To discover is to see.*

Encounter

The final step is to move from knowing the truth about the divine to encountering it. This too is a personal act.

It is, in fact, interpersonal, for to encounter is to interact with the Other. It is the climax and consummation of a process that began as information-gathering. We turn from examining the evidence to examining ourselves. Do we personally reach out to the divine once we discover its presence and action? From studying the phenomenon, we move to experiencing it.

Can there be proof, can there be certainty? We respond that it is encounter, it is seeing, it is knowing. But it is also believing. "In a very real sense, I perceive God who reveals himself; but I perceive him in such sort that I am not dispensed from believing that he reveals himself. To perceive the reality of the revelation and to perceive the obligation to believe are one and the same thing.'"

*Henri Bouillard, *The Logic of Faith* (New York: Sheed and Ward, 1967), 21–22.

Third, although inadequate on their own, records are still indispensable for our purposes.

If God did reveal himself in history, it is reasonable to believe that he would have to preserve the memory of his actions in a text and/or a tradition of some kind. And, of course, the text and the tradition would need some kind of authority. A work of history by a Tacitus or some modern historian would have no special authority. Only a living witness could provide this kind of authority.

Fourth, we have to approach this inquiry from a radically skeptical standpoint. To be radically skeptical is to be skeptical especially of the skeptics. Is it possible that the skeptics in their skepticism are blind to what is obvious? The history of philosophy and theology show that speculative flights of fancy take precedence over hard facts of experience—although fashionable thought-forms are regularly replaced by newer variations as their vacuity becomes obvious to the next generation. Above all, our study cannot be influenced or directed by the speculation of scholars or by the kind of conspiracy-theory thinking found in books like *The Da Vinci Code* and *The Passover Plot*. Speculation without any grounding in data is to be avoided simply because there is no assurance that it has any bearing at all, and in general it is a waste of time and energy because there is no way to verify its postulates. Conspiracy theories will be rejected because, to work, they must explain away facts that are obvious. (As an aside, let us note that never before has there been as much insanity and fraud as today in the conspiracy theory business. From *The Jesus Papers* and *The Da Vinci Code* to *The Gospel of Judas* and *The Jesus Tomb*, we have been treated to an all-out assault on the Jesus phenomenon, which has created a new genre of historical fiction. Whereas traditional historical novels at least try to operate within a historically sound frame of reference, these new fantasies simply create their own histories.)

Our fifth and final guardrail is that of being aware of arbitrary a priori and self-imposed straitjackets. We must remember that any theory built on skepticism-despite-all-the-evidence-to-the-contrary can be made to sound plausible and persuasive. Thus, D. F. Strauss's nineteenth-century *Life of Jesus, Critically Examined*—the book that allegedly caused Nietzsche to lose his faith with its claim that the happenings narrated in the Gospels are "myths"—may seem compelling to the average reader.[102] But later historians have pointed out that Strauss had no real idea of the nature of historical research let alone any clue to the Jewish world of Jesus.

The point here is that what appears to be all the rage among skeptical scholars today may be disowned by its most ardent promoters tomorrow. To give an example from a different domain, the same logical positivist who once said, "all metaphysics is nonsense," admitted within a decade or so that "to say that metaphysics is nonsense is nonsense."[103] The wisest course of action is to reject arbitrary a priori assumptions and simply evaluate the evidence on its own merits.

FACT AND FICTION—THE JESUS OF HISTORY AND THE CHRIST OF FAITH

Here we must draw attention to one of the oldest ploys of all, that of erecting a wall between the Jesus of history and the Christ of faith. The idea was that a critical investigation of the texts helps us to determine the historical core of what can be known about Jesus and to separate this from the later theological additions of the disciples that were inserted purely on the basis of their faith. Not to put too fine a point to it, the goal is to separate fact from fiction.

This tactic has been the primary weapon deployed by skeptics from the nineteenth through the twenty-first centuries to wall off the "real" Jewish mystic from the faith-created Christian Messiah. Any statement about Jesus' miracles or his divine status, they say, is not true in a historical sense: it is true for those who believe in it in a metaphorical or mythological sense.

The affirmation that Jesus was the Son of God is simply a statement of faith and piety made by Jesus' followers; it is not something that is factually the case in the manner understood by councils and creeds. This approach is what we might call the Dr. Jekyll and Mr. Hyde mode of scholarship. Dr. Jekyll, Jesus as portrayed in the New Testament and in Christian history, is the individual under study; Mr. Hyde is the "real" Christ as re-created by the scholars and shorn of the imaginary creations of the potion of faith. As should be obvious, such Jekyll-and-Hyde scholarship cannot but end up in a vicious regress.

If you declare that your arbitrary criteria should be applied in determining which accounts and affirmations of the New Testament are factual, then other scholars can introduce their own criteria and apply them as they please in making their own determinations. This indeed is what has happened. The study of the texts has become a free-for-all of competing arbitrary criteria and equally arbitrary subjective interpretations. Dr. Jekyll gradually disappears until, ironically, only the illusory Mr. Hyde is left, the scholar's newly created Christ.

The fundamental problem with the Jekyll-and-Hyde ploy is that it simply cannot account for two events that cannot be denied—the death of Jesus and the transformation of the apostles. Jesus was put to death, and his death simply could not have been for teaching moral truths. He said and did something that infuriated his contemporaries enough to have him killed. And the account and meaning of his passion and death were central to doctrine and worship from the start. Likewise, the transformation of his apostles and other followers cannot be denied and can only be explained by something extraordinary— something as extraordinary as the resurrection claims.

In both instances, we cannot apply a distinction between fact and faith, history and myth, reality and metaphor. What we have to say is that *it is these two events that grounded the faith of the church rather than the faith of the church that grounded the events*.

Our approach here, to emphasize again, is to hold to what is obvious, no matter who denies it, while critically analyzing speculation, no matter who proposes it. "The apostles did not simply attach to Jesus certain characteristics and ways of behavior subsequent to Easter which he never had on earth (nor claimed to have)," writes the Tübingen scholar Peter Stuhlmacher. "On the contrary, the post-resurrection confession of the Christian Church in Jesus as Son of God and Messiah confirms and recognizes who Jesus historically wanted to be and who he was and remains for faith. God's history in and with Jesus, the Christ of God, is the basis for the Christian faith from the beginning. This history bears and determines this faith; faith does not initially create this history."[104]

TWO CHALLENGES — "All in Our Heads" and Wishful Thinking

We must acknowledge two genuine challenges to any effort to accept the ancient affirmations of the followers of Jesus. First, we have to confront the skepticism that tells us that this whole business is simply something going on in our minds or—what should concern us even more—the minds of a few first-century Jewish peasants and fishermen. Why on earth should we believe that something so dramatic as is claimed took place in our three-dimensional world? In the light of the noonday sun, this whole story seems simply too ethereal and unreal to merit serious consideration. These beliefs are all "in our heads," and that's all there is to them. This is a common refrain of the skeptics.

But before we succumb to this lethal line of reasoning, we should remember that the story does have certain three-dimensional effects. After all, we do have a teaching church that, over nearly two millennia, has instituted an enduring edifice of doctrine and discipline; we have liturgies and devotions that seek to put us in touch with the objects of our belief here and now; we have numerous texts that attest to events and experiences shared by individuals from diverse backgrounds; we have conversions by the million of those who claim to have experienced their Lord for themselves. All of these concrete states of affairs at least need to be explained with something more substantial than a simple dismissal that "it's all in the head."

Just as important: the whole Christian narrative is focused on the physical, three-dimensional world. The claim that Jesus rose from the dead and that we will rise from the dead is an affirmation that we are not complete without our bodies. Again, the sacraments, which are vehicles of the divine life, are physical. Christianity will not shy away from the physical because it affirms that God acts in and through the physical and tries to show how the evidence supports this affirmation.

The second challenge is the allegation that Christianity is simply wishful thinking. The whole story is too good to be true. Yes, it promises us the possibility of endless happiness, of living with the divine life, of receiving all that we ask. But this is precisely why we should be suspicious of its provenance. We humans, from the Stone Age to the present, are too prone to believe what we want to hear, of falling for pie-in-the-sky superstitions.

The skeptic does not deny that the gospel is good news, but it is precisely because it is good news that the skeptic thinks of it as a game of self-deception. To this line of reasoning we have no choice but to point to the story in its entirety. For there is clearly another side to the gospel: heaven and happiness are possible only for those who seek holiness and moral purity, who have faith in what they have received of the revelation of God and try to live up to its demand of taking up the cross. The Christian story is as much a story of suffering and the possibility of hell as it is about joy and heaven. It is true to life because it is all-encompassing, shedding light as it does on all thoughts, choices, acts, events, realities.

A MAP FOR THE JOURNEY

So now we continue our journey with a new map that lays out the contours of the landscape ahead.

Let's consider the data first. Essentially, there are five hard facts underlying the phenomenon of Jesus that need to be assembled, explained, and understood.

1. The life and mission of Jesus as understood from the New Testament texts and other documents about the world of Jesus that we have from first-century Greeks, Romans, and Jews.

2. The claim that Jesus rose from the dead, the transformation of the first witnesses of the reported resurrection, and the unanimous acceptance of the resurrection in the early church.

3. The teaching mission of the Church as seen in popes, fathers, synods, councils, and creeds along with the divinizing mission of the church as reflected in liturgies, sacraments, devotions, and exorcisms.

4. The Jesus of martyrs, saints, mystics, and converts and the world of apparitions, visions, and miracles.

5. The religious history of humanity and the themes of incarnation, sacrifice, redemption, and resurrection with a special emphasis on the milieu of Second Temple Judaism. (The original Temple of Jerusalem was destroyed by the Babylonians. A second temple was constructed

over its site by 515 BC and lasted until AD 70, when it was destroyed by the Romans. The Judaism of the era between 515 BC and AD 70 is, appropriately enough, called Second Temple Judaism.)

Each one of these elements is an integral ingredient of the Jesus phenomenon, but understandably enough, the New Testament accounts seem to attract almost all the attention, sometimes with virtually no study of the other items on the list. However, we will review all five hard facts while considering the New Testament narratives at three different levels: as written texts subject to literary analysis, as historical accounts held to the same standards as other historical claims, and finally, as a purported revelation of God's actions.

Counterexplanations include the following:

- The Jesus who did not exist
- The Jesus about whom we know nothing
- The Jesus of the Gnostics
- Jesus the teacher of timeless truths
- Jesus the healer
- Jesus the magician
- Jesus the prophet
- Jesus the purveyor of harmful religious superstitions
- The Jesus hoax

Our inquiry will compare the various explanations and see which of them make sense of all the data.

If we opt for one of the counterexplanations, there is not much more spadework to be done. But if we come to the conclusion that the standard explanation sounds plausible or at least merits further investigation, then there is more exploring and assimilating ahead.

Chief among all of these questions is the question that Jesus himself asked: who do you say that I am? These are questions only we can answer—none of the scholars or critics can answer them for us because, just as only we can open our eyes and see, so also only we can open our minds and grasp the truth.

Beyond discernment and recognition there is the final step of touching and feeling. This ranges from such simple acts as prayer to the subtlety and depth of mystical union with God. This is a well-trodden path, but at the end of the day it is again we who must take the plunge.

CHAPTER 12

A History of the Historical Jesus Quest

You can read and enjoy the works of William Shakespeare without having to wade through the commentaries of generations of literary critics. The same is true of the Gospel accounts of Jesus in relation to the commentaries they inspired. Nonetheless, there are good reasons for reviewing what historical and theological researchers have said about the New Testament portrait of Jesus. Among other things, they illustrate various possible ways of responding to the phenomenon. We will start this inquiry with a brief outline of major milestones in the attempt to study and explain Jesus in the scholarly world.[105]

Modern New Testament studies began in the eighteenth century with what is called the quest for the historical Jesus. It was concerned with the sources and genesis of the New Testament documents and with the question of which parts stem from real events and which are simply embellishments. Not surprisingly, this quest generated myriad opinions on the life, mission, and teachings of Jesus.

There have, in fact, been several major variations of the quest to date: the first quest, the no quest (Rudolf Bultmann), the new quest, and the third quest. By and large, the most influential of the New Testament critics have not only denied traditional affirmations about Jesus but also claimed that we can know very little about him.

Paradoxically the search for the Jesus of history has yielded multiple Christs of faith since each researcher has created a portrait of Christ in his or her preferred image. This curious result is consequently reflected in the third category below, "The Christ of Their Faith."

Era	Movement/Individual	The Christ of Their Faith
1694–1768	**Hermann S. Reimarus** (first) quest for the historical Jesus	Jesus seen as a Jewish revolutionary whose mission failed and whose body was stolen by the disciples, who then concocted various stories about him. The miracle stories were mere fictions. Reimarus was a Deist, and his writings must be seen against the background of the antisupernaturalism of the Enlightenment, which had begun to take root in Europe. According to Albert Schweitzer, he was the first to draw a distinction between the historical Jesus on one side and the Jesus of the Gospels and the Christ of faith on the other. (It is today accepted that Reimarus was not the first to introduce the idea; nevertheless, he is the first to have successfully popularized this train of thought.) His objective was not so much to find out more about the historical Jesus as to show that Christianity rested on superstitions that would not survive historical inquiry. He declared, in fact, that "Christianity was a fabrication created out of the conniving minds of Jesus' followers."[106] It has been said that Reimarus substituted dogmatic orthodoxy with dogmatic skepticism.
1808–74	**David F. Strauss**	In his *Life of Jesus, Critically Examined*, Strauss claimed that what "was once sacred history for the believer is, for the enlightened portion of our contemporaries, only fable." Most of the stories in the Gospels, especially the miracles, he said, were "myths." The depiction of Jesus as the miracle-working Son of God was simply mythological. Strauss sought to recreate Christianity on Hegelian lines. The philosopher Friedrich Nietzsche gave up Christian belief after reading Strauss's book in 1864. He remarked that "if you give up Christ, you give up God also," and was later to postulate the dictum "God is dead."
1841	**Bruno Bauer**	In three volumes Bauer sought to show that Jesus never existed. This view had some influence for two generations after him in German universities, and in fact, Marx and Engels made the nonexistence of Jesus a dogma of Marxism. Although Bauer's thesis has been revived in recent years, even prominent atheists do not take it seriously today.
1823–92	**Ernest Renan**	Renan was a famous French philosopher whose *Life of Jesus* was first translated into English in 1863. He argued that Jesus was a moral teacher whose mission failed and whose teachings have been misrepresented by a repressive church.

Era	Movement/Individual	The Christ of Their Faith
1832–1910	H. J. Holtzmann/ source criticism	Drawing on the work of Friedrich Schleiermacher and Christian Herman Weisse, Holtzmann, in a book published in 1863, established the theory of Markan priority: Mark, along with a missing document with the sayings of Jesus called "Q" (from the German *Quelle* for "source"), was the first of the Gospels to be written. The other Gospels are based on Mark and Q. In his view Mark and Q were more historical than theological and mythological. He considered Jesus to be simply a teacher of timeless ethical truths. Holtzmann's Markan priority is today the dominant view among biblical scholars, but because of serious flaws in the original theory, some critics talk of a missing proto-Mark that preceded the current Mark. The method of analyzing a text so as to determine the sources of information used in creating it has come to be called source criticism. It is presumed that the text can be better understood by identifying the sources used by its author. Source criticism has been complemented by redaction criticism, which seeks to determine the process by which the editor or redactor edited material from different sources to create the final work.
1859–1906	Georg Friedrich Eduard William Wrede	Wrede argued that the Gospel of Mark (on which Markan priority rested) was largely fictional. In his 1901 book *The Messianic Secret*, he alleged that Jesus never claimed to be the Messiah and that Mark's community came up with this idea after the execution of their leader.
1875–1965	Albert Schweitzer	Author of *The Quest of the Historical Jesus* (1906), Schweitzer took seriously the apocalyptic dimension of the teachings of Jesus. He criticized the various lives of Jesus that had emerged from the quest for the historical Jesus, pointing out that these reflected their authors more than they did Jesus. In his view Jesus expected the end of the world and the coming of God's kingdom. According to him, the Gospels rightly reflect Jesus' proclamation of the kingdom—although he also said that Jesus' life ended as a failure. Schweitzer accepted the essential historicity of the Synoptics and held that Jesus instituted baptism and the Eucharist and taught the doctrine of the atonement. Schweitzer's approach was so influential that it helped bring down the curtain on the initial search for the historical Jesus.

Era	Movement/Individual	The Christ of Their Faith
1894	Jesus in India	Another theory is that Jesus went to a Buddhist monastery in India before he was thirty and learned to perform miracles there. Also, Jesus is alleged to have come to India after the crucifixion and married a princess in the kingdom of Kashmir. Like most other such extraordinary theses, this one has no evidence to support it—only prodigious speculation. But quite apart from the lack of evidence, the thesis has major holes. Paradoxically, Swami Devananda Saraswati, a Hindu critic of Christianity, points out that the monastery in which Jesus is supposed to have studied was only built in the sixteenth century; the first promoter of the Jesus in Kashmir story, Nicholas Notovich, was a Russian forger who published this piece of fiction in Paris in 1894; the tomb where Jesus is allegedly buried actually contains the body of an ambassador from the Moghul empire to Egypt who became a Christian; and tenth-century Nestorian missionaries who came through Kashmir are responsible for the crosses found there.
1910s	The New Theology	Reverend R. J. Campbell, in his New Theology, proclaimed that "Jesus was God but so are we" and that humanity and divinity were two sides of one great consciousness. A contemporary rebirth of this view is found in the New Age Christ (see below).
1884–1976	Rudolf Bultmann/ form criticism	Like many of the scholars before him, Bultmann held that the Gospels do not give us a reliable portrait of Jesus. Bultmann popularized form criticism, which is a method for trying to identify the oral traditions, be they stories or legends, that lie behind a text. His focus was on the faith of the early church as reflected in the "Jesus stories." In his view the stories and sayings relating to Jesus were transmitted in oral pericopes; when reduced to writing these reflected the beliefs of second- and third-generation churches and of the individual writer and not the historical record. At best they were church-created "propaganda." In *Jesus and the Word*, he said, "In my opinion we can sum up what can be known of the life and personality of Jesus as simply nothing."[107]

Era	Movement/Individual	The Christ of Their Faith
1950s–1970s	New (second) quest for the historical Jesus	This quest began with a 1953 lecture, "The Problem of the Historical Jesus," by the German theologian Ernst Käsemann. It focused on the "sayings" of Jesus as opposed to his deeds. With the application of certain criteria, you could separate authentic sayings of Jesus from later accretions. Some popular criteria for judging authenticity were: embarrassment (a saying that would have embarrassed the early church); discontinuity (sayings and actions not obviously connected to Judaism or the early church); multiple attestation (sayings and actions found in more than one source); coherence (words and actions that fit in with other words and actions that are accepted as historical); and rejection and execution (sayings or actions that may have been responsible for his crucifixion). Most of the scholars associated with this quest agreed that the New Testament documents were produced by AD 70. Günther Bornkamm, a pioneer of the second quest, argued in *Jesus of Nazareth*[108] that the miracles stories of Jesus were creations of the early church, as was the idea that Jesus was the Messiah. The Jesus Seminar of the 1980s was, in certain respects, a resuscitation of this school.
1965	The Passover plot	In *The Passover Plot*,[109] a book subsequently made into a movie, the Jewish theologian Hugh Schonfield laid out yet another version of the theory that the disciples had stolen the body of Jesus: Jesus was a religious Jew who suffered from the delusion that he was the Messiah; he planned his crucifixion in such a manner as to ensure that he would not die but could then claim that he had risen from the dead; his plan goes wrong when one of the soldiers spears him to death; the tomb was empty because Jesus' disciples removed his body; the risen Jesus was actually the apostle John masquerading as Christ! (John Lennon of the Beatles, who rejected Christianity, said in an interview that his views on Christ were directly influenced by this book.)
1971	Jesus did not exist	In such books as *The Jesus of the Early Christians* (1971)[110] and *Did Jesus Exist?* (1975),[111] G. A. Wells, a professor of German based in England, rekindled the old idea that Jesus never existed. Although no historian has taken his views seriously and he himself has now recanted his previous position, a few other thinkers (e.g., Robert Price, Earl Doherty) have taken up the cause.

Era	Movement/Individual	The Christ of Their Faith
1970s	**The Gnostic Jesus**	According to the Gnostic worldview, prevalent in different forms since the second century, the physical world is evil and was created by an evil god. Salvation comes from liberation from this world; this liberation comes from the knowledge (*gnosis*) of secret mysteries or wisdom; the key secret is realizing that the divine is present in us; Jesus came from the "spiritual" world to reveal this secret to a chosen few. Gnostic sects were prevalent in the second century, and such apocryphal texts as the self-styled *Gospel of Thomas* and *Gospel of Peter* are creations of the Gnostics. Early-twentieth-century critics argued that the theology of some of the New Testament Gospels and epistles originated in Gnosticism. Bultmann, for one, held that the beliefs of the early church had Gnostic roots. In recent years, Helmut Koester, Elaine Pagels, Burton Mack, and John Dominic Crossan have claimed that early Christianity sprang from Gnostic sources.
		In her 1979 work *The Gnostic Gospels*[112] and her later *Beyond Belief: The Secret Gospel of Thomas*,[113] Elaine Pagels argued that there were many interpretations of early Christianity, which the leaders of the church suppressed as heresies, and one of these was the Gnostic view (although today she says that some of the books she called Gnostic Gospels are not Gnostic). The Gnostics, as she saw it, undermined the authority of church leaders because they held that those who received "gnosis" (enlightenment) were not subject to ecclesiastical leadership; they did not believe that Jesus had been physically resurrected from the dead; and they taught women had a higher role, as in the case of Mary Magdalene. Consequently, according to Pagels, they were denied positions of authority. The Gnostics propagated a maverick idea of God as an "oversoul" with male and female aspects (a mother God). They saw Jesus not as the incarnation of God but as an instrument of the oversoul, who sought to enlighten those who followed him (as opposed to redeeming them); enlightenment came from looking within and liberating oneself from the physical world. Pagels lauded Gnosticism for planting the seeds of many modern ideas such as the rejection of institutions and traditions and the understanding of religion as the exploration of the psyche. The claims of orthodox Christianity, in her view, are politically motivated.

Era	Movement/Individual	The Christ of Their Faith
	The Gnostic Jesus continued	N. T. Wright has noted that these Gnostic ideas are nothing new and were highlighted long ago in the decisive refutations produced by church fathers like Irenaeus. Moreover the Gnostics believed that only the elite would be enlightened and had no concern with humanity as a whole. They thought of women as inferior to men who could be perfected if they were made male—hardly a modern idea!
1970s	**Secret Mark**	Columbia professor Morton Smith authored two books in which he claimed to have discovered a letter from Clement mentioning a longer version of the Gospel of Mark. Clement allegedly urged that this work should be suppressed because a heretical sect had used it to introduce "carnal doctrine." The letter (around which the thesis revolves), however, disappeared—if it ever existed—and in recent years it has been alleged that the whole idea was a hoax perpetrated by Smith, who died in 1991. Smith's former student and admirer Rabbi Jacob Neusner recently described the "Secret" Gospel of Mark as "an outright fraud" and added, "As to the scholarly fraud, who speaks of it any more, or imagines that the work pertains to the study of the New Testament at all?"[114]
1977	**Jesus is not God incarnate**	Seven British theologians published *The Myth of God Incarnate*—edited by John Hick—in which they claimed that the idea that Jesus is God incarnate or the second person of the Trinity is simply "a mythological or poetic way of expressing his significance for us." Jesus is seen as the "Man of Universal Destiny."[115] The authors forcefully rejected the belief that Jesus is God incarnate.
1985–1990s	**The Jesus Seminar**	The Jesus Seminar revived the focus on the sayings of Jesus. Various theologians voted on various levels of probability regarding the authenticity of the sayings. In one of their books, *The Five Gospels*, the majority voted that 82 percent of the sayings are inauthentic.[116] Robert Funk (1926–2005), who started the Jesus Seminar, held that Jesus was an itinerant sage who taught of the coming of the kingdom but in a nonapocalyptic manner. John Dominic Crossan and Burton Mack saw Jesus as a Cynic philosopher who rejected conventional beliefs and values. Crossan claims Jesus was put to death but did not rise again. Mack views the Gospels as "imaginative creations" and not "historical accounts"; Mark's Gospel simply created a myth of Jesus' life.

Era	Movement/Individual	The Christ of Their Faith
1992	Jesus and the Dead Sea Scrolls	Australian Barbara Thiering, in *Jesus the Man*, claims that Jesus married Mary Magdalene, had three children, then divorced her and married the Lydia who is mentioned in the Acts of the Apostles.[117] Jesus did not die on the cross but lived on in Rome. According to Acts, "The Lord opened her [Lydia's] heart" (16:14), and this is evidence enough for Thiering that Jesus married her! The quality of the evidence for the book as a whole is no better (and, in fact, worse). Her only evidence for her extraordinary thesis is her allegorical interpretation of the Gospels using the Dead Sea Scrolls. She claims with no evidential support at all that the Gospels are coded descriptions of events in the life of the Dead Sea community. The Dead Sea sect, of course, flourished around 150 BC, and as N. T. Wright has pointed out, no scholar to date—with the sole exception of Thiering—has suggested that the scrolls make any mention of Christianity.[118] Consequently scholars of every religious or nonreligious background who have examined her thesis have rejected it.
1999	Jesus a pagan myth	In *The Jesus Mysteries: Was the "Original Jesus" a Pagan God?* Timothy Freke and Peter Gandy claim to unearth the true foundations of Christianity, based to a great extent on the Nag Hammadi Gnostic Gospels.[119] Among its theses: Jesus did not exist; the persistent theme in pagan mystery religions of a dying-and-rising god-man was adapted by a Gnostic sect to create the story of Christ; those on the outskirts of the sect who had not been initiated into the inner mysteries later supplanted the original Gnostics and, arrogating to themselves the role of church, taught that the Christ story was literally true. The scholarship on which the book relies is hopelessly out of date; the authors themselves are more interested in promoting their own New Age agenda than in engaging contemporary New Testament scholarship; and like other conspiracy theories, the book has not been endorsed by any New Testament scholar or historian of the ancient world. We will be reviewing in more detail the idea that the story of Jesus was created from pagan myths.
1990s–present	The third quest for the historical Jesus	Whereas influential members of the Jesus Seminar saw Jesus in the context of the Greco-Roman Mediterranean environment and its associated

Era	Movement/Individual	The Christ of Their Faith
	The third quest for the historical Jesus continued	philosophies, the third quest locates Jesus fairly and squarely in Jewish terrain. The interests of third quest scholars have ranged from the archaeology of Israel to the theological architecture of Second Temple Judaism as reflected in its texts. Jesus' announcement of the kingdom of God is seen in this context. One of the most famous works in this school is E. P. Sanders's *Jesus and Judaism*.[120] The quest includes Jewish writers like Jacob Neusner and Geza Vermes. The best-known contributor has been N. T. Wright, with his Christian Origins and the Question of God series, which so far includes *The New Testament and the People of God*,[121] *Jesus and the Victory of God*,[122] and *The Resurrection of the Son of God*.[123]
2005	**Altered Bible**	In *Misquoting Jesus: The Story Behind Who Changed the Bible and Why*, Bart Ehrman claims that Jesus was simply an apocalyptic prophet who was turned into the divine Son of God by the mistakes and intentional alterations of the scribes who wrote the Bible.[124] His book is primarily an overview of textual criticism of the Bible with several samples of variants in the text—but almost none of these variants deal with the sayings of Jesus. The title is therefore misleading. Daniel B. Wallace of the Center for the Study of New Testament Manuscripts points out that two of the three controversial verses involving Jesus that Ehrman cites (Jesus' anger in Mark 1:41 and the Son's ignorance of the end in Matthew 24:36) have parallels in other texts (Mark 3:5; 13:32), over which there is no controversy. The third is a Trinitarian passage in the First Epistle of John (5:7–8), but this particular passage does not appear in any modern translation. It is clear from a study of Ehrman's catalog that he has not provided any evidence for his thesis of doctrine being created from disputed texts. Ehrman's book is a popular version of his *Orthodox Corruption of Scripture*,[125] which was subjected to sharp criticism from peers. Ben Witherington notes, "As I remember Bruce Metzger saying once (who trained both Bart and myself in these matters) over 90% of the NT is rather well established in regard to its original text, and none of the remaining 10% provides us with data that could lead to any shocking revisions of the Christian credo or doctrine. It is at the very least disingenuous to suggest it does, if not deliberately provocative to say otherwise."[126]

Era	Movement/Individual	The Christ of Their Faith
2006	The New Atheism	The so-called New Atheism, promoted by Richard Dawkins, Sam Harris, and Christopher Hitchens among others, sees all religion as both false and harmful. Belief in Jesus and his teachings is identified with blind-faith fundamentalism that is not simply irrational but inimical to civilized norms. In *God Is Not Great*, Hitchens holds that Jesus did not exist.[127] Dawkins has claimed that there is a case to be made for the nonexistence thesis. Critics have pointed out that these books have not even taken a serious look at the evidence for such claims as the resurrection. In a debate with the Christian mathematician John Lennox, Dawkins makes the egregious charge that belief in the salvific death and resurrection of Jesus is parochial and petty when compared with the majesty of the universe. This line of thinking simply shows ignorance of the nature of the Christian claim: Jesus is the eternal Logos, the Alpha and the Omega, the ultimate matrix of the creation of the universe; moreover, one human soul is more majestic and mysterious than the entire universe; Jesus came to redeem every human person. Even if you reject these claims, you can hardly describe them as petty and parochial.
2008	The New Age Christ	In the same year, the self-help guru Deepak Chopra published two books on Jesus, *The Third Jesus*[128] and *Jesus: A Story of Enlightenment*.[129] They had nothing to do with history and everything to do with self-help therapy. They are Chopra's reinvention of the Jesus story to promote the ultimate form of self-help—"finding God-consciousness through your own efforts." The first book presents the paradigm that there are three Jesuses: the historical Jesus of the Gospels (a "sketchy historical figure"), the Jesus supposedly created by the church to further its agenda (an "abstract theological creation"), and finally the real Jesus, the cosmic Christ who has found enlightenment and wishes to share it with all. The second book is a novel that speculates on Jesus' life between the ages of twelve and thirty, complete with tutelage under a Himalayan guru. Since all the optional reinventions of Jesus have already been offered (however briefly) over the last two thousand years, Chopra had little hope of presenting something original. At best, his "Jesus" is nothing but a reincarnation of the Gnostic Jesus; in fact, Chopra calls this the "Third Coming" of Christ. Some critics have said that Chopra is

Era	Movement/Individual	The Christ of Their Faith
	The New Age Christ continued	promoting a Hindu message. But in point of fact, Chopra's advaitic Hinduism (which originated only in the eight century AD), with its ideas of monism and pantheism (everything is God), is just one of six schools of Hinduism. All the other (more ancient) schools teach plurality, or a distinction between God and creation. But these finer points of detail should not distract us from the central fact that Chopra is giving us not a work of history or theology but of re-creation in his own image. It is a contemporary Gnostic "Gospel," which, as Chopra himself admitted in an interview with *Time*, belongs in the category of "religious fiction."
2008	**The Jesus cover-up thesis**	In *How Jesus Became Christian*, Barrie Wilson repackages the old argument that Jesus never intended to start a new religion and that Christianity as we know it is a creation of the apostle Paul. According to his "thesis," Jesus was a faithful rabbi and wanted his followers simply to adhere to Jewish law so as to bring about the kingdom of God. After Jesus' death, James continued his mission by leading the Jesus movement. But this movement was "hijacked" by the Christ movement created by Paul. Wilson's theses are hardly original, and we will be reviewing a number of works that have made the same claims. But what is different in the present day is that this approach has been repudiated by contemporary Jewish scholars. Jon Levenson, professor of Jewish studies at Harvard, has recently criticized the old canards about the apostle Paul that are central to Wilson's argument. Levenson notes, "This is simplistic if not wrongheaded. In his own mind, Paul was not turning away from Judaism or founding a new religion but following out the logical implications of living in a period when the biblical promises of messianic redemption were in the process of being fulfilled, especially the promises centered on the Gentiles. His arguments with Judaism were based, for the most part, on his reading of the Hebrew Bible, which he quotes abundantly and interprets using methods familiar to the Jews of the time. Yes, Paul thought that the God of Israel had done something new through the advent of Jesus that voided the Mosaic commandments (which never applied to the Gentiles anyway)."[130]
present–future		Newer variations on the same old theories.

THE SCHOLARS WHO WOULD BE CHRISTS

What is apparent from this survey, and from any long-range view of the matter, is that in every decade of the modern era—including the present—there is a band of supposedly daring scholars who take on the establishment with their radical new views. But the merry-go-around never stops. Before you know it, there is a changing of the guard and it's time to move on to the next daring thesis. The with-it views become yesterday's news.

For anyone who wishes to return to their senses, it is important to step off the merry-go-round to see why it keeps spinning endlessly in circles.

There is a reason why we have said that the historical Jesus of the New Testament scholars turns out in the end to be their Christ of faith. These worthies of every recent generation have decided which parts of the New Testament can be taken as historical, and it is the Jesus that emerges from their dissection that they proclaim to be the real Jesus. But since the whole exercise is based simply on their application of their own subjective criteria, we have to treat their "Jesus" as an object of faith, faith in their criteria and its application. And since the criteria vary across multiple scholars, we end up with multiple Christs of faith.

Albert Schweitzer's wise observation remains as true today as when he first made it over a hundred years ago: "It was not only each epoch that found its reflection in Jesus; each individual created Him in accordance with his own character. There is no historical task which so reveals a man's true self as the writing of a life of Jesus."[131]

Let us consider the critics' litany of affirmations that were supposedly invented by the early church:

- Jesus claimed to be the Messiah.
- Jesus claimed to be divine.
- Jesus claimed that he would give up his life in atonement for sin.
- Jesus instituted the Lord's Supper.
- Jesus rose from the dead.

We are supposed to believe that a confused band of fisher folk scattering in all directions after the horrific death of their master somehow managed to hatch a plot where they reinvent their dead leader's persona in the most unbelievable representation imaginable. All of this in a short span of time when they are desperately evading their Jewish and Roman enemies and trying to earn a living, and all of this while many of their contemporaries who actually knew their leader were alive. Despite these insuperable obstacles they manage to pull it off. The hoax stays in place for nearly two thousand years until, finally, the first sensible investigators arrive on the scene and pinpoint the culprits. With that, the game is up and it is time for us all to move on.

This is the story that the critics have managed to sell. But it is a story that has no claim to credibility. Just a narration of its presuppositions (see above) is enough to demonstrate its absurdity. As Schweitzer put it, "The Jesus of Nazareth [of the critics] . . . never had any existence. He is a figure designed by rationalism, endowed with life by liberalism, and clothed by modern theology in an historical garb."[132] Charlotte Allen said it best: "Ironically, the quest for the 'historical' Jesus in the end has yielded a figure who is not historical at all, and to whom historical reality is quite irrelevant."[133]

In one sense, to be sure, we can say, yes, there is a great divide between the Jesus of history and the Christ of faith. But this is the divide between, on one side, the Jesus who emerges from the earliest narratives, apostolic traditions, liturgies, creeds, councils, and accounts of Christian experience and, on the other, the multiple Christs created by various New Testament theologians in their own images with a little help from the ancient Gnostics.

CHAPTER 13

The Three Amigos—
Species of Skeptics We Will Always Have with Us

Our initial survey of the quests for the historical Jesus indicates that a good many of the "quests" were skeptical from start to finish with respect to the Gospel narratives and historic Christian affirmations. Three species of New Testament skeptics have repeatedly shown up along the way:

- The fundamentalist skeptic, who holds it as an article of faith that Jesus never existed.

- The traditionalist skeptic, who believes that pretty much everything said about Jesus was concocted by the early church: consequently we only have later traditions that have no relation to what actually happened.

- The nihilist skeptic, who says that nothing is true and we can believe whatever we wish.

Interestingly, these three amigos are critical not only of the historic affirmations of Christianity but even more so of each other.

Paradoxically, a study of each species of skepticism and the skeptics' past and present arguments and methods helps us think more clearly in this domain. (Manure often serves as a very effective fertilizer!) If nothing else, the skeptics can help us better understand the nature of the phenomenon that is Jesus of Nazareth by showing us the right and wrong ways of coming to grips with it. So we move on now to these three amigos.

THE FUNDAMENTALIST SKEPTIC

Not even the most ferocious early critics of Christianity argued that its founder did not exist. But that is precisely the position taken by the modern fundamentalist in the teeth of all available evidence. Of course this faith in the nonexistence of Jesus is today professed mostly by fringe writers and not by any influential New Testament scholar, no matter how radical. In point of fact, no major atheist historian denies the existence of Jesus. But the nonexistence theory is an obsession of certain kinds of tabloid thinkers—the sort of wild-eyed sensationalists who spend their lives unearthing the conspiracies of the establishment and re-creating history in the image of some esoteric theory or other.

NEWSFLASH—

DISBELIEVER IN JESUS' EXISTENCE NOW ACCEPTS IT

We should note here that the Jesus-did-not-exist school of thought sustained a head wound in 1999, when its best-known modern spokesman, G. A. Wells, a British professor of German, grudgingly admitted in his work *The Jesus Myth*[134] that a real Galilean Jewish prophet of the early first century named Jesus did indeed exist. Despite three decades of publications denying Jesus' existence, Wells had remained open to the evidence, and it was the evidence that led him to change his mind. Atheist apologist Jeffery Jay Lowder of the website Internet Infidels reports: "There is simply nothing intrinsically improbable about a historical Jesus; the New Testament alone (or at least portions of it) are reliable enough to provide evidence of a historical Jesus. On this point, it is important to note that even G. A. Wells, who until recently was the champion of the Christ-myth hypothesis, now accepts the historicity of Jesus."[135]

Although, with this, the Jesus-did-not-exist school has now all but ended with a bang, it continues to whimper along with a few diehards who heroically try to resurrect the nineteenth-century Jesus-as-product-of-mythology thesis. This desperate thesis has been repeatedly discredited by present-day scholars of comparative religion.

HOW THE JESUS-DID-NOT-EXIST MOVEMENT CAME TO EXIST

The idea of Jesus' nonexistence,[136] according to the French historian Maurice Goguel, first arose among the followers of the eighteenth-century English Deist politician Henry Bolingbroke and was taken up by some of their French Enlightenment contemporaries. Thomas Paine, the American "freethinker" of note during the lead-up to the Revolutionary War, jumped on this bandwagon with nothing to back him but his own pontifical pronouncements.

In the nineteenth century, Bruno Bauer, a German philosopher, tried to explain history and Christianity through the lens of his teacher G.W.F. Hegel. History, in his view, was a manifestation of the development of the human spirit, and Christianity had to be left behind for humanity to reach the next level of autonomous self-consciousness. Bauer's philosophical agenda led him to reject the historical existence of Jesus, which he did by denying the veracity of the New Testament documents; and he rejected not just the existence of Jesus but also the authenticity of Paul's writings. The Gospels, he said, were simply expressions of human religious consciousness and not historical narratives of any kind.

The next generation of Jesus-did-not-exist purveyors was the late-nineteenth-century radical Dutch School of the University of Amsterdam, which claimed that the Gospels were poetry, legend, and Gnostic philosophy; the Epistles were second-century constructs; and Jesus himself was simply a symbol of the essence of the people of Israel. This theory did not gain much of a following.

They were followed by J. M. Robertson (d. 1933), a British journalist, politician, and "rationalist" who held that the Old and New Testaments were accounts of various pagan myths drawn from ancient cults and rites. The Gospels were Gnostic writings, Jesus never existed, and the account of his passion was simply an ancient Palestinian mystery drama. "It was by reason of a similar failure to find a historic footing," wrote Robertson, "that the present writer was gradually led, on lines of comparative hierology and comparative mythology and anthropology, to the conception of the evolution of the Jesus-cult from the roots of a 'pre-Christian' one."[137] Like other standard-bearers of the Jesus-as-myth movement, Robertson was so concerned to propound his thesis that he simply ignored the canons of historical study and the evidential value of the Gospels themselves.

Robertson's chief successors were an American mathematician, William Benjamin Smith (d. 1934), and a German philosopher, Arthur Drews (d. 1935). Smith said belief in Jesus' existence can be traced to a pre-Christian Jewish cult (influenced by the Hindu religion) that worshiped a pre-Christian divinity called Jesus and led a protest against polytheistic idolatry. Drews asserted that Christianity was a variation of the many Mediterranean and Persian dying-and-rising god-man myths; Jesus is the pre-Christian deity Joshua; the Passion narratives come from Plato and Jewish Wisdom poetry; the Gospels are nonhistorical; and Christianity sprang from Jewish Gnosticism.

The arguments of the mathematician and the philosopher had no historical basis or bearing, and so their theological conclusions were simply expressions of personal faith. Not for nothing did a contemporary atheist, Joseph McCabe, describe Robertson, Smith, Drews, and others as a "hotch-potch of amateur historians."[138]

THE MYTH OF THE DYING-AND-RISING-GOD MYTH

The primary explanation for the rise of Christianity offered by the Jesus deniers has been the Jesus-mythology thesis, the claim that the story of Jesus is simply a Jewish cultic version of pagan dying-and-rising-god myths (Greek, Egyptian, Persian, and others). Curiously, Archibald Robertson, a British atheist of yore, would have no truck with this thesis. He spoke of "the proclivity of mythicists to overstate their case, and while demanding mathematical certainty from their opponents, themselves . . . indulge in hypothetical flights every whit as fanciful and as incapable of proof as those which they attack."[139]

The history of the Jesus-mythology thesis shows that it is a playground for nonhistorians who want to draw attention to themselves or their theories by offering their own reconstructions of history. More than anyone else, they resemble the nonphysicists who tell us why Einstein's theory of relativity is mistaken. Of course, everyone has a right to free speech and, occasionally, amateurs turn out to be right and the experts wrong. But to be taken seriously when you propound a sensational idea, especially one that proudly proclaims all specialists to be mistaken, you need to provide sensational evidence.

On this score, the mythology proponents are at a factual disadvantage. They have no evidence to speak of—let alone sensational evidence. But what they lack in expertise and evidence they make up for with passionate rhetoric, riveting melodrama, and continuing speculation. Conspiracy-theory thinking is endemic to the radical fringe of New Testament studies, and it reaches its logical culmination in the Jesus-mythology view of the world—a view other radical critics hold in disdain because of its plebian origins.

What sets the story of Jesus apart from the mythological motifs is clear from the start:

- He lives and dies in a definite place and time.
- He is portrayed as a man on a mission.
- He explicitly gives up his life to fulfill his mission.
- His sacrifice of his life is a one-time event not an annual cycle.
- He performs miracles and prophesies his rising from the dead.
- He entrusts his followers with teachings and practices that are to be transmitted to all.
- His resurrection from the dead was unexpected and does not tie in either with pagan ideas of life after death (as most recently shown by N. T. Wright in his *The Resurrection of the Son of God*) or with Jewish expectations that centered on collective and not individual resurrection.

While some of the pre-Christian myths can arguably be cited as preparations of the human psyche for the historical incarnation of God in Christ, there can be no doubt that there is nothing quite like the life, death, and resurrection of Jesus in pre-Christian mythology.

Some of the mythologists have argued that the Jesus story is reconstructed from Old Testament prophecies. This again is most unlikely because the life and death of Jesus conflicted with conventional expectations of the coming of the Messiah. Maurice Goguel notes that the Jews were bewildered by the life story of Jesus because it was incompatible with their idea of the Messiah. Paul initially could not believe in Jesus because of the curse associated with the cross. In later years, the Jewish Trypho was willing to concede to the Christian Justin that the Messiah is called to suffer, but he could not accept the punishment of the cross since it seemed contrary to Deuteronomy 22:23.[140] (Paul points out, of course, that Jesus redeemed us from the curse of the Torah by becoming a curse for us.)

FIRST THINGS FIRST

To the question of Jesus' existence, we note that there are several primary reasons traditionally given for believing that Jesus existed:

- The Gospel accounts, which are treated as historical;
- The transformation of the apostles of Jesus after his alleged resurrection from the dead;
- The personal experience of Jesus in the lives of his followers; and
- The extrabiblical evidence available from near-contemporary historians and the undeniable fact that Christianity spread rapidly across the Roman Empire at a very early date.

In studying the historical evidence for Jesus, we are naturally led to ask if there are any extrabiblical sources that speak of him, preferably contemporaneously. The two obvious sets of candidates would be Jewish and Roman historians of Jesus' time. But right at this point, we have a problem. Within a generation of Jesus' death, the Jewish people faced one of the greatest calamities in their history. It has been estimated that over two million Jews died as a result of famine, disease, and war in that time. For instance, according to the contemporary historian Josephus, over a million Jews died in the war against Rome and one million were exiled. If that were not catastrophe enough, there is the parallel problem of the loss of all Roman historical writings in the period contemporaneous to Jesus.

Despite these challenges, it is startling to find that not only do we find mention of Jesus in extrabiblical Jewish and Roman writings; but also these references come principally from two individuals who were, respectively, the greatest of the Roman and Jewish historians, Cornelius Tacitus (ca. AD 56–120) and Flavius Josephus (ca. AD 37–100).

In his *Annals*, his last work, Tacitus writes,

> Consequently, to get rid of the report, Nero fastened the guilt and inflicted the most exquisite tortures on a class hated for their abominations, called Christians by the populace. Christus, from whom the name had its origin, suffered the extreme penalty during the reign of Tiberius at the hands of one of our procurators, Pontius Pilatus, and a most mischievous superstition, thus checked for the moment, again broke out not only in Judaea, the first source of the evil, but even in Rome, where all things hideous and shameful from every part of the world find their centre and become popular.[141]

Referring to the passage, Daniel Schowalter, in an essay in *The Oxford History of the Biblical World*, remarks that "it is significant that Tacitus—making one of the earliest direct references to Jesus' followers outside the New Testament—uses the popular name *Christiani* to describe them. The name *Christian* is not used in the earliest New Testament literature, the letters of Paul, and the Gospels."[142] About Josephus' references to Christ, the historian James Charlesworth observes that "we can now be as certain as historical research will presently allow that Josephus did refer to Jesus."[143]

About the evidence as a whole, another historian, Michael Grant, points out that in recent years, "no serious scholar has ventured to postulate the non-historicity of Jesus."[144] In any event, if Jesus did not exist, we would expect the first enemies of Christianity to have broadcast this embarrassing fact. The fact that such an argument was never deployed is seen by many as the final nail in the coffin for the Jesus deniers. Goguel says that "the importance of this fact is considerable," given that Jewish opposition to Christianity began in Jesus' own land.

> How is it possible to suppose that the first antagonists of the Church could have been ignorant of the fact that the entire story of Jesus, His teaching, and His death corresponded to no reality at all? That it might have been ignored in the Diaspora may be admitted, but it appears impossible at Jerusalem; and if such a thing had been known, how did the opponents of Christianity come to neglect the use of so terrible an argument, or how, supposing they made use of it, does it happen that the Christians succeeded in so completely refuting them that not a trace of the controversy has been preserved by the disputants of the second century?[145]

HOW OLD IS THE NEW TESTAMENT?

A key foundation for the Jesus-mythology thesis is the claim that the New Testament books, and especially the Gospels, were written toward the end of the first century and into the second century. The writing of them is too far removed from the events that they describe to be historically accurate, the critics say.

When were the various New Testament books written? Since the books are not "date stamped" and there is no technological method for dating them (even were we to have the autographs—i.e., the original documents—which we do not), scholars have relied mostly on guesswork in fixing dates for their composition. In addition to the guesswork, we have three other more reliable sources—the available fragments of ancient manuscripts of New Testament books, the references to these books in the earliest Christian writers (such as Ignatius of Antioch), and the traditions of the church fathers.

Let's turn first to the guesswork, which relies primarily on literary analysis. Most scholars today believe that:

- Paul's epistles to the Romans, Corinthians, Galatians, and Thessalonians were written in the fifties (of the first century AD);
- Ephesians, Philippians, Colossians, Timothy, Titus, and Philemon in the sixties;
- Hebrews and Jude in the sixties;
- James anywhere from the fifties to after the seventies;
- First and 2 Peter in the sixties;
- The Acts of the Apostles anywhere from the sixties to the eighties;
- First, 2, and 3 John between the eighties and nineties; and
- The book of Revelation in the nineties.

As to the Gospels, most take Mark to have been written between 65 and 75, Matthew between 70 and 85, Luke between 80 and 95, and John between the 80s and 90s.

There have been prominent dissident voices in the scholarly communities. For instance, John A. T. Robinson, a noted liberal scholar, shocked his colleagues with his assertion that the whole of the New Testament was complete before the destruction of the Jerusalem temple in AD 70. Robinson pointed out that if the New Testament had been written after the fall of the temple, the writers would have referred to this event as a fulfillment of the prophecies in Matthew 24 and Luke 23.

Turning to sources other than literary guesswork, we start with the earliest manuscripts of the New Testament books. There are now nearly six thousand ancient Greek manuscripts of the New Testament as well as nearly twenty thousand copies in Syriac, Latin, Coptic, and other languages. Manuscripts are principally dated on the basis of the handwriting style. The earliest copies of individual books date back to at least AD 200, while copies of complete manuscripts of the New Testament are available from AD 350. The P52 fragment of the Gospel of John copied in Egypt is dated at around AD 125 (some say AD 100). This suggests that this Gospel was written in the first century since, by the time this manuscript was written, copies of the Gospel had apparently been circulating for some time.

It might be asked why the autographs of the New Testament are not available. The answer is to be found in an ancient custom: "In the East when documents and books are worn out they are copied exactly and the originals are burned. This is due to the belief of the Eastern people that it is a sin to allow a book to fall to pieces."[146]

The second method of dating the New Testament is from the writings of the earliest church fathers. A letter from Clement of Rome, written in AD 96, to the church in Corinth refers to ten of the New Testament books. Ignatius of Antioch (d. 110) referred to 1 Corinthians and arguably to the Gospel of Matthew and other New Testament books. Polycarp of Smyrna (d. 155), who was a disciple of the apostle John, has references to the three synoptic Gospels and various Epistles. Justin Martyr (d. 165) quoted from the Gospels and other New Testament books. Irenaeus of Lyons (d. 180) quoted extensively from the New Testament books. So did Clement of Alexandria (d. 212).

With regard to the order of the books, Clement of Alexandria (cited by Eusebius) points to a tradition "on the order of the Gospels" handed down by "the elders who lived in the first days."[147] According to these elders, the two Gospels with genealogies (Matthew and Luke) were written first, followed by Mark and John; later commentators said that Mark did not include a birth narrative because it was already found in the earlier Gospels. All the early church fathers who wrote about this matter held to Matthew as the first Gospel.

SUMMING UP THE HISTORICAL EVIDENCE

Our study of the evidence indicates that, from the standpoint of historical methodology, the available data points unmistakably to the existence of Jesus as a historical person. Those who deny his existence cannot offer even a remotely plausible case for their thesis.

But it is not just conventional historical methodology that is our concern here. Rather, we have to study the evidence on its own terms. We have to grasp the phenomenon in its fullness if we are to understand and explain it. The historical Jesus of the scholars is as artificial as any product of an academic exercise can be. The Jesus mythologists are simply the logically inevitable products of the kind of thinking adopted by most of the pioneers of the quest for the historical Jesus.

The historicity of Jesus does not rest on a few stray comments from Tacitus or Josephus or a fragment or two of ancient manuscripts of the New Testament books. These are certainly helpful as far as they go. But neither these nor the works of the New Testament scholars can serve as adequate foundations for an assertion of the existence of Jesus. What we have to do is to step back and look at the entire panorama. Of course, we see the thousands of manuscripts of the New Testament that spread across the ancient world. But quite apart from these tangible products, something else becomes evident.

What we see is a story, a proclamation, a testimony, a call to thought and action that creates a new kind of community. It is a community with its own leadership structure, its own rules and rituals, its own raison d'être. And it is a community centered on the life and message as well as the death and resurrection of a singular individual. Jesus was not simply embedded in the very life of the community, but the community believed itself to embody Jesus. They spoke with his authority, acted on his behalf, made present on a continuous basis his climactic sacrifice, and transmitted his very life to all who responded to their call. It was, and is, an utterly unique community, one that changed lives and that, by changing lives, changed empires.

This community called itself "the church." As we have seen, it was already active in Rome quite early in the first century. It was present right from the start. Its affirmation and proclamation was transmitted through the ancient liturgies, liturgies that are celebrated to this day. To attempt to "prove" the historicity of Jesus by reference to the accounts in the New Testament narratives is to put the cart before the horse. We must first account for the existence of the ancient community that is the church and then turn to the book it gave the world. The central messages of the New Testament were the central messages of the preaching, teaching, and acting of the church.

Consider a remarkable testimony to the power of the Jesus of the Gospels—a testimony that came from a fellow Jew, Albert Einstein. When asked by G. S. Viereck whether he accepted the historical existence of Jesus, Einstein replied, "Unquestionably. No one can read the Gospels without feeling the actual presence of Jesus. His personality pulsates in every word. No myth is filled with such life. How different, for instance, is the impression which we receive from an account of legendary heroes of antiquity like Theseus. Theseus and other heroes of his type lack the authentic vitality of Jesus."[148]

THE TRADITIONALIST SKEPTIC

Among the most ardent defenders of Jesus' existence is the traditionalist. But the traditionalist gives with one hand and takes away with the other. While strongly affirming the existence of Jesus, the traditionalist is equally adamant in denying the factuality of the Gospel narratives. All we know about Jesus are traditions about him created by the early church.

Historically the traditionalist position has paralleled the development of source, redaction, and form criticism, collectively known as the historical-critical method. The historical-critical method itself is theologically neutral, but the Enlightenment gave rise to two parallel movements of traditionalist skepticism. On the one hand you had those like Reimarus who dismissed the veracity of the New Testament as a whole because they could not accept the historicity of its narratives. On the other, you had those like Bultmann who admitted that the Bible did not work as history but then went on to abstract from it certain timeless truths that they held to be applicable even in the present day.

GNOSTICISM

The traditionalist's besetting sin is often a kind of Gnosticism. The temptation is twofold. On one level, several of the traditionalists are ardent devotees of the second- to fourth-century Gnostic Gospels, which they take to be more reliable and inspiring than the first-century New Testament documents. On another level they are Gnostic in intellectual temperament. (*Gnosis* is the Greek word for knowledge.) They believe they have access to a secret knowledge hidden from the masses.

These characteristics might well be applied to many of today's traditionalist skeptics. Everything that was said about Jesus to date is wrong, but not to worry, we now have the real story, the true message. Only the enlightened know the actual truth about Jesus, but by joining their august ranks, you too can be liberated from the bondage of superstition and mythology. Be suspicious of everything you have heard about Jesus, everything that had seemed obvious. At the same time, broaden your mental horizons to accept the latest new revelation about Jesus, no matter how seemingly bizarre or lacking in concrete evidence it might be. Exchange the Christ of faith for the real Jesus.

This can be interpreted as the conspiracy-theory view of history, and it is the common thread that ties together traditionalist skeptics from Reimarus and Bultmann to *The Da Vinci Code*. Strangely enough, crusty old German New Testament scholars, baby boomer North American leaders of the Jesus Seminar, and assorted fantasy history sensationalists all coexist in a parallel universe of feverish speculation, paranoid fears, and bizarre beliefs. Nightmares of crafty priests and fiery fundamentalists who suppress the truth and invent legends to perpetuate their power structures keep these poor souls tossing and turning through an endless dark night. But their phobias and obsessions cannot dictate the agenda for rational inquiry.

A conspiracy theorist, in this ecosystem, is someone who refuses to take a hard fact seriously on its own terms, creates speculative theories that principally rely on arbitrary presuppositions, and insists on viewing all available data through the lens of a pet theory. You cannot change the theorist's mind with facts: facts that do not fit in with the theory are discarded, and all others are somehow subsumed into the body of the theory. It is even difficult to carry on a discussion with conspiracy theorists because they give new meanings to the very terms you use. Ask them if they believe if Jesus is God, and they will say yes and then explain that this means "you encounter God through Jesus." Like termites, they eat away at the meaning of words until all you have left is a stream of vibrations in the air. Their Christ of faith supersedes any evidence, physical or otherwise.

THEOLOGY BECOMES AUTOBIOGRAPHY

The traditionalist arguments are alternative explanations for the Jesus phenomenon. These arguments tend to be variations on themes that keep emerging, although they have repeatedly been decisively refuted. The underlying errors remain the same in all the attempted counterexplanations of the traditionalists:

- They fail to consider the phenomenon in its fullness.
- The presuppositions they use in criticizing historic views are their own conclusions. (In other words, they do not first prove their positions but take them as starting points.)
- They only select data that support their theory.
- Their attempt to explain the facts about Jesus relies on speculation for which there is no evidence beyond the proponent's authority.
- They create a Christ of faith whose mission and message reflects their own ideology.

Charlotte Allen has chronicled this correlation:

Jesus scholarship has been shaped by nearly every intellectual fashion of the past three centuries: English deism, Enlightenment rationalism, philosophical Idealism, Romanticism, Darwinism, existentialism, Marxism and feminism. The liberal Protestant outlook of the nineteenth century, the "social gospel" of the early twentieth century, the "God is Dead" movement of the 1960s, and the liberation theology of the 1970s and 1980s have all cast long shadows on the search for Jesus. In 1909, the Modernist Catholic theologian George Tyrell complained that the liberal German biblical scholars of the day had reconstructed a historical Jesus who was no more than "the reflection of a liberal Protestant face, seen at the bottom of a deep well." In other words, the liberal searchers had found a liberal Jesus. The same can be said of the Jesus-searchers of every era. . . . The "scientific" quest for the historical Jesus has nearly always devolved into theology, ideology and even autobiography.[149]

If there is any dichotomy between the Jesus of history and the Christ of faith, it is really one between the Jesus of historical fact and the Christ of scholarly fiction. We can illustrate this by considering two prominent examples of neo-Gnosticism: the fountainhead of modern traditionalist skepticism, Rudolf Bultmann, and the Jesus Seminar.

RUDOLF BULTMANN

Rudolf Bultmann (1884–1976) was one of the intellectual celebrities of the twentieth century. He was to biblical criticism what Einstein was to physics, Darwin to biology, and Freud to psychology. But in terms of enduring influence, the closest analogue is probably Freud. Freud may be revered as the father of psychoanalysis, but he is now considered a literary figure rather than a scientific one because, as one recent biographer put it, he turned out to be wrong in every particular of his theories. The same is true of Bultmann. Today, his methodologies for the study of the Gospel documents are seen to be fundamentally flawed, his dogma of demythologization is viewed as naively mechanistic, and the philosophy of existentialism with which he reclothed Christianity is as dead as the Hegelianism of his forebears.

Bultmann was a Lutheran minister who was a son and grandson of Lutheran pastors. His professors at the University of Marburg promoted certain fashionable ideas of the time that formed Bultmann's views on Jesus and the Gospels. These were the following: the real Jesus did not claim any of the titles endowed on him by his followers; early Christians had built their Christ of faith around the redeemer of Hellenistic myths; and the modern world made it impossible to believe in the articles of the Christian creed.

Bultmann brought three direct influences to bear on New Testament studies:

- The form criticism inaugurated by Martin Dibelius;
- A self-declared scientism that ruled out any trace of the transcendent or the supernatural; and
- The existential philosophy of Martin Heidegger, which became for Bultmann the key to understanding the message of the Gospels.

Originally developed by Hermann Gunkel in studying the Old Testament, form criticism was applied by Martin Dibelius to the New Testament. Dibelius argued that the Gospels were made up of oral traditions and that an analysis of its various literary forms (e.g., parables, sayings, healing narratives) would help us determine when these were orally transmitted. He believed that Jesus' sayings derived from him but that the narratives were constructed by the disciples. Bultmann took Dibelius's ideas one step further and not only denied the historicity of the deeds attributed to Jesus but also the words.

In his most famous work, *History of the Synoptic Tradition* (1921), Bultmann said, "The aim of form-criticism is to determine the original form of a piece of narrative, a dominical saying or a parable. In the process we learn to distinguish secondary additions and forms, and these in turn lead to important results for the history of the tradition."[150] Form criticism thus understood determines the authenticity and accuracy of various New Testament texts by analyzing their literary form (parables, sayings, healing narratives) so as to pinpoint the original oral or written sources from which they derive. It is assumed that each text is a mountain created from a molehill. The molehill is an original oral tradition of a saying or event; the mountain is created by various retellers and writers who add successive layers that reflect their own theological agendas.

As Bultmann saw it, the task was to recover the original kernel of meaning by stripping away the overlay of mythic accretions. In other words, even when we get to the bottom layer of the Jesus stories in the Gospel, we find not the real Jesus but another representation of him. In Bultmann's view the Gospels were devotional and apologetic works of the church and not biographies of Jesus. He almost entirely rejected the historicity of the Gospels of Matthew, Mark, and Luke (John, to which he devoted another book, was not even in the running) and conceded only that a person named Jesus lived and was probably crucified. In *Jesus and the Word* (1926) he said we can know virtually nothing about the actual life and personality of Jesus.

Although he authored several other major books, Bultmann's second-most-influential work was his essay "The New Testament and Mythology" (1941). Here he held that our reading of the New Testament should be informed by an understanding of a clash of civilizations, that between the first-century Jewish Christians, with their primitive conceptions of a three-story universe, and twentieth-century thinkers guided by modern science, philosophy, and historical studies.

There is a kerygma, or proclamation, of religious truth at the core of the Gospel traditions, but this can be retrieved only by "demythologization." What he called demythologization was a program of stripping away the mythical outgrowths that had sprung up around the Gospel stories so as to get down to their core message. This message was nothing less than existentialism: "Heidegger's existentialist analysis of human existence seems to be only a profane philosophical presentation of the New Testament view of who we are," Bultmann wrote.[151]

The criteria for demythologization were modern science and existentialism: "What is involved here, is not only the criticism that proceeds from the world picture of natural science, but also—and even more so—the criticism that grows out of our self-understanding as modern persons."[152] The Christian life of the Spirit does not involve anything supernatural but is "a genuine human life," which gives up "all self-contrived security."[153]

Among the Christian beliefs Bultmann rejected as "myths" were the ideas of the virginal conception, resurrection, ascension, and second coming of Christ. Also rejected were the notions of the incarnation of God in Christ, the atonement effected by the death of Christ, and the doctrine of the Trinity. Christianity, according to Bultmann, was "a remarkable product of syncretism."[154]

In the sections that follow we will meet many standard-bearers of the Bultmannian mind-set, as well as the overall skeptical challenge, on all these fronts.

THE JESUS SEMINAR

The now defunct Jesus Seminar was an assembly of like-minded New Testament scholars who, by voting among themselves, "decided" which statements and deeds attributed to Jesus are authentically his. Since most of the participants already shared the same skeptical views about the New Testament sources and the Jesus story, it was not surprising that they reached the same skeptical conclusions.

What was different with this enterprise was the fact that these "majority" conclusions were instantly broadcast to the media with the implicit suggestion that they represented mainstream research. But if you had asked a group of fifty evangelical New Testament scholars to take a vote on which of Jesus' statements and deeds in the New Testament were historical, the results would have been fairly predictable. In neither of these cases would the poll have a bearing on what is the majority view of "mainstream" scholarship. At best the Jesus Seminar offered a snapshot of the opinions of a few radical scholars at a certain time.

Interestingly, the seminar's principle for determining which of Jesus' words originated from him was not based on a set of peer-reviewed criteria. Rather, the participants started with their own picture of Jesus and on the basis of this picture they determined what he was likely to say. Burton Mack, one of its leaders, said that the standard criterion of dissimilarity is replaced with "the criterion of plausibility, given what can be reconstructed of social life and thought in the Galilee of the times."[155]

Mack is notoriously skeptical about the New Testament. In his view Christianity is a creation of Mark. The real Jesus was a Cynic sage who began a movement of social protest. N. T. Wright notes that "the huge development necessary for Mack's theory to work is almost entirely (since there is no real evidence for it whatsoever) an exercise in creative imagination." He concludes, "Mack's proposal, in short, is a historical hypothesis, to be verified according to the normal canons; and by those canons it fails."[156]

For Mack, as also John Dominic Crossan, the idea that Jesus is a Cynic philosopher influenced by the Greco-Roman intellectual milieu is crucial. But specialists on first-century Palestine such as Eric Meyers find this assumption to be implausible. Meyers "considers the Hellenistic influence on Galilee in the time of Jesus to be on a much smaller scale than Mack or Crossan envisages." Meyers cannot, in fact, "in the Galilee at the time of Jesus find traces of the Mediterranean and Hellenistic traditions of the Cynic philosophers that Mack and Crossan suggest." His conclusion is that "Jesus' Galilean context was first and foremost a Jewish one both in context and in its political, administrative form."[157] Moreover, recent archaeological studies[158] indicate that the city of Sephoris near Nazareth was culturally Jewish during the time of Jesus and became a Hellenistic center only one to two centuries later. This finding significantly undermines the Jesus-as-Cynic thesis of Crossan, Mack, and the Jesus Seminar.

N. T. Wright concludes that what the Jesus Seminar gives us "is not the detailed objective study of individual passages, leading up to a new view of Jesus and the early church. It is a particular view of Jesus and the early church, working its way through into a detailed list of sayings that fit this view."[159] The Seminar proclaims that it has found "what Jesus really said," but the presumptuous claim of finding the "real" Jesus is the favorite superstition of every card-carrying skeptic. Perhaps the most perceptive critique of the Jesus Seminar comes from a non-Christian, the eminent Jewish scholar Rabbi Jacob Neusner: "I think that the Jesus Seminar is a scholarly hoax in which people are pretending to know things that we cannot possibly know and no scholarly issue is settled by having scholars vote. At first I thought it was a joke, but it isn't a joke. They really take themselves very seriously and they pretend to have informed opinions about issues that are very hard to settle. They also pretend to settle these by voting. I think that is absurd." Rabbi Neusner noted that if the Seminar was not a hoax then this meant that New Testament studies has become intellectually bankrupt because those who pursue it "have used up all of the capital of rationality, logic and rigorous argument that sustains scholarship. You cannot give up on all of the rules and still be a going concern."[160]

THE NIHILIST SKEPTIC

The nihilist skeptic is perhaps the most pleasant of the three amigos. Unlike the fundamentalist and the traditionalist, the nihilist does not have a position to defend. Nonetheless, he is the deadliest of the three because nihilism (from the Latin *nihil*, "nothing") is the chief enemy of rationality and truth in modern thought, the annihilation of all thinking and knowing.

In the latter half of the twentieth century, the dogmas of the Enlightenment were followed by the chaos of postmodernism. Under this new dispensation, the historical-critical method beloved of the traditionalists was ejected and replaced by newer methods shaped by literary, cultural, and sociological considerations. For instance, instead of simply trying to determine the history of texts or communities, narrative criticism tried to focus on the text itself and the world built into the text. This led to strategies of reading such as structuralism, where you examined texts in a quest for embedded universal structures, and reader response criticism, where you studied the role of the reader in constructing meaning.

The question of whether biblical texts concern real-world happenings is of no interest to these critics since they do not believe we can ever know anything. It is not simply the fact that they do not believe in the stories and sayings relating to Jesus. Rather, they do not believe in any stories and sayings.

JOHN DOMINIC CROSSAN

Today's best-known New Testament nihilist is John Dominic Crossan. He is not a pure nihilist because he takes a traditionalist approach to some questions. Crossan himself would deny that he is a skeptic and affirm that he is a Christian who believes the Bible to be the Word of God. But what makes Crossan so devastating is his pattern of ceremoniously giving with one hand while innocuously taking away with the other—all this without the average observer being any the wiser.

Like any good magician, the suave theologian is so subtle and swift with his sleight of mind that a gullible audience will think that the improbable and the implausible are natural and normal. Ask him if he believes that Jesus rose from the dead or that Jesus is the Messiah or the Son of God, and he will say yes. Ask him why he believes all this or whether Jesus physically rose from the dead in the course of history or if Jesus is actually what the traditional titles affirm him to be, and he will evade a direct answer.

The sayings of Jesus and the sayings about Jesus, he will reply, originate in evolving traditions that reflect the faith of the early communities; for those who have faith, for those who experience God in a certain way, Jesus is known through these categories. But is Jesus actually what his followers believe him to be?

At that point, we are given discourses on metaphors and told how the Gospels themselves were produced long after the purported events had taken place; each author later "created" events and words that reflected his faith. All we know about Jesus is that he had taken a stand against unjust power structures and paid the price. The accounts of his passion, death, and resurrection are clearly not historical; they were just ways of using Old Testament prophecies and themes to express the faith of his followers. They were hermeneutical and not historical events.

Crossan's most prominent work is *The Historical Jesus: The Life of a Mediterranean Jewish Peasant.*[161] In it, Crossan denies the following:

- The objective existence of a God who exists whether or not there are people who believe in his existence
- The existence of a life after death
- The virginal conception of Jesus
- Jesus as the source of most of the sayings attributed to him in the Gospels
- The natural miracles of Jesus including the raising of Lazarus from the dead—although he accepts some healings
- The passion of Jesus, the burial of Jesus, the empty tomb of Jesus, the physical resurrection of Jesus
- The divinity of Jesus as affirmed by Christians

It is hard to see how anyone who denies all of the above can, in all seriousness, describe himself as a believing Christian—but that is precisely what Crossan does.

Crossan deploys three complementary strategies:

- From his magic hat, he adroitly produces his own sequence of the pre-Gospel literary sources used in creating the Jesus story: this is, at best, a conjuring trick because there is no historical or literary evidence supporting Crossan's ingenious sequence, and it has consequently not been endorsed by any major New Testament scholar, mainstream or otherwise.
- He provides a study of the social anthropology and cultural setting of Jesus' era and alleged environment and applies his own mix of the data in "locating" Jesus' mission and life. Given the largely subjective nature of his selection of the data and its application, Crossan's results

here have been sharply disputed, and he himself has revised some of his claims.

- He then generates his historical reconstruction of what we can know about Jesus.

Crossan's Jesus is a Cynic philosopher and social revolutionary. But Crossan's Cynic thesis is now seen to be fatally flawed. For example, there is no evidence that there were Cynics in first-century Palestine. Also, Cynics were generally from towns. His critics have said that Crossan, like Bultmann and the older German critics, has entirely missed the Jewish dimension of Jesus' culture and agenda just like he misunderstood the apocalyptic nature of Jesus' teaching. As we shall see, these are insights that have been recognized in the third quest for the historical Jesus.

Crossan seems clear when he says, "I am seeking an understanding of the Jesus tradition. . . . What is of supreme interest to me is not the content of the Jesus voice but the nature of the Jesus tradition."[162] His method of reconstructing the historical Jesus is essentially one of picking, choosing, and in some instances creating the data he needs to support his preconceived portrait of Jesus.

He admits that his image of the historical Jesus is dependent on his particular ordering of the New Testament sources, and "if wrong today or disproved tomorrow, everything I have done on the historical Jesus would need review."[163] In fact, Crossan's inventory of New Testament sources, built almost entirely on guesswork, has not been accepted by any major New Testament scholars. Consequently, there is no good reason to accept his rendering of "the historical Jesus."

But Crossan is important in the present context because he demonstrates the dangers of nihilism and its sibling, Gnosticism. He replaces the standard accounts of the historical Jesus with his own speculative version of the life, mission, and death of Jesus. This speculative version is dependent on an endless regress of sources and traditions that are hypothesized into being so as to support a particular picture of Jesus: Cynic philosopher, wisdom teacher, social revolutionary, egalitarian. This is the Christ of Crossan's faith, who must be accepted without any historical evidence.

BEYOND NIHILISM

The nihilist loss of intellectual nerve paralyzes the mind and reduces reality to a maze of smoke and mirrors. Nihilism was most clearly embodied in the philosophy of Friedrich Nietzsche, who claimed: "Every belief, every considering something-true, is necessarily false because there is simply no true world."[164]

Nietzsche's denial of reality and truth seems to have hypnotized one European philosopher after another, from Martin Heidegger to Jacques Derrida. Everything thus became perspective, interpretation, narrative, rhetoric, including the assumption that, not only was there no such thing as truth, but there was also no need to even bother to deny the existence of truth.

Instead, or in contrast, the goal of reasonable, thoughtful, people is to find out what we can know about Jesus from all available and reliable sources. But such exploration inherently assumes that we can make judgments, discern patterns, and draw inferences, that we are capable of—yes—knowing. In fact, these assumptions are fundamental to the whole framework of data, explanation, understanding, discovery, and encounter. But these are the very assumptions that nihilists deny and—by extension—their New Testament–studying fellow travelers. Consequently we have to both identify their presuppositions—which we have done—and show why these are wrong.

Ultimately, in a journey such as ours, the only enduring response to nihilism is a fundamental recognition and acceptance of the facts that we *do* know and of the fact that we *can* know. Pause for a moment and consider some of the things of which you are certain. You know that at this very moment you are reading, that this essay had at least one author, that the print marks on these pages contain a message, that this message may well describe your own experience accurately.

At virtually every instant of our lives, we perform actions that show the nihilists to be dead wrong. We engage in conversations, we write e-mails, we read newspapers. What do all these things have in common? They assume that we can understand and that we can "mean" things. We "see something to be the case" or say, "I know what you mean."

To know is to see something to be the case, and the best analogy is physical seeing. No proof can show that the activity of "seeing" exists. You have to "see" to believe in seeing. Dom Illtyd Trethowan put it very well:

"Knowledge is basically a matter of seeing things [and] arguments, reasoning processes, are of secondary importance and this not only because without direct awareness or apprehension no processes of thought could get under way at all, but also because the point of these processes is to promote further apprehensions."[165]

When we turn to a study of the phenomenon of Jesus, we are called to make a certain kind of judgment. We have to determine for ourselves whether or not the data makes sense in the light of what is being claimed. It's a matter of assembling, explaining, understanding, and perhaps, discovering. We have to judge, infer, synthesize, recognize. This requires both an openness and confidence in our self-evident capability of assessing and judging.

And so, as the three amigos ride into the sunset, it would be fitting to end this section with Albert Schweitzer's century-old admonition, which remains as valid today as when he first uttered it:

> Modern historical theology has more and more adapted itself to the needs of the man in the street. More and more, even in the best class of works, it makes use of attractive headlines as a means of presenting its results in a lively form to the masses. Intoxicated with its own ingenuity in inventing these, it becomes more and more confident in its cause, and has come to believe that the world's salvation depends in no small measure upon the spreading of its own "assured results" broadcast among the people. It is time that it should begin to doubt itself, to doubt its "historical" Jesus, to doubt the confidence with which it has looked to its own construction for the moral and religious regeneration of our time. Its Jesus is not alive.[166]

CHAPTER 14

A Return to the Roots of the Jesus Story

The preceding survey may seem to suggest that historical investigations into Jesus are all dead ends. This is not always or necessarily the case. We will now consider what can be known about the life and teaching of Jesus on the basis of historical studies that take the phenomenon on its own terms.

We have thus far outlined the range of views of the New Testament to highlight the nature of the problem we face when it comes to knowing Jesus. Our exploration of these views shows that neither historical analysis nor critical studies of the texts can solve the problem in any definitive sense. But that is not the same as saying that there is no solution possible. In fact, we affirm that a study of the "hard facts" does provide us with a solution. And the sooner we recognize the self-imposed constraints that come from relying only on texts, the sooner we can pursue all the "leads" available.

At this point the skeptic will protest that we falsely assume a solution is possible. The moral of this whole exercise, says the skeptic, is that the relativists are right after all. Everything in this business is a matter of opinion, and we can never hope to transcend such an inherent self-limitation. But instead of cursing the darkness, let us light a candle. Historical-critical studies may not yield any definite answers, but they do lay out various possibilities, some of which are more probable than others.

So here we are—lost in darkness so thick that even the candles we think we light are projections of our mind, nocturnal mirages. Does our quest then stop here? Since blind literalistic belief is not an option for those who wish to study the evidence, do we simply choose to "believe" one of the myriad theories, knowing full well that we cannot know anything for certain? Instead of believing in nothing, we pretend to believe in something, all the while knowing that we are pretending!

The answer offered in this book, an answer consistent with the beliefs of the earliest followers of Jesus, is entirely different. The process of explanation and understanding considers exegesis and historical analysis, but it also studies the thinking and acting church as well as the sense of the supernatural embedded in the experience of the followers of Jesus and the apparent pointers to a pattern of divine action in history. To be sure, a study of the New Testament narratives is essential because it is both a primordial and present-day testimony to the experience of Jesus. Moreover, most critiques of the claims of Jesus and his followers take these narratives as their starting point. But there are other sources as well.

In the context of these considerations, our study of the Jesus phenomenon proceeds down parallel paths. We set out to:

- Amass the results of various serious historical studies into the life of Jesus and extant historical evidence relating to his Jewish forebears and contemporaries;
- Consider the beliefs and practices of the Christian community from its earliest days as embodied in the writings of the early church fathers, the liturgies, and the early creeds;
- Sift through traditions about the teachings of the apostles and the churches they started;
- Study the history of councils and synods and the remarkable body of sophisticated doctrines they generated;
- Analyze the accounts of miraculous events and encounters through the centuries; and
- Map the main themes sounded in the major religions that preceded the coming of Christ.

For the most part, these are the paths we traverse. In the course of this chapter, we hope to complete the phases of compiling, explaining, and understanding the data, thus opening the door to the possibility of discovery and encounter. Our approach requires us to take seriously the results of New Testament scholarship while distinguishing data from speculation. We will rely on three rational and universally acceptable principles that should guide all research relating to Jesus:

- We should study the Jesus phenomenon on its own terms without inserting our own a priori dogmas.

- We should study the phenomenon in its entirety and not just those areas (e.g., the texts) with which we are comfortable.

- We should anchor ourselves in the data at hand—the Gospels, the transformation of the apostles, or the acting church, for instance—instead of creating and swearing by an infinite regress of hypothetical documents and traditions for which there is no evidence other than our own fervor.

THE GOSPELS AS BIOGRAPHY

The word *gospel* is derived from the Old English *gōdspel,* for "good tale" or "good news." One of the major breakthroughs in New Testament studies over the last two decades has been a better understanding of the literary structure of the Gospels. Most scholars had accepted the Gospel according to Bultmann: his view that the literary form of the Gospel was unique, sui generis, and each of the four Gospels had been assembled from bits and pieces of oral tradition. In this Bultmannian universe, the Evangelists were less writers in their own right than they were collectors of traditions.

In a dramatic turnabout, it is today widely recognized that the sui generis theory was mistaken and the Gospels belong to a biographical genre common in the Greco-Roman world. Charles Talbert's 1977 book *What Is a Gospel?* explicitly stated that the Gospels belong to the genre of Greco-Roman biographies. This line of thought came to a head with the publication in 1992 of *What Are the Gospels? A Comparison with Greco-Roman Biography* by Richard Burridge.

Burridge's work had an enduring impact. "Very few books on the Gospels have influenced scholarly opinion more strongly," wrote Cambridge New Testament scholar Graham Stanton in his introduction to the second edition. "I do not think it is now possible to deny that the Gospels are a sub-set of the broad ancient literary genre of 'lives,' that is, biographies."[167] Talbert, who pioneered the new approach, noted that "this volume ought to end any legitimate denials of the canonical Gospels' biographical character."[168] This new perspective on the Gospels represents an irreversible breakthrough in our study of Jesus. It lifts us out of the quicksand of an endless regress of prior traditions and allows us to shelve futile and unverifiable speculation about the origins of the sayings of Jesus. We realize now that we are dealing with what were seen as standard biographies of Jesus rather than quilts of sayings and traditions.

In building his case, Burridge shows that the biographical genre of the ancient era, which is very different from the modern biography (hence he prefers the Greek term *bioi*), had elements of historiography, rhetoric, encomium, polemic, and moral philosophy. There are four standard elements that constitute these works: opening features, subject, external features, internal features. Using these as his template, he analyzes ten Greco-Roman biographies, five written before the Gospels and five contemporaneous with or after, and finds that they fit a definite genre. For the most part, these biographies were about statesmen, philosophers, and poets. He then applies the same template (using computer analysis of verb forms among other things) to the synoptic Gospels and the Gospel of John and concludes that each of the Gospels clearly belongs to the same genre of Greco-Roman biography. Within this genre, the Gospels most closely resemble the biographies of philosophers.

Burridge's study offers a treasure chest of insights, as noted in a review article:[169]

- Greco-Roman biographies have internal and external features. Internally, these biographies center on the ancestry, birth, education, character traits, deeds, death, and influence of its subjects. From an external standpoint, they tended to be prose narratives with a length of 11,000–19,000 words and chronological accounts with topical material. In its internal and external features, the structure and content of the Gospels match those of the Greco-Roman biographies.

- The protagonist's last days and death were a key part of the Greco-Roman biographies: Plutarch (17.3 percent), Nepos (15 percent), Tacitus (10 percent) and Philostratus (26 percent). It is no surprise then that the Last Supper, trial, passion, and resurrection of Jesus takes up between 15 and 19 percent of the Gospels.

- Luke 1:1–4 is a formal preface that is "a significant attempt to relate his work to contemporary Greco-Roman Literature" (188).

- Jesus is the subject of the verbs in a quarter to a sixth of all the instances in the Synoptics and in John. This is the same proportion as that of other biographies.

- The dialogues and speeches in John (which are longer than in the Synoptics) are similar to other biographies "especially those of philosophers and teachers."

The very literary structure of the Gospels is a testimony to the Evangelists' central claims about Jesus. The literary form employed communicates how "writing a biography of Jesus implies the claim that not only is the Torah embodied, but that God himself is uniquely incarnate in this one life, death and resurrection."[170]

The writers of the Gospels intended to convey historical fact in their work. David Aune observes that the biographies of the day emphasized praise of their subjects but were nevertheless rooted in historical fact and not literary fiction. Consequently, the fact that the Evangelists chose to deploy the Greco-Roman biographical format indicates that their intention was to communicate what they thought had actually happened.[171] The Evangelists emphasize their historical intent with a focus on the role of eyewitnesses and testimony. Luke says, "Just as those who were eyewitnesses from the beginning and ministers of the word have handed them down to us, I too have decided, after investigating everything accurately anew, to write it down in an orderly sequence for you" (1:2–3). "It is this disciple who testifies to these things and has written them, and we know that his testimony is true" (John 21:24).

THE GOSPELS AS HISTORY

Another startling development comes from renewed ways that the Gospels themselves are accepted as historical documents. In the past, critics had sought to brush aside the surface credibility of the Gospel narratives by offering their own highly speculative accounts of what (in their view) actually took place. But now, as E. P. Sanders highlighted in his influential *Jesus and Judaism*, the dominant view is that we not only know what Jesus set out to accomplish and what he said but also that both of these fit into the world of first-century Judaism.[172] Peter Stuhlmacher of Tübingen points out that as a Scripture scholar his inclination was to doubt the Gospel stories, but as a historian he is obliged to take them as reliable. In fact, as he sees it, the biblical texts are the best hypotheses for explaining what really happened.[173]

Even such Jesus Seminar skeptics as Robert Funk and Marcus Borg accept some of the healings and exorcisms of Jesus. Funk comments that Jesus' reputation as a healer made it probable that he did engage in healing. Borg holds that there is a historical core behind the picture of Jesus as healer and exorcist, especially given that there are more healing stories about Jesus than about anyone else in Jewish tradition.[174] The fact that exorcisms were attributed not just to Jesus but also to his followers suggests to scholars that Jesus did perform exorcisms. Josephus, the first-century Jewish historian, wrote that Jesus was "a doer of startling deeds." As to the claims of Jesus bringing the dead back to life, it is striking that the town of Bethany was renamed as el-Azariyeh, "the place of Lazarus," by the Arabs after its destruction by the Romans in AD 70.

No longer manacled by the Bultmannian dogma that the miracle stories belong to mythology, scholars have begun to take a second look at their historical basis. Craig Evans reports that Jesus scholars now both treat seriously and generally accept the miracle stories as deriving from Jesus' ministry.[175]

Likewise, many non-Christian historians even accept the crucifixion of Jesus as historical. In a remarkable passage, the Jewish scholar Paula Fredriksen writes, "What do we *know* about Jesus of Nazareth, and how do these facts enable us to start out on the road to a solid and plausible historical portrait of him? The single most solid fact about Jesus' life is his death: he was executed by the Roman prefect Pilate, on or around Passover, in the manner Rome reserved particularly for political insurrectionists, namely, crucifixion."[176] Fredriksen notes that it is unfashionable to talk about "facts," but a reconstruction of Jesus' mission and message must address "what we *know* to have been the case."

THE DISCOVERY OF THE JEWISH JESUS

But perhaps the greatest breakthrough of all in biblical studies over the last two decades has been the discovery of the Jewish Jesus. A May 2008 *Time* story described this as one of the "ten ideas that are changing the world."

To understand what Jesus said and did and how he was perceived, we must understand first the theological thought world and symbol-universe in which he lived, spoke, and acted. He was Jewish and lived in the world of Second Temple Judaism. Now, this might seem to be a mere truism, but incredibly, most of the leading lights in the history of New Testament criticism have seemed entirely oblivious to it. Among other things, eminent scholars portrayed him as an enemy of Judaism, a purveyor of platitudes, a sixties hippie, and a nineteenth-century liberal revolutionary. ("Historical criticism became, in the hands of most of those who practised it, a secret struggle to reconcile the Germanic religious spirit with the Spirit of Jesus of Nazareth," said Schweitzer.[177]) These portrayals were little more than anachronistic flights of fancy, but they proved to be irresistible to the best and the brightest.

In this period of the third quest for the historical Jesus we have seen an emphasis on the Jewishness of Jesus and the need to understand his life and teaching in relation to the Judaism of his time. "With its emphasis on the continuity between the Jewish worlds of Jesus and the Judaism-infused theology of a crucified Messiah," says Charlotte Allen, "the Third Quest seems to promise some results of lasting value—perhaps because it represents a full-circle return. Jews and Christians will probably never reach a consensus on who Jesus was, but the importance placed by the third questers on the ancient prophetic tradition offers a way in which Jews and Christians might reach a consensus on what Jesus *was like*."[178]

N. T. Wright, who is one of the third quest's best-known representatives, identifies at least twenty major historians and theologians whose work can be situated in this quest. They range from George Caird and Martin Hengel to E. P. Sanders and James Charlesworth. Although the conclusions of the various authors vary dramatically, there are certain key approaches and assumptions they hold in common. Jesus is placed within "apocalyptic Jewish eschatology." This apocalyptic eschatology had nothing to do with the end of the space-time world; rather, it concerned the end of the present world order and the coming of the kingdom of God, which is the restoration of God as king of the world. The Jewish people saw their history coming to a climax through the action of God as promised by their prophets and laid out in the covenant. Jesus, in this frame of reference, saw the climax taking place in and through him.

Scholars, now guided by first-century sources and by a study of Judaism of the day, evaluate Jesus' message in terms of what it would mean to its hearers, not for its timeless significance. There is no attempt to detach Jesus' sayings from the rest of the evidence and to downplay the Jewishness of Jesus—both mainstays of earlier quests for the historical Jesus. The dissimilarity criterion of the previous quests walled Jesus off from both Judaism and the early church. The new approach locates Jesus within Judaism and also sees continuity between him and his followers.

The focus on history means that Jesus has to be studied not simply in terms of his sayings but also in the context of his actions and mission. Instead of simply creating arbitrary criteria (to determine, for instance, which sayings of Jesus derive from him), scholars now apply such standard methods as hypothesis and verification, which are deployed in the study of any historical figure. Thanks to this welcome development, the study of Jesus can move from ideology into history. "All these things have enabled the study of Jesus to rejoin the mainland of historical work after drifting, for more years than was good for it, around the archipelago of theologically motivated methods and criteria."[179]

We've also made progress in learning about the world of Jesus. We see this especially in the case of the 1947 discovery of the Dead Sea Scrolls, a collection of two-thousand-year-old Jewish religious documents, in the Wadi Qumran. Charlotte Allen notes that the accounts of Judaic beliefs and practices in the scrolls were dramatically similar to those portrayed in the New Testament narratives. These include the notion of "living water," a sacred meal of bread and wine, and eschatological meditations on the coming of someone seen as the Messiah, who "will be called the son of God; they will call him the son of the Most High."[180]

The similarities between Qumran and Christian ideas were close enough for some writers to speculate that the Qumran community was made up of

Christians. But when the Israeli Department of Antiquities performed state-of-the-art carbon-14 testing of the scrolls in 1991, they found "that most of the documents in question dated to the second and first centuries BCE with only one text dating to the period after Jesus' birth."[181] The scrolls are nevertheless important in showing that the New Testament sayings of Jesus are not alien creations of various communities constituting the "early church" but the kind of teaching one would expect from a Jewish apocalyptic prophet of the first century. Scholars see the Dead Sea Scrolls as providing reliable information on the Judaism of the first century.[182]

Additionally, we know more about the cultures and philosophies that were prominent at the time of Jesus. These insights in tandem with what we know of the thought-structure of Judaism in first-century Palestine help us assess the significance of the teachings and actions of Jesus reported in the New Testament accounts. In themselves, such critical studies cannot tell us whether or not the reported events and statements actually took place, but they can help us appreciate the nature and implications of what was being claimed.

A major breakthrough has also been the willingness over the last century for leading Jewish thinkers to look beyond the polemics of the past and consider the claims and mission of Jesus. Startling is the passion with which some of them accept and celebrate Jesus as a devout fellow Jew.

One thinks here in particular of Martin Buber, Joseph Klausner, Sholem Asch, Schalom Ben-Chorin, and Harvey Falk. At the same time we have the work of scholars like Rabbi Jacob Neusner and Jon Levenson, who pinpoint the precise areas of divergence between Jewish and Christian understandings of the Torah and Jesus and other foundational issues. Moreover, prominent Jewish scholars of today, such as Geza Vermes, Paula Fredriksen, and Amy-Jill Levine, have specialized in New Testament and life-of-Jesus studies.

Judaism is obviously important when we consider the life and mission of Jesus. This is because Jesus was a Jew who lived in the intellectual and cultural universe of Second Temple Judaism and described himself and his mission in its vocabulary. Likewise, his apostles and the leaders of his church were all Jewish and viewed their proclamation of the kingdom of God as the fulfillment of Judaism rather than as a separate religion. This obvious connection was somehow missed by the life-and-teaching-of-Jesus establishment and has only recently become part of mainstream New Testament studies.

While there is a central nonnegotiable point of difference between Judaism and Christianity, we cannot discount the importance of "locating" the life and teaching of Jesus in its true theological and historical home, the people of Israel. And in this respect the renaissance of Jewish studies of Jesus has made an incalculably important and profoundly moving contribution to the deeper understanding of Yeshua, whom Christians acclaim as the Messiah of Israel.

A few excerpts from the writings of the Jewish admirers of Jesus will make this abundantly clear.

Professor Joseph Klausner in *Jesus of Nazareth*:

Jesus was a Jew and a Jew He remained until His last breath. His one idea was to implant within His nation the idea of the coming of the Messiah and by repentance and good works, hasten the "end." . . .

From the standpoint of general humanity, He is, indeed, "a light to the Gentiles." His disciples have raised the lighted torch of the Law of Israel . . . among the heathen of the four quarters of the world. No Jew can, therefore, overlook the value of Jesus and His teaching from the point of view of universal history. This was a fact neither Maimonides nor Yehuda ha-Levi [medieval Jewish scholars] ignored.[183]

Martin Buber:

Since my youth I noticed the figure of Jesus as that of my great brother. That Christianity should consider, has considered him and considers him as God and Redeemer, has always seemed to me a fact of great seriousness, that I must try to understand for his love and for my love. . . . My open brotherly relationship with him always got stronger and got purer more than ever. And for me, it's more certain than ever that he will have an important place in the history of faith in Israel and that this place cannot be circumscribed with any of the usual categories of thought.[184]

Schalom Ben-Chorin in *Brother Jesus: A Jewish Point of View on Nazareth*:

Underneath the Greek face of the Gospels there hides, so to speak, an original Jewish tradition, in that Jesus and his disciples were Jewish, purely and solely Jewish.[185]

Rabbi Stephen S. Wise, founder of the Jewish Institute of Religion:

Neither Christian protest nor Jewish lamentation can annul the fact that Jesus was a Jew, an Hebrew of the Hebrews. Surely it is not wholly unfit that Jesus be reclaimed by those who have never unitedly nor organizedly denied him, though oft denied by his followers; that Jesus should not be so much appropriated by us as assigned to the place in Jewish life and Jewish history which is rightfully his own. Jesus was not only a Jew but he was the Jew, the Jew of Jews. . . . In that day when history shall be written in the light of truth, the people of Israel will be known not as Christ-killers, but as Christ-bearers; not as God-slayers, but as the God-bringers to the world.[186]

Professor David Flusser in *Christianity: A Jewish Religion*:

As long as no Christian New Testament scholar [had] begun to doubt this—and even declared that the life of Jesus was "non-messianic" (what does the life of a messianic person look like?)—it never entered the mind of any Jew to doubt the messianic self-consciousness of Jesus. . . . Over the last years I have expended much strength and diligence to show in Hebrew as well as in English that Jesus really understood himself as Messiah and as the coming Son of Man.[187]

Sholem Asch in *One Destiny*:

A little less than two thousand years ago, there came into our world among the Jewish people and to it a personage who gave substance to the illusion perceived by our fathers in their dream. Just as water fills up the hollowness of the ocean, so did he fill the empty world with the spirit of the one living God. No one before him and no one after him has bound our world with the fetters of law, of justice, and of love, and brought it to the feet of the one living Almighty God as effectively as did this personage who came to an Israelite house in Nazareth in Galilee—and this he did, not by the might of the sword, of fire and steel, like the lawgivers of other nations, but by the power of his mighty spirit and of his teachings.

He, as no one else before him, raised our world from "the void and nothingness" in which it kept losing its way and bound it with strong ties of faith to the known goal, the predetermined commandment of an almighty throne so as to become a part of the great, complete, everlasting scheme of things. He, as no other, raised man from his probationary state as a beast, from his dumb, blind, and senseless existence, gave him a goal and a purpose and made him a part of the divine. He, as no other, works in the human consciousness like a second, higher nature and leaves man no rest in his animal state, wakens him, calls him, raises him, and inspires him to the noblest deeds and sacrifices. He, as no other, stands before our eyes as an example and a warning—both in his divine form and in his human one—and demands of us, harries us, prods us to follow his example and carry out his teachings.[188]

CHAPTER 15

The Aims and Claims of Jesus

We have outlined some of the remarkable developments in our understandings of Jesus. This leads us inevitably to questions about the aims and claims of Jesus. What was his mission, and who did he say he was? In this area too there has been a major breakthrough, particularly with respect to our understanding of what Jesus intended and why.

Here we should pay attention not simply to the words of Jesus but to his acts and their symbolic significance. His mission was inextricably tied to the vocation of Israel, and his ministry was oriented entirely toward the divine promise of salvation.

JESUS' MESSIANIC CLAIMS

What is meant by "Messiah" and other titles applied to Christ in the New Testament? "Messiah" is Hebrew and "Christ" Greek for "the anointed one." As we will see, any claim that Jesus never saw himself as Messiah stands in conflict with the texts as they stand.

In the texts, the accounts of Jesus' baptism and temptation show that he has a messianic role to play, as does the Transfiguration, with the two messianic figures Moses and Elijah. Simon Peter's confession that Jesus is the Messiah at Caesarea Philippi (Matt. 16:13–21; Mk. 8:27–31) is an explicit affirmation of his messianic role because Jesus commends Peter for stating this truth. Jesus' triumphant entry into Jerusalem, recorded in all the Gospels, is again messianic in its relation to Old Testament prophecy. Most important, the main charge against Jesus at his trial was his claim to be the Messiah, a claim he did not deny and that led to his condemnation: "Again the high priest asked him and said to him, 'Are you the Messiah, the son of the Blessed One?' Then Jesus answered, 'I am'" (Mk. 14:61–62).

One of the greatest contemporary authorities on Jesus' messianic claims, Tübingen scholar Martin Hengel, points out that Jesus lived in the world of the Old Testament and its Jewish-Galilean environment. He acted with the apocalyptic right to inaugurate God's reign over Israel and all nations as the "Anointed to God." His death, which Jesus consciously affirms, was the seal of confirmation on this right. Hengel goes so far as to say: "that Jesus conducted himself in this manner, I hold to be provable by the methods of historical-critical research."[189]

Jesus' self-understanding of his prophetic role is evident as well. There can be no doubt that Jesus also saw himself as a prophet, as did his contemporaries. He presented himself, in fact, as an eschatological prophet announcing the kingdom of God.

JESUS' DIVINE CLAIMS

At the center of the Christian proclamation are the claims of divinity made about Jesus. Here an understanding of Jesus' Jewish milieu is indispensable in making sense of his purported statements and actions. For a Jewish perspective we turn to Rabbi Jacob Neusner.

In his *A Rabbi Talks with Jesus*, Neusner develops the following train of thought: Jesus' claim to fulfill the Torah ("Think not that I have come to destroy the law, or the prophets—I have come not to destroy but to fulfill" [Matt. 5:17 KJV] gives him a status equal to that of Moses. But Jesus in his statements also claims to supersede the Torah when he says that he is Lord of the Sabbath and that his followers have to choose him even over their own parents. In the Sermon on the Mount he repeatedly says, "You have heard that it was said [in the Torah]. . . . But I say unto you . . ." These utterances show that he sees himself as superior to the God-given Torah, which gives him a status equal to that of God. "Christ now stands on the mountain, he now takes the place of Torah."[190]

In several incisive statements, Neusner goes to the heart of what Jesus claimed in his teachings: "Jesus was not just another reforming rabbi out to make life 'easier' for people. . . . No, the issue is not that the burden is light. . . . Jesus' claim to authority is at issue."[191]

The issue that divides Neusner and the Christian is fundamentally the question of who Jesus is. But both agree that Jesus claimed to be God. The Christian affirms that Jesus indeed was God and man. In a commentary on Neusner's book, Pope Benedict XVI writes that Jesus' interpretation of the fourth commandment goes beyond the parent-child relationship to the social structure of the people of Israel. Such a restructuring derives from "Jesus' claim that he, with his community of disciples, forms the origin and center of a new Israel. Once again we stand before the 'I' of Jesus, who speaks on the same level as the Torah itself, on the same level as God." The two dimensions of "the opening up of the 'eternal Israel' into a new community" and "Jesus' divine claim" are directly connected.[192] As Messiah, Jesus

> has brought the God of Israel to the nations, so that all the nations now pray to him and recognize Israel's Scriptures as his word, the word of the living God. He has brought the gift of universality, which was the one great definitive promise to Israel and the world. This universality, this faith in the one God of Abraham, Isaac, and Jacob—extended now in Jesus' new family to all nations over and above the bonds of descent according to the flesh—is the fruit of Jesus' work. It is what proves him to be the Messiah. It signals a new interpretation of the messianic promise that is based on Moses and the Prophets, but also opens them up in a completely new way.[193]

Let's encapsulate what is integral to the first-century Jewish milieu and review the claims of Jesus in this light:

- Judaism had a strong sense of God incarnating himself in history. In Judaism, the role of the temple and the language used of Shekinah, Torah, wisdom, Word, and Spirit in the Old Testament shows us a transcendent God who is also immanent, active in the world and especially in Israel. This was the language used by the first Christians (who were of course Jewish) when they developed Christology.[194]

- Jesus saw himself through the lens in which the Jewish people saw God's action in the world.[195]

- As R. T. France, R. H. Stein, and others have shown (see below), Jesus identifies himself with the God of Israel in an astonishing variety of contexts:

  - He forgives sins (Mk. 2:1–12)—something only God can do.

  - He gives rest to those who embrace his yoke (Matt. 11:28–30) —Judaism saw this as a function of the divine wisdom.

- He had the right to cleanse God's temple (Mk. 11:27–33).
- His words have eternal validity (Mk. 13:31)—like God's (Isa. 40:8).
- His words had greater authority than the Old Testament (Matt. 5:31–32).
- He is the Lord of the Sabbath (Mk. 2:28).
- He decides the eternal destiny of every person, and his decision is based on the state of their relationship with him (Matt. 7:21–23; Mk. 8:34–38).
- He is the ultimate judge; he is king of an everlasting kingdom (Matt. 25:31–46).
- To accept or reject him is to accept or reject God (Matt. 10:40).
- He is the Good Shepherd who seeks and saves the lost (Lk. 19:10; Jn. 10:11)—like God, who is shown as a shepherd in Ezekiel 34.
- He is the stone on which people stumble (Lk. 20:18)—an image for God in Isaiah 8.
- He compares John the Baptist (Mk. 9:12) to Elijah, who prepares the way for the coming of God in judgment (Mal. 3:1).
- His depiction of himself as judge (Matt. 24:31) is comparable to the depiction of God as judge in the Old Testament (e.g., Dan. 7:9).
- He portrays himself as shepherd, bridegroom, and sower in his parables—roles assigned to God in the Old Testament.
- The title "Son of Man" is the one Jesus applied to himself most often. In the Old Testament it is used to refer both to "man" (Ps. 8:5) and, more commonly, to a heavenly figure (Dan. 7:13) who will judge all people at the end of time. Jesus uses the title both to emphasize his authority (Mk. 2:10; Lk. 12:8) and his humility (Mk. 10:45).
- "Son of God" is the title by which a voice from the heavens refers to Jesus at his baptism and transfiguration, and he is addressed thus by Peter (Matt. 16:16), demons, and a centurion. Although the Old Testament has different understandings of this title, where it refers to Israel and to her king, in the Gospels the meaning of this title is especially evident in the special relationship between Jesus and his

Father: "No one knows the Son except the Father, and no one knows the Father except the Son." (Matt. 11:27).

- The identification of Jesus with the God of Israel is amplified in the rest of the New Testament. Jesus is:
  - The Lord of creation (Phil. 2:9–11; Col. 1:16–17; 1 Cor. 15:27)
  - Identified with Yahweh of the Old Testament (e.g., Rom. 10:9–13 and Joel 2:32; 2 Thess. 1:7–10 and 1 Cor. 5:5 with Isa. 2:10–19)
  - Recognized as having always existed (2 Cor. 8:9; Phil. 2:6)
  - The "form" (Phil. 2:6) and "image" of God (Col. 1:15)
  - Referred to as "God" (Rom. 9:5; 2 Thess. 1:12; Titus 2:13; Heb. 1:5–8; 1 Jn. 5:20; Jn. 1:1)
  - The fullness of deity incarnate (Col. 2:9)

We can now finally see the disconnect between the Jesus of history and the Christ of faith as a non sequitur. We cannot understand Jesus' work or his passion story unless we accept the New Testament account of his claiming to be the messianic Son of Man sent to Israel by God. His words and acts would have led his listeners to ask who he was![196]

Last, in perhaps the most moving dimension of the claim to divinity, we have Jesus' use of the term *Abba*. This usage of *Abba*, which means "Papa" or "Daddy," to refer to God is unique in religious literature and indicates an equality of nature. In fact, throughout the Gospels, he refers to God only as "Father" except on the single occasion when he quotes from the twenty-second psalm. Jean Galot notes that this invocation of God as *Abba* was unheard-of in Jewish religious language given the Jews' reverence for God's transcendence.[197]

The implications for the identity of Jesus are monumental. "We certainly do not get in the Hebrew Bible any teacher speaking of God as 'Father' . . . like the Jesus of Matthew. And this habitual and concentrated use rightly produces upon us an impression. . . . We are moved by it to wish that we too could feel that doctrine, even as Jesus teaches that we ought to feel; and that we, too, could order our lives in its light and by its strength." Fatherhood implicitly points to both generation and similarity of nature. In fact "Abba" contains a theology that led to the proclamation of the Son as being consubstantial with the Father. As with Jesus' identification of himself with the covenant and the Bridegroom, here too he implicitly affirms his divine identity. But "this divine identity was not detached from the human reality of Jesus. Rather, it was perfectly incarnated. Indeed, Abba expressed a human experience of divine sonship."[198]

JESUS AS SAVIOR

The Evangelists Matthew and Luke make the startling announcement that Jesus is a Savior: "You are to name him Jesus, because he will save his people from their sins" (Matt. 1:21). "For today in the city of David a Savior has been born for you" (Lk. 2:11). The declarations are further developed in the Gospels and the rest of the New Testament by reference to the Suffering Servant of Isaiah and other Old Testament prophecies. These programmatic directives come to a head with Jesus' unambiguous pronouncement in Mark 10:45: "For the Son of Man did not come to be served but to serve and to give his life as a ransom for many."

The Gospels and the Epistles and the entire New Testament center on the salvific mission of Jesus: his life and his acts, primarily his passion, death, and institution of the Eucharist, were oriented toward salvation. Historically Christians have proclaimed that Jesus made atonement for the sins of humanity through his death: he voluntarily gave up his life that we might be saved. This proclamation is embodied in the liturgies and sacraments of the church. Salvation lies at the center of the life of Christ.

There is a new willingness today to pay attention to what is obvious in the texts. Even skeptical historians now acknowledge that the narratives of the Passion in the four Gospels, the accounts of the suffering and death of Jesus, are remarkably consistent. They are willing to admit that there is a core of historical truth here. Likewise, they are open to acknowledging a redemptive dimension to Jesus' mission.

In an introduction to the second edition of her *From Jesus to Christ*, Paula Fredriksen writes,

I incline now to see the message of biblical redemption itself as *the* fundamental factor shaping Jesus' mission and his supporters' response to him. Both he and they exist as points along an arc that stretches roughly from the Maccabees to the Mishna, which passes from the prophecies of Daniel through the letters of Paul, from the later books of the classical prophets—Isaiah, Jeremiah, Ezekiel—in the Jewish canon to the Book of Revelation, which concludes the New Testament. It is the arc of a biblical perspective on God and history that scholars have labeled *apocalyptic eschatology*: the belief that God is good, that he will not countenance evil indefinitely, that in the End he will act to restore and redeem.

This is what binds Jesus together with his predecessors (like the Baptizer), his supporters, and his later apostles (like Paul). No sketch of the economic conditions of the Galilee can have a sufficient or convincing explanatory effect on all the data . . . in the way that these biblical apocalyptic commitments do.[199]

So how does Jesus understand the significance of his death, and why do the texts as well as the early church speak so clearly about a link between Jesus and atonement? Nowhere is this link clearer than in the emphasis given to Isaiah 53 in the Gospels. Did Jesus see himself as the Savior and, if so, in what sense? Can he be construed as the Suffering Servant of Isaiah? Did he consciously offer himself as the "ransom for many" (Mk. 10:45)?

In the Judaism of Jesus' day it was already believed that the death of an innocent person had the power of atonement for others. In this context, when Jesus identifies himself with the paschal lamb in the Last Supper he is expressly stating that his death will have a saving effect.

Contemporary scholars have shown that if we consider Jesus in terms of his Jewish milieu, many of his statements take on a meaning that may not be apparent to those living in other cultures and times. The prophets had said that there will be a time of eschatological tribulation. Jesus, a prophet steeped in Jewish eschatology, sees himself as the Messiah who will not only bring about this tribulation but also suffer and perish in it. By his suffering (as Brant Pitre notes) he will "ransom" the lost tribes of Israel from the nations in which they are dispersed and thus bring about the end of the exile. This tribulation is an eschatological Passover from which Israel is delivered by Jesus' "prophetic sign"; the new Passover sacrifice is followed by a new Exodus. After the Last Supper, Jesus cites Zechariah's prophecy about the shepherd being struck and the sheep falling away: it is his death that begins the tribulation. But Jesus also says here, "After I am raised up, I will go before you to Galilee" (Mk. 14:28 ESV). Brant Pitre concludes that "Jesus, speaking of himself as both Son of Man and Messiah, deliberately took the sufferings of the tribulation upon himself in order to atone for the sins of Israel, sins which had led them into exile. Because he saw this tribulation as nothing less than an eschatological Passover, he sought to inaugurate it in both word and deed, thereby, to bring about the End of the Exile and the restoration of the twelve tribes in a New Exodus."[200]

The discovery of the Jewish Jesus has enabled us to see Jesus and his mission in the context of the history of Israel. He is the Messiah. He is the embodiment of Word, wisdom, Spirit, temple. He is the Passover sacrifice. All of this inescapably roots his mission in the destiny of Israel. And the idea of the atonement is intrinsically related to the Jewish dimension of the mission of Jesus.

THE "LAST" SUPPER

From the earliest days, Christians affirmed that on the last night of his life Jesus instituted a sacred meal that would be a continuing manifestation of his redemptive death, covenant renewal, and sacramental presence. All his followers were commanded to celebrate this act of ascent and descent in perpetuity.

This injunction of the Lord was faithfully recorded in the first writings of the New Testament, the Letters of Paul, as well as in all the Synoptics, with a parallel version in John 6. In other words, it passed the tests typically applied by critics:

- multiple attestation (it is found in Paul and the Gospels),
- coherence (ties in with Jesus' aims), and
- discontinuity (from Jewish and early church practice [see below]).

Many scholars agree that Jesus celebrated a final meal with the disciples the night before his death and that it took place in the context of the Jewish feast of the Passover.[201]

Much has been made about apparent discrepancies relating to the precise timing of the Last Supper. The Synoptics speak of Jesus celebrating the

Passover a day earlier than John, who shows Jesus being crucified on the day the lambs were slain for Passover. This has been explained in several ways. In the Synoptics Jesus is shown following the calendar of the Pharisees, while John follows the calendar of the Sadducees, who moved Passover forward if it fell on a Friday—thus the Passover meal would be on Friday night. Others have said that Jesus followed the Essene calendar. Historians take John's passion story seriously in light of Josephus's accounts of the Passover and other such considerations. If indeed the Last Supper took place on the eve of the Passover sacrifice it would still be on the "day" of Passover, which begins the evening before the feast.[202]

The absence of a Passover lamb is significant. "The biblical accounts," writes Pitre, "strongly suggest that Jesus is replacing the 'flesh' of the Passover lamb (Exod 12:8) with his own body and the 'blood' of the Passover lamb (Exod 12:13, 22–27) with his own blood. Hence, by means of this final enacted sign, Jesus is *prophetically reconstituting the Passover sacrifice around his own suffering and death*, with himself as the new Passover lamb."[203]

It might be asked how Jesus apparently seems to violate the Old Testament injunction against drinking blood. The prohibition on eating blood was directly tied to atonement: "For the life of a creature is in the blood, and I have given it to you to make atonement for yourselves on the altar; it is the blood that makes atonement for one's life. Therefore I say to the Israelites, 'None of you

TABLE 15.1

Datum accepted by scholars	How skeptics "explain" it
YES, the urgency of participating in the Lord's Supper was laid out in the most ancient New Testament documents, the Pauline Epistles.	BUT this meant Paul invented it.
YES, the accounts of a regular celebration of the paschal meal met their criterion of discontinuity with Jewish traditions.	BUT this simply meant the New Testament writers adopted it from the pagans.
YES, it has multiple attestation because all the Synoptics, as well as John, contain an institution narrative.	BUT this simply meant that the Evangelists applied the Jewish Sabbath meal to their theological agenda.

may eat blood, nor may an alien living among you eat blood'" (Lev. 17:11–12 NIV). The atoning death of Jesus replaces the atonement offered through the animal sacrifices of the temple. It is his blood that atones for our sins. And in drinking his blood at his express command, we receive his life.

Despite these historical foundations, which meet skeptics' criteria for reliability, some skeptics refuse to recognize the obvious. In their view there was no Last Supper, and the idea of a ritually celebrated paschal meal originated not in Jesus but in the liturgical "creativity" of the early Christian communities. Some even allege that the ceremony had its roots in contemporary Greco-Roman cults. On closer examination, however, we find that none of these pronouncements are based on any historical or theological evidence: they are simply products of the "creativity" of armchair analysts who change the rules at random and rely only on speculation. Table 15.1 gives a few examples relevant to the present discussion.

Certainly, in view of Old Testament prohibitions against drinking blood, all Jews would have been shocked by Jesus' commandment to drink his blood. But Joachim Jeremias points out that this very fact should show that the institution came from Jesus. Whatever seems scandalous is by that very reason likely to be historical.[204] More recently it has been shown that since the Jews were forbidden to drink blood, this command can only be attributed to Jesus and not the early church.[205]

Additional skeptical escape route

(Of course, if it was not in the Epistles, the skeptics would then say that the Pauline "silence" proved it was a later invention.)

(Needless to say, if it was continuous with Jewish traditions this too would mean it did not originate in Jesus.)

(Of course, if it was included in only one or two of the Gospels, then this would mean it really didn't happen.)

A FOOTNOTE ON THE END OF THE WORLD

Among the most controversial of the teachings of Jesus in the Gospels are his sayings about the end times. The critics who say that none of Jesus' sayings in the Gospels actually came from him are willing to make an exception when it comes to these particular statements; they add triumphantly that he was, of course, wrong since the world did not end when he thought it would. Here are a few excerpts from the passages in question:

> As he was making his way out of the temple area one of his disciples said to him, "Look, teacher, what stones and what buildings!" Jesus said to him, "Do you see these great buildings? There will not be one stone left upon another that will not be thrown down." . . . "And then they will see 'the Son of Man coming in the clouds' with great power and glory, and then he will send out the angels and gather (his) elect from the four winds, from the end of the earth to the end of the sky. Learn a lesson from the fig tree. When its branch becomes tender and sprouts leaves, you know that summer is near. In the same way, when you see these things happening, know that he is near, at the gates. Amen, I say to you, this generation will not pass away until all these things have taken place." (Mk. 13:1–2, 26–30)

> Jesus left the temple area and was going away, when his disciples approached him to point out the temple buildings. He said to them in reply, "You see all these things, do you not? Amen, I say to you, there will not be left here a stone upon another stone that will not be thrown down." . . . "Amen, I say to you, this generation will not pass away until all these things have taken place." (Matt. 24:1–2, 34)

Jesus is talking about two things: the destruction of the temple and the ensuing tribulation on the one hand and the end of the world and his second coming on the other. The judgment of God and the vindication of his Messiah are the primary themes.

There is a remarkable level of agreement among scholars that Jesus did prophesy the destruction of the temple. At one time it was popular to say that these passages were penned after the destruction of the temple of Jerusalem since it was simply unthinkable that Jesus could predict the future. But this view could not survive the discovery of the Jewish Jesus.

Not only were Jesus' words uttered in the language of the great Jewish apocalyptic prophets but also statements of his such as the "abomination of desolation" parallel Old Testament texts on temple destruction. And since there is no one-to-one match between the actual destruction of the temple and the details of the prophecy, it is hard to argue for a postdated account.

Brant Pitre points out that most of the prophetic texts can be understood in terms of what actually happened in the generation that followed Jesus' sayings—that is, the prophecies were fulfilled:[206]

- The events in question were predicted to take place within one "generation." A generation is supposed to be forty years. The Romans destroyed both Jerusalem and the Temple in AD 70, that is, within forty years.
- Josephus (*Antiquities of the Jews* 20.8.6) reports that false Messiahs arose between AD 40–70 and that civil war raged in the Roman empire (*Jewish War* 4.8.1).
- Eusebius (*Church History*) reported worldwide famine under Emperor Claudius.
- Colossae and Pompeii were destroyed by earthquakes (AD 50s–60s).
- Both Jews and Gentiles (the Jerusalem Sanhedrin and Nero) persecuted Christians between AD 30–70.
- There was apostasy, as many Christian gave up their faith when persecuted (Rev. 1–3).
- As for the evangelization of the world, Romans 1:8 says the faith "is proclaimed in all the world."
- "For then there will be *great tribulation*, such as has not been from the beginning of the world until now" (Matt. 24:21): Romans crucified five hundred or more Jews each *day* (*Jewish War* 5.11.1).

The apocalyptic language of these sayings uses imagery found in the Old Testament:

- During the destruction of Babylon, the "sun, moon, and stars" are darkened (Isa. 13).

- When wicked nations are destroyed, stars "fall" from heaven (Isa. 34).
- When Egypt is destroyed, the "sun," "moon," and "stars" go dark (Ezek. 32).
- The "coming" of God refers to the judgment of a city or nation: "The Lord is coming" (Isa. 26) in judging a land; the Lord "comes" on a cloud (Isa. 19) in judging Egypt; when Jerusalem is judged, "*he comes up like clouds*, his chariots like the whirlwind" (Jer. 14:13); and the Son of Man is "at the very gates" of Jerusalem.
- In Daniel we read that "a Messiah shall be cut off, and shall have nothing; and the people of the prince who is to come *shall destroy the city and the sanctuary. Its end* shall come with a flood; and *to the end there shall be war*; *desolations are decreed*. . . . He shall cause sacrifice and offering to cease; and upon the wing of *abominations* shall come *one who makes desolate*" (Dan. 9:26–27). In Luke "desolation" refers to the destruction of Jerusalem: "But *when you see Jerusalem surrounded by armies*, then know that its desolation has come near" (Lk. 21:20).

It seems clear in Matthew 24–25 that Jesus is talking about two separate events, the first being the destruction of the temple and the second the end of the world. Commentators like Pitre have pointed out that the destruction of the temple that is Jesus' body in AD 30 prefigures the destruction of the Jerusalem temple in AD 70. And since the latter temple was seen as a microcosm of the universe, its destruction in turn prefigured the passing away of heaven and earth.

CHAPTER 16

Comeback—"On the Third Day"

The last chapter looked at the aims and claims of Jesus. But one particular claim deserves a chapter all its own.

An integral element—*the* integral element—of the Jesus story is the claim that he rose from the dead. Is there any way to confirm or justify it? Interestingly, many of the skeptical attacks on Christianity hardly pay attention to the evidence adduced in favor of the Resurrection. Skeptics dismiss it without further ado, along with all other claims of the supernatural in the New Testament, as a prescientific superstition or hoax.

Many a revisionist has piously paid homage to the resurrection "experience" and described the accounts of the risen Jesus as metaphorical representations of the changed lives of the disciples. Revisionists will always want to revise, of course, but we in the twenty-first century have grown up; no one in their right (modern) minds would take the primitive legendary accounts to be literally true. And yet they are "true" in the sense of reflecting the mental states of the disciples. Now here the matter may have ended and the case been brought to a close if not for one unavoidable consideration: the claim that Jesus physically rose from the dead is fundamental to Christianity no matter how you want to spin it. If Christians are mistaken on this point, then any historically continuous profession of the Christian faith has a problem.

If Jesus did not rise from the dead, if his body never left its tomb, if his corpse was devoured by scavengers, then Christianity itself is definitively dead. Crossan, Borg, and others blithely declaim that the "truth of Easter" does not depend on "whatever happened to the corpse of Jesus" and that the "powerfully true metaphorical narratives" simply tell us that the community experienced the "power of the Spirit they had known in Jesus continuing to be and to operate." Crossan, Borg, and the nihilist skeptics might well be sincerely convinced that Jesus did not physically rise from the dead and that it is still possible to believe in Christianity.[207] But no church father or council, Christian martyr or mystic would have found this curious juxtaposition intelligible. If there was one thing on which Christendom was unanimous for more than a millennium and a half, it was the affirmation that a Christianity not grounded in the physical resurrection of Jesus is unthinkable. Even the fundamentalist and traditionalist skeptics recognize this to be the case. At best it is simple self-deception to suggest that you can still believe in the conclusions reached by Christians while denying their central premises.

We have studied the skeptical mind long enough by now to recognize why the nihilists perform these kinds of intellectual balancing acts. For them the Jesus story is an entirely immanent, wholly horizontal operation. There is no room in their thinking for any intrusion of the transcendent in the space-time continuum. This world is all we are allowed to talk or think about.

Nowhere more than in the claim of Jesus' resurrection is there an ineluctable supranatural stake in the ground. The other world is suddenly in this world: concrete events and individuals here and now are "touched" by the Other. The revisionists can huff and puff and tut tut all they want about literalism and crude physicality, about the need to focus on "experiences" rather than on "facts." But everything about Christianity is flesh and blood and testimony to the truth and the transcendent in the immanent. Granted, the Christian story may be false, but let us not pretend this was not the story. If you want to rewrite the story, call it something else.

In brief, all of Christianity starts with three assumptions:

- Jesus is alive and acting in history.
- He is alive not as an idea but a definite person, an agent who takes specific and concrete actions.
- We know the first two assumptions to be true because he appeared physically to his disciples after his death.

THE RESURRECTION OF THE RESURRECTION

So how do we determine whether or not the Resurrection story is true? The main criticisms of the claim are summarized here:

- Resurrections do not take place as a matter of natural law, and no amount of evidence would suffice to show that the impossible took place.

- We do not know if the tomb of Jesus was empty.
- The disciples of Jesus concocted a fraud.
- The accounts of the appearances of Jesus were the product of hallucinations.
- The first accounts of the Resurrection were written years after they took place.
- The accounts have contradictions and discrepancies.
- Recently the tomb of Jesus with his remains has been found in Jerusalem.

Most of these critiques have been around for some time and have been regularly refuted. But one remarkable feature of today's trends is what we might call the intellectual resurrection of the Resurrection story. After languishing in the outer darkness of the Enlightenment, this claim that is fundamental to any possibility of coherent Christianity is back on the agenda of scholarly inquiry. Five monumental works have helped drive this dramatic turnabout:

- In *The Events of Easter and the Empty Tomb* (1952), Hans von Campenhausen defended the historical basis of the empty tomb claim.
- In *Jesus—God and Man* (1968), Wolfhart Pannenberg, one of Germany's leading theologians, argued that from the evidence for the empty tomb and the appearances of Jesus it is possible to rationally conclude that Jesus' resurrection from the dead took place in history.
- In *The Resurrection of Jesus: A Jewish Perspective* (1983), the Jewish scholar Pinchas Lapide held that no vision or hallucination is sufficient to explain the revolutionary transformation of the peasants, shepherds, and fishermen who had followed and then denied Jesus.
- In the epochal work *The Resurrection of the Son of God* (2003), N. T. Wright tied together the historical arguments in favor of the bodily resurrection of Christ. As noted in an Associated Press story, Wright seeks to answer the question "Why did Christianity emerge so rapidly, with such power, and why did believers risk everything to teach that Jesus really rose?" (Richard N. Ostling, April 19, 2003). The best explanation, argues Wright, is that the early Christians "all

believed that Jesus was bodily raised, in an Easter event something like the stories the gospels tell; the reason they believed that he was bodily raised is because the tomb was empty and, over a short period thereafter, they encountered Jesus himself, giving every appearance of being bodily alive once more."[208]

- In *The Resurrection of God Incarnate* (also 2003), noted Oxford philosopher Richard Swinburne argued that Jesus' resurrection from the dead is what you would expect if Jesus is God incarnate, that the accounts of his appearances were such as would be expected if there were real appearances, and that the available evidence is what would be expected if the tomb was indeed empty.

The different varieties of skeptics have obviously not gone away. In the old days, they professed their faith in philosopher David Hume's dogma against miracles. According to Hume, miracles do not happen because the laws of nature cannot be broken, and therefore, any claim of a miracle, no matter how well substantiated, has to be rejected. This of course is nothing more than a dogma to be believed in faith, and numerous were the skeptics who subscribed to it.

But the Humean approach is now found only among nonspecialists. The more common rejection of the Resurrection is that of the nihilist: the Resurrection as simply a metaphor. The bodily resurrection of Jesus, writes John Dominic Crossan "is a metaphorical parable about the meaning of Jesus' life and death and not an historical account about the status of Jesus' corpse and tomb."[209] In *The Last Week: A Day-by-Day Account of Jesus's Final Week in Jerusalem*,[210] Crossan and Marcus Borg argue that the "historical reports" of the empty tomb and Jesus' resurrection are purely and simply parables and metaphors, not historical facts.

The fatal flaw of the nihilists seems to be that they are often in the position of explaining away what is obvious and plausible. Two recent debates involving John Dominic Crossan, one with N. T. Wright and the other with William Lane Craig, illustrate the problem.

In a debate with Crossan, Wright clarified that the distinction should not be between literal and metaphorical, as Crossan would have it, but between concrete and abstract. The revisionists like Crossan are really saying that what happened at Easter was not a concrete event. Wright also pointed out that Crossan's hypothesis cannot account for the transformation of beliefs required for the first Christians to move out of Judaism or other religions and cultures. To Crossan's response that this change came from the announcement of the kingdom of God, Wright noted, "I don't think those by themselves would have been sufficient to generate anyone saying, 'He has been raised from the dead.'"[211]

Second, the published version of a debate between Crossan and William Lane Craig shows that Crossan does not choose to challenge the foundations of the traditional claims for the historicity of the Resurrection. In his concluding statement, Craig noted that he "summarized several lines of evidence with respect to each of the four putative facts. Fully expecting these points to be vigorously disputed by Dr. Crossan, I came to the debate prepared to defend each of them; but Dr. Crossan, to my surprise, failed to contest a single piece of evidence which I adduced in support of the four main facts." Even more astonishing is the fact that he does not attempt to defend the foundations of his own skeptical position. Craig again: "I came to the debate fully expecting a lively exchange concerning those presuppositions, but my preparations proved superfluous, as Dr. Crossan made almost no effort to defend his presuppositions."[212]

Another apparent attempt to refute the Resurrection was the 2007 Discovery Channel program "The Lost Tomb of Jesus." According to the program, a tomb found in 1980 in Jerusalem's East Talpiot region contained the ossuaries, or bone boxes, of Jesus, Mary Magdalene, allegedly Jesus' wife, and Judah, allegedly Jesus' son. Virtually every major archaeologist, Jewish, Christian, and nonbeliever, dismissed this sensational theory for various reasons. First, the inscription that is said to read "Mary Magdalene" actually says "Mariamene." Second, the names Jesus, Joseph, Judah, and Mary were among the most common Jewish names in Jesus' time. In fact, the name Joseph is used on forty-five known ossuaries that have been dug up, Judah on forty-four, Mary on forty-two, and Jesus on twenty-two. A January 2008 symposium of some of the world's leading archaeologists held in Jerusalem concluded among other things that the Mariamene listed on the ossuary is not

Mary Magdalene and that "the probability of the Talpiot tomb belonging to Jesus' family is virtually nil if the Mariamene named on one of the ossuaries is not Mary Magdalene." A panel of experts on the subject of Mary in the early church "dismissed out of hand the suggestion that Mary Magdalene was married to Jesus, and no traditions refer to a son of Jesus named Judah (another individual named on an ossuary from the Talpiot tomb). Moreover, the DNA evidence from the tomb, which has been used to suggest that Jesus had a wife, was dismissed by the Hebrew University team that devised such procedures and has conducted such research all over the world."[213]

ONLY THE UNBELIEVABLE WILL WORK

Before reviewing the arguments supporting the factuality of the Resurrection, we should—as in all areas of the study of Jesus—examine our expectations and accordingly align our assumptions. Often the empty tomb, the posthumous appearances of Jesus, and the transformation and worldwide witness of the apostles are cited as "proving" the Resurrection. But the claim of the Resurrection is too unbelievable to be supported by any and all of these. The fundamental starting point has to be the very origin of the Christian phenomenon. The pitiless processes of nature before which all must yield, the inexorable march of cosmic history, the drop-in-the-ocean insignificance of our planet relative to the multibillion-galaxy universe, the oblivion to which every living being is consigned at death—against this backdrop the only defense is something so decisively extraordinary as to transcend all that is earthly.

Even the skeptics' counterexplanations of hallucination or fraud concede too much because they assume that the Gospel accounts are accurate up to a point. In the interest of honesty, we have to be more radically skeptical than the most radical skeptics because we have to come to grips with the utterly merciless, relentless tidal wave of annihilation represented by the black hole of nonbeing, the wiping out of everything in death's dateless night. Only when we have realized the desperateness and wretchedness of our plight are we in the right frame of mind to consider the question before us.

What we are looking for is something so altogether extraordinary as to unmistakably bear witness to the extraordinariness of what is being claimed. Given this, we realize that we can never know what is true about the Resurrection until we are able to recognize the power and the glory of the three principal witnesses to this momentous claim:

- The Gospel narratives in their raw simplicity
- The universal and unchanging witness of the church
- And the voice of the Spirit of God within us

There is of course much rational evidence, but by itself such evidence does not suffice because the claim it tries to support is too extraordinary to rest simply on a structure of premises and inferences. But if the narratives are startling in their almost embarrassing matter-of-factness, if the message and practice of the church is shocking in its immediacy and universality, and if one's own heart is driven by a compelling sense of the presence of the risen one that is remarkable in its own right, then all three witnesses together can lead us to the universal Christian affirmation that the Lord *is* risen.

But to recognize what needs to be recognized is a far cry from actually making the leap. Nevertheless, only with this sensitized state of mind can we begin the pilgrimage to the empty tomb. No one put this more poignantly than the philosopher Ludwig Wittgenstein, who wrote the following:

What inclines even me to believe in Christ's resurrection? It is as though I play with the thought. If he did not rise from the dead, then he is decomposed in the grave like any other man. HE IS DEAD AND DECOMPOSED. In that case he is a teacher like any other and can no longer HELP; and once more we are orphaned and alone. So we have to content ourselves with wisdom and speculation. We are in a sort of hell where we can do nothing but dream, roofed in, as it were, and cut off from—heaven. But if I am to be REALLY saved, what I need is CERTAINTY—not wisdom, dreams or speculations—and this certainty is faith. And faith is what is needed by my HEART, my SOUL, not my speculative intelligence. For it is my soul with its passions, as it were with its flesh and blood, that has to be saved, not my abstract mind. Perhaps we can say: Only LOVE can believe the Resurrection. Or: It is LOVE that believes the Resurrection.[214]

MEANWHILE, BACK AT THE TOMB

Once our minds have been attuned to the enormity of the Resurrection claim, we are ready to do justice to the evidence, to assess the arguments that are relevant and to weigh the alternatives. We have noted David Hume's influential argument against miracles. Richard Swinburne, a leading philosopher of science, has shown the limitations of the Humean dogma. Swinburne notes that Hume's worst mistake concerned his assumption of the relevant background information, what might be called a "background" theory of the world's operations. Hume's error was to assume that only scientific data was relevant to such a background theory. But what is crucially relevant is a theory that can tell us whether the laws of nature studied by science are ultimate or if they depend on something "higher" to be operative. Here the fundamental issue is whether or not there is a God. If there is no God, then the laws of nature are the ultimate determinants of all events. But if there is a God, then when and how the laws of nature operate depends on God. This is especially the case if there is evidence not simply for a God but for a God who might occasionally intervene in the natural order. This will provide sufficient ground to expect occasional suspensions of the laws of nature.

Swinburne then applies this insight to the claim of the Resurrection. Such a claim of a "violation of natural laws," he suggests, would have to be supported by one or more of three kinds of evidence: apparent memories, testimony, or physical trace. What we have with respect to the Resurrection is apparent testimony of witnesses of an indirect kind. Such indirect testimony to historical events has to be considered as real testimony if there is no evidence to the contrary. "In this case there are several indirect witnesses and two at least of them claim to have heard their news from more than one direct witness. In such circumstances positive counter-evidence is needed for not believing the news."[215]

It has often been pointed out that the Resurrection claims are very ancient and therefore unlikely to have been the product of legend. First Corinthians 15:3–8 and Luke 24:34 are two of the most ancient creeds of the church, and both affirm the Resurrection; the appearances recorded in Matthew are also ancient in origin. In 1 Corinthians, Paul writes,

For I handed on to you as of first importance what I also received: that Christ died for our sins in accordance with the scriptures; that he was buried; that he was raised on the third day in accordance with the scriptures; that he appeared to Cephas, then to the Twelve. After that, he appeared to more than five hundred brothers at once, most of whom are still living, though some have fallen asleep. After that he appeared to James, then to all the apostles. Last of all, as to one born abnormally, he appeared to me.

(The terms "handed on" and "what I also received" are rabbinic terms referring to a sacred tradition; hence the conclusion that these verses come from a creed.) In Luke we see, "The Lord has truly been raised and has appeared to Simon." More details about the appearances are given in the Acts of the Apostles, showing the significance of the Resurrection for the early church.

Traditionally, the historical evidence for the physical resurrection of Jesus has been grouped under three categories: the existence of the empty tomb, the reports of the appearance of Jesus to his disciples and others, and the origin of the Christian church. These categories of evidence are summarized below.

The empty tomb:

- Jesus was buried: 1 Corinthians 15; Gospel accounts; no other claims made about Jesus' body.
- Tomb was guarded: even enemies acknowledged this.
- Historical core: sequence of discovery described differently in the Gospels but common threads; Joseph of Arimathea buried Jesus; women discovered the tomb was empty; angel seen outside.
- Women shown as first witnesses: Jewish law does not recognize women as witnesses: if the accounts were invented men would have been the witnesses.
- No fanciful description, as in the apocryphal accounts. No description of the actual Resurrection.

The appearances of Christ:

- In 1 Corinthians, Paul reports that Jesus appeared to him, Peter, the apostles, and five hundred others. The epistle was written when many of those who had seen the risen Jesus were still alive, and so it is unlikely to have been concocted. The Gospels show Jesus appearing to Mary Magdalene and other women, to ten of the apostles, and then to all eleven and also to the disciples on the road to Emmaus.

- Did the appearances in fact occur? The legend hypothesis is implausible because 1 Corinthians 15 is dated very early.

- Were the witnesses simply hallucinating? William Lane Craig gives reasons why this hypothesis doesn't work: hallucinations are individual in nature and are experienced only by one person, but the appearances of the risen Jesus were witnessed by hundreds; those who hallucinate usually expect to see the object of their hallucination, but the terrified disciples did not expect to see their master again after his crucifixion and burial; hallucinations are sometimes induced by drugs or mental illness, but the appearances were witnessed by people who were generally recognized to be simple, sober folk with differing personalities.

- Were they lying? This is implausible because the apostles literally staked their lives on the claim that they had seen the risen Jesus. Almost all of them died horrible deaths—but they went to their deaths proclaiming the Resurrection. It is unreasonable to suggest they were willing to die for a lie. Also, at least one witness was initially a skeptic, Saul of Tarsus. He had no reason to "invent" the Resurrection since it contradicted his previous beliefs.

Origins of Christianity:

- The explosion of Christianity in first-century Palestine cannot be explained without reference to the Resurrection. From the very beginning, as even Bultmann acknowledged, the message that Jesus had risen from the dead lay at the heart of the Christian gospel. The affirmation that Jesus was the Messiah would have been impossible if he had not been resurrected because for all practical purposes his mission would be considered a failure if it ended with the cross.

- The claim that Jesus had risen from the grave is not something that could have been extrapolated from any belief system. Although some

Jews believed in the idea of resurrection, such a resurrection is one that involved the entire human race and that took place at the end of history. Jesus' resurrection, however, involved one individual, and it took place within the historical process.

The claim of the resurrection of Jesus can no longer be dismissed as a pious legend or an afterthought as the nineteenth- and early-twentieth-century New Testament critics made out. It is a claim that anyone who wants to be taken seriously must at least consider. Even the hardiest of today's skeptics acknowledge the fact that the earliest Christians had experienced something. What remains in dispute is the nature of that "something."

THE RISING SON

Today, the claim of Jesus' resurrection from the dead is taken more seriously than ever before in the last two hundred years. Above all else, the rising Son of God is seen in the witness of the church, which was created in the decades after the Resurrection. N. T. Wright explains:

> I have examined . . . all the alternative explanations, ancient and modern, for the rise of the early church, and I have to say that far and away the best historical explanation is that Jesus of Nazareth, having been thoroughly dead and buried, really was raised to life on the third day with a new *kind* of physical body which left an empty tomb behind it because it had "used up" the material of Jesus' original body, and which possessed new properties which nobody had expected or imagined but which generated significant mutations in the thinking of those who encountered it. If something like this happened, it would perfectly explain why Christianity began and why it took the shape it did.[216]

Two other perspectives will be of interest here. Wolfhart Pannenberg, one of Germany's most important twentieth-century theologians, was once an atheist. He underwent an intellectual conversion to Christianity and affirmed that it is rationally untenable to deny that the resurrection of Christ was a historical event. He considered the empty tomb to be a strong argument in its favor. He noted that it is well known that there were early disputes between Christians and Jews concerning the Resurrection:

> The Jews accepted that the tomb was empty. The dispute, however, was about how this is to be explained. The Jews said the disciples had removed the body. But they did not question the fact that the tomb was empty. That, I think, is a very remarkable point. And then, of course, my main reason is a general reflection, given the concreteness of the Jewish understanding of a resurrection from the dead. It would hardly be conceivable that the earliest Christian congregation could have assembled in Jerusalem of all places, where Jesus had died and was buried, if His tomb was intact.[217]

Another unique perspective comes from Rabbi Pinchas Lapide, who caused a sensation with his argument that Jesus actually did rise from the dead. About the idea that Jesus' appearances to his disciples were simply the products of self-delusions, Lapide writes that in none of the accounts of such visions in rabbinic literature is there a change in the life of the person resuscitated or those who witnessed it. The vision was often embellished, but there were no other consequences.

> It is different with the disciples of Jesus on that Easter Sunday. Despite all the legendary embellishments, in the oldest records there remains a recognizable historical kernel that cannot simply be demythologized. When this scared, frightened band of the apostles which was just about to throw away everything in order to flee in despair to Galilee; when these peasants, shepherds, and fishermen, who betrayed and denied their master and then failed him miserably, suddenly could be changed overnight into a confident mission society, convinced of salvation and able to work with much more success after Easter than before Easter, then no vision or hallucination is sufficient to explain such a revolutionary transformation. For a sect or school or an order, perhaps a single vision would have been sufficient—but not for a world religion which was able to conquer the Occident thanks to the Easter faith. . . . If the defeated and depressed

group of disciples overnight could change into a victorious movement of faith, based only on autosuggestion or self-deception—without a fundamental faith experience—then this would be a much greater miracle than the resurrection itself.[218]

The post-Easter change in the disciples "was no less real than sudden and unexpected" and can only be explained with a concrete foundation like the physical Resurrection.[219] Lapide points out that for the first Christians the immediate historicity of the Resurrection "was not only a part of that happening but the indispensable precondition for the recognition of its significance for salvation."[220]

WE'VE ONLY JUST BEGUN

Those who come to recognize the factuality of the Resurrection do so because they find the evidence overwhelming and/or become increasingly aware of divine action in history.

Although we have concerned ourselves with the various arguments for the Resurrection, it should be said that a study that remains exclusively focused on answering the skeptics is misguided. If we do not recognize the claim of the Resurrection for what it is, we will neither take it seriously nor grasp its ultimacy.

The Resurrection is perceived as the most extraordinary event in human history not simply because it is miraculous nor only because it represented Jesus' victory over the forces ranged against him. Rather, it is especially significant because it is the key to human destiny; it is the organizational matrix of the human species.

Thus, the billions of years of cosmic history and the billions of galaxies that stretch across the cosmic spaces pale before the revelation that this unique union of matter and spirit we call the human person will last forever. Indeed, the very cosmos is ordered toward a new state of being mirrored in and modeled on the risen Jesus.

The claim of the Resurrection is a claim about Jesus, but it is also a claim about human destiny. Above all, it is an affirmation that God is working in human history through the laws of nature, drawing all of creation to a climax.

It is one small step for humanized divinity and a giant leap for divinized humanity.

CHAPTER 17

Who Do I Say That You Are?

Now that the questions of history are behind us, we confront the question that Jesus asked nearly two thousand years ago: "Who do you say that I am?" The very fact that he put such a question is intriguing. It's almost as if he wants his hearers to discover who he is. And when Peter answers that he is the Son of the living God, Jesus states that this is a revelation from on high; it is neither a lucky guess nor a logical deduction.

Jesus is a phenomenon that is to be examined in its entirety, explained, understood, discovered, and finally encountered. Now we face the challenge of saying who he is, of moving toward discovery and encounter. Inevitably, the answer is a deeply personal one.

The dynamic underlying the spread of Christianity, ultimately, was one of personal discovery and encounter. To be sure, the trappings of empire and social acceptance helped its growth. And, of course, most Christians today are Christian because they were born into a Christian family or environment. But the rise and expansion of Christianity and its corresponding sociocultural influence are grounded ultimately in discovery and encounter. The converse is also the case. Where discovery and encounter have ceased, the Christian faith eventually ceases to have an influence, and this is especially apparent in those societies described today as post-Christian. Nevertheless, the opportunity to discover and encounter is always available.

Our survey has shown the different options that are possible with respect to the identity of Jesus:

- Jesus did not exist, and the whole story of his life and mission was concocted by clever Galileans.
- There was a Jesus, but we know next to nothing about his actual life and teaching since his followers overlaid their accounts with later beliefs and traditions.

- Jesus was a first-century rabbi who falsely claimed to be the Messiah and was put to death.

- Jesus was a prophet of God superseded by later prophets.

- Jesus was a political revolutionary.

- Jesus was a wisdom teacher.

- Jesus was a Cynic philosopher.

- Jesus' earliest followers never claimed that he was divine.

We have already seen why some of these options simply cannot get off the ground.

TABLE 17.1

Verdict on Jesus	Historical reality
Jesus did not exist	The accepted antiquity of the Epistles of Paul, the references to Jesus in the writings of both the greatest Jewish and the greatest Roman historians, and the explosive growth of the Christian church within the Roman Empire within a decade of Jesus' reported death put the burden of proof on those who "believe" in Jesus' nonexistence. No prominent historian, Christian or non-Christian, denies the existence of Jesus, and the leading contemporary proponent of the Jesus-does-not-exist school, G. A. Wells, has now retracted his position.
Nothing can be known about Jesus' life or teachings because there are no reliable records	Mainstream historians and New Testament critics have discounted this nineteenth- and early-twentieth-century contention— especially after the recognition of the genre of the Gospels and the discovery of the Jewish Jesus. Although critics today have different interpretations of Jesus' identity, they do not deny the historical reality of the central sections of the Gospel narratives.
Jesus was a reform rabbi who mistakenly thought he was Messiah	Not only have New Testament scholars discovered the Jewish Jesus, but Jewish scholars have also "reclaimed" Jesus. While they have rightfully identified Jesus' faithfulness to his Jewish heritage, some have ignored or discounted his larger claims. But other Jewish scholars have equally rightly pointed out that he was not just a reform rabbi but that he claimed to be both Messiah and the Lord of the Torah. In their view, these claims are incompatible with Judaism.
Jesus was a political revolutionary	If he was simply a political revolutionary, he would not have been accused of blasphemy. As noted, perceptive Jewish thinkers of our day find that Jesus' claims were theological not political.
Jesus was a wisdom teacher	If he was just a wisdom teacher there is no reason why he would be crucified.
Jesus was a Cynic philosopher	It has turned out that there is no evidence of Cynic philosophers being active in first-century Palestine.

Verdict on Jesus	Historical reality
Jesus was a prophet of God superseded by later prophets	Jesus did not claim to be a prophet. His claims were to divinity and messiahship. Whether or not there is good reason to believe these claims is a different matter, one which we address in this chapter. But if he were truly a prophet of God he would not make a blasphemous claim—of being God. And if he is truly God and man then he is the ultimate and definitive revelation of God.
Jesus' followers never claimed that he was God and man	It has been said that the proclamation of the divine nature of Jesus may have been a later invention rather than one that originated either in Jesus or in his first followers. The evidence, however, indicates that early followers did make these connections:

1. New Testament documents date back to the first century with some of the Epistles of Paul being the earliest. The divine personhood of Jesus is proclaimed either explicitly or implicitly in these documents. Colossians says, "In him dwells the whole fullness of the deity."

2. Among the Gospels, the latest one, the Gospel of John, is obviously very clear in its proclamation of the divinity of Jesus: "And the Word was God." But the synoptic Gospels—as we have seen—are just as explicit, with Jesus affirming his divine status in a variety of contexts as confirmed by contemporary Jewish scholars.

3. If Jesus was not spoken of as divine, the new movement would have been incorporated into Judaism as a sect.

4. Even the earliest skeptics did not use the argument that Jesus made no claim to be divine.

5. The earliest church fathers, those who taught right after the apostles in the first and second centuries, are unanimous in proclaiming Jesus as God incarnate.

6. The Eucharist, which was celebrated from the first century, included the command to eat of the body of Christ and drink of his blood. This Eucharistic practice is implicit acceptance of divinity because, as noted, only God "can give us his own blood, the symbol of his own life, to drink."

7. All those churches that claimed to have an apostolic origin, those that were formed in the first century, proclaimed Jesus as God and man. This was especially true of the church begun by Peter and Paul and the mother church of all the others.

8. The Christians were persecuted by pagans precisely because of the nature of their nonnegotiable commitment to Jesus as God. If they were willing to worship the Roman emperor, they would have been left alone. Also, they were called cannibals because they were said to consume the body and blood of their Savior.

9. The ancient liturgies and creeds of the church bore ample witness to the faith of the first Christians in the divinity of their founder.

10. In general, the ancient veneration of Mary testified to the Christians' beliefs about her Son. The dogmatic definition of Mary as the Mother of God (in 431) bears witness to the common conviction that Jesus was God incarnate.

In this next phase of our inquiry, we will proceed in five stages.

WHAT DID THE FIRST CHRISTIAN FATHERS SAY?

Already in the Gospel of John we see Jesus addressed explicitly as God: "My Lord and my God!" (Jn. 20:28). Clement of Rome in his epistle of AD 96 speaks of "Our Lord Jesus Christ, the Scepter of the majesty of God," who "did not come in the pomp of pride or arrogance, although He might have done so, but in a lowly condition, as the Holy Spirit had declared regarding Him."[221] The affirmation that Jesus is God and man is constantly reiterated by all the fathers thereafter. This testimony of the fathers is extraordinarily important because it shows us that, in addition to the New Testament claims, the entire edifice of Christianity from its inception rested on the affirmation that Jesus was human and divine. This was the engine driving the followers of Jesus in their preaching and teaching, their praying, and their celebration of the Eucharist.

Ignatius of Antioch

> For our God, Jesus Christ, was conceived by Mary in accord with God's plan: of the seed of David, it is true, but also of the Holy Spirit. (*Letter to the Ephesians* 18.2 [AD 110])

Justin Martyr

> For if you had understood what has been written by the prophets, you would not have denied that He was God, Son of the only, unbegotten, unutterable God. (*Dialogue with Trypho* 121 [AD 155])

Irenaeus

> Nevertheless, what cannot be said of anyone else who ever lived, that he is himself in his own right God and Lord . . . may be seen by all who have attained to even a small portion of the truth. (*Against Heresies* 3.19.1 [AD 189])

Clement of Alexandria

> The Word, then, the Christ, is the cause both of our ancient beginning— for he was in God—and of our well-being. And now this same Word has

appeared as man. He alone is both God and man, and the source of all our good things. (*Exhortation to the Greeks* 1.7.1 [AD 190])

Tertullian

The origins of both his substances display him as man and as God: from the one, born, and from the other, not born. (*The Flesh of Christ* 5.6–7 [AD 210])

Origen

Although he was God, he took flesh; and having been made man, he remained what he was: God. (*De Principiis* [The Fundamental Doctrines], 1.1.4 [AD 225])

Hippolytus

Only [God's] Word is from himself and is therefore also God, becoming the substance of God. (*Refutation of All Heresies* 10.33 [AD 228])

Cyprian of Carthage

One who denies that Christ is God cannot become his temple [of the Holy Spirit]. (*Letters* 73.12 [AD 253])

Gregory Thaumaturgus

There is one God, the Father of the living Word, who is his subsistent wisdom and power and eternal image: perfect begetter of the perfect begotten, Father of the only-begotten Son. There is one Lord, only of the only, God of God, image and likeness of deity, efficient Word, wisdom comprehensive of the constitution of all things, and power formative of the whole creation, true Son of true Father . . . immortal of immortal and eternal of eternal. . . . And thus neither was the Son ever wanting to the Father, nor the Spirit to the Son; but without variation and without change, the same Trinity abides ever. (*Declaration of Faith* [AD 265])

WHAT THE COUNCILS AND CREEDS OF THE CHURCH TAUGHT ABOUT JESUS

From the beginning, the major forums for the church's teaching mission included councils and creeds. The first seven councils of the church reflected on the witness to Jesus that had been received from the apostles and the first followers of Jesus. The councils took the fundamental truths handed to them as starting points and confirmed, clarified, and amplified their attendant implications and inferences. This meant excluding certain views as incompatible with the primordial body of truth and defining explicitly what was implicit.

In table 17.2 are the principal conclusions from these councils, and in the text below are excerpts from two of the creeds.

TABLE 17.2

Council	Date	Doctrines Taught
Nicaea I	325	Jesus Christ is of the same substance (*homoousios*) as God. The Nicene Creed was developed to teach this and other truths of the Christian faith.
Constantinople I	381	The Holy Spirit is consubstantial with the Father and the Son. The Nicene Creed confirmed and further refined.
Ephesus	431	There is only one person in Christ, a divine person, although he has two natures, divine and human. Mary is therefore Theotokos, the Mother of God.
Chalcedon	451	Jesus is truly God and truly man and the two natures exist in him "without confusion, without change, without division, without separation." In his divinity, Christ is "consubstantial with the Father" and in his humanity he is "consubstantial with us in manhood."
Constantinople II and III	553 and 680	Ratification of previous councils, particularly of Chalcedon.
Nicaea II	787	Ratification of the previous councils and a defense of the practice of venerating sacred images.

Creed of Nicaea I

The Council of Nicaea is remembered not simply as the first of the post–New Testament councils but as the council that definitively articulated the affirmation that Jesus was divine. This affirmation was spelled out with such specificity ("begotten not made," "of the substance of the Father") as to leave no room for alternate interpretations of its underlying teaching. The creed it laid out for the faithful became the first normative statement of belief for Christians.

> We believe in one God, the Father Almighty, maker of all things visible and invisible; and in one Lord Jesus Christ, the Son of God, the only-begotten of his Father, of the substance of the Father, God of God, Light of Light, very God of very God, begotten not made, being of one substance with the

Doctrines Condemned

Arianism the Son is a creature and neither preexistent nor of the same substance as God.

Semi-Arians the Son is like the Father but not in essence.
Pneumatomachians the Holy Spirit is a creation of God but not God.
Eunomians Arians who believed in a form of polytheism (three deities).
Sabellians denial of three divine persons: the view that Father, Son, and Holy Spirit are simply three modes of one divine person.
Apollinarians Christ had no human soul or mind.

Nestorianism the view that there are two persons in Christ, one human and one divine.

Monophysitism Christ has only one nature, a divine nature, although he took on human flesh.

Repeated condemnation of the heresies mentioned above.

Condemnation of iconoclasm, the view that the veneration of sacred images is equivalent to idolatry.

Father. And whosoever shall say that there was a time when the Son of God was not or that before he was begotten he was not, or that he was made of things that were not, or that he is of a different substance or essence [from the Father] or that he is a creature, or subject to change or conversion—all that so say, the Catholic and Apostolic Church anathematizes them.

Creed of Constantinople

The Council of Constantinople in 381 expanded and finalized the Nicene Creed and is known for emphasizing the divinity of the Holy Spirit. The finalized version is known today as the Nicene-Constantinopolitan Creed.

Our Lord Jesus Christ must be confessed to be very God and very man, one of the holy and consubstantial and life-giving Trinity, perfect in Deity and perfect in humanity, very God and very man, of a reasonable soul and human body subsisting; consubstantial with the Father as touching his Godhead and consubstantial with us as touching his manhood; in all things like unto us, sin only excepted; begotten of his Father before all ages according to his Godhead, but in these last days for us men and for our salvation made man of the Holy Ghost and of the Virgin. . . .

We glorify two natural operations indivisibly, immutably, inconfusedly, inseparably in the same our Lord Jesus Christ our true God, that is to say a divine operation and a human operation, according to the divine preacher Leo, who most distinctly asserts as follows: "For each form does in communion with the other what pertains properly to it, the Word, namely, doing that which pertains to the Word, and the flesh that which pertains to the flesh."[222]

ANCIENT LITURGIES ON JESUS

Right from the beginning of Christianity, the celebration of the Eucharist was the central act of worship of those who called themselves Christians. The earliest records of these liturgies were the *Didache* and Justin Martyr's *Apology*, from the first and second centuries. The celebration of the Eucharist, as detailed in those documents, was an explicit affirmation of, first, Jesus' divinity—because only God can give us his life through the vehicle of matter—and, second, Jesus' humanity—because it is the body and blood of the Jesus who lived, died, and rose again in human history. And whereas Yahweh was the center of Jewish worship, the triune God lies at the heart of the Christian liturgy.

These ancient liturgies, shown in table 17.3, testify to the universal Christian belief in the divinity and humanity of Jesus. Each text comes from liturgies across the Christian universe of the first five centuries. These include the Roman liturgy found in the work *Apostolic Tradition* by the presbyter Hippolytus, which goes back to AD 215; the liturgy of St. James, celebrated in the Antiochean Church; the liturgy of the apostles Mar Addai and Mari that found its home in the Chaldean Church; the liturgy of St. Mark, celebrated by the Coptic Church; the liturgy of St. John Chrysostom (which is believed to have its roots in the liturgies of St. James and St. Basil), of the Byzantine Church; and the liturgy of St. Basil.

TABLE 17.3

Hippolytus, Rome (approximately 215)	He is your Word, inseparable from you, through whom you have created everything and in whom you find your delight.*
Liturgy of St. James, Antiochean (between second and fourth centuries)	O Christ our God, Who by Your death trampled our death and destroyed it. You Who are One of the Holy Trinity, and are worshiped and glorified in unity with Your Father and Your Holy Spirit, have compassion on us all.†
Addai and Mari, Chaldean (approximately third century)	That all the inhabitants of the earth may know you, that you alone are true God the Father and that you have sent our Lord Jesus Christ, your son and your beloved, and he our Lord and our God taught us in his life-giving gospel.‡

* "Anaphora of St. Hippolytus of Rome," *Sancta Liturgia Blog,* http://sanctaliturgia.blogspot.com/2005/10/anaphora-of-st-hippolytus-of-rome.html, accessed December 21, 2010.

† "The Public Celebration of the Liturgy of the Catechumens," Syriac Orthodox Resources, http://sor.cua.edu/Liturgy/Anaphora/PubCeleb.html, accessed December 21, 2010.

‡ Thomas Elavanal, *The Memorial Celebration: A Theological Study of the Anaphora of the Apostles Mar Addai and Mari* (Alwaye, India: MCBS, 1983), 33.

TABLE 17.3 continued

Liturgy of St. Mark, Coptic (approximately fourth century)	O Prince of Life and King of Ages, God unto whom every knee bows, of those in heaven, of those on earth, and of those under the earth; to whom everything is subject and in the bond of servitude, bowing their heads to the scepter of Thy kingdom.*
Liturgy of St. John Chrysostom, Byzantine (fifth century)	O Only-Begotten Son and Word of God, Who, being immortal, deigned for our salvation to become incarnate of the Holy Mother of God and ever-Virgin Mary, and became man without change. You were also crucified, O Christ, our God, and by death have trampled death, being one of the Holy Trinity, and glorified with the Father and the Holy Spirit, save us.†
Liturgy of St. Basil (fourth century)	Let us give thanks to the beneficent and merciful God, the Father of our Lord, God and Savior, Jesus Christ, for He has covered us, helped us, guarded us, accepted us to Him, spared us, supported us, and has brought us to this hour. Let us also ask Him, the Lord our God, the Pantocrator, to guard us in all peace this holy day and all the days of our life.‡

THE MARTYRS AND MYSTICS ON JESUS

The most touching testimonies of faith in Jesus are to be found in the numerous accounts of the deaths of martyrs in the first three centuries of Christianity. The best-known historian of the martyrs was Eusebius (260–339). The two excerpts below describing martyrs facing death for their faith in Christ are believed to date from the reign of Marcus Aurelius in AD 177:[223]

Sanctus was another who with magnificent, superhuman courage nobly withstood the entire range of human cruelty. Wicked people hoped that the persistence and severity of his tortures would force him to utter something improper, but with such determination did he stand up to their onslaughts that he would not tell them his own name, race, and birthplace, or whether he was slave or free; to every question he replied in Latin, "I am a Christian."

---

* "The Coptic Liturgy of St. Mark the Apostle, Commonly Known as the Liturgy of St. Cyril," Coptic Orthodoxy Church Network, http://www.copticchurch.net/topics/liturgy/liturgy_of_st_cyril.pdf, accessed December 21, 2010.

† Adapted from http://www.wordiq.com/definition/Incarnation, accessed December 21, 2010.

‡ *St. Basil Liturgy Reference Book,* ed. Abraam D. Sleman, Coptic Church Network, http://www.coptic church.net/topics/liturgy/liturgy_of_st_basil.pdf, accessed December 21, 2010.

Blandina was hung on a post and exposed as food for the wild beasts let loose in the arena. She looked as if she was hanging in the form of a cross, and through her ardent prayers she stimulated great enthusiasm in those undergoing their ordeal, who in their agony saw with their outward eyes in the person of their sister the One who was crucified for them.

From the martyrs we turn to the mystics. The supernatural is the warp and woof of Christianity. From the miracles in the Gospels and Acts to the miracle traditions of the apostles on their worldwide journeys, to the countless other supernatural events associated with Christianity, we are dealing with a phenomenon that unashamedly and unambiguously has a foot in two worlds. This is not the place for a detailed exposition or defense of claims concerning such supernatural events. Rather, we will simply present some historically well-known claims of the visions of Jesus while noting that they represent the tip of the iceberg when it comes to such phenomena.

In the Acts of the Apostles, we read about the vision of Saul (who later became the apostle Paul): "On his journey, as he was nearing Damascus, a light from the sky suddenly flashed around him. He fell to the ground and heard a voice saying to him, 'Saul, Saul, why are you persecuting me?' He said, 'Who are you, sir?' The reply came, 'I am Jesus, whom you are persecuting. Now get up and go into the city and you will be told what you must do'" (9:3–6). In the book of Revelation, we see Jesus again in the first of John's visions: "A sharp two-edged sword came out of his mouth, and his face shone like the sun at its brightest. When I caught sight of him, I fell down at his feet as though dead. He touched me with his right hand and said, 'Do not be afraid. I am the first and the last, the one who lives. Once I was dead, but now I am alive forever and ever. I hold the keys to death and the netherworld'" (Rev. 1:16–18).

These visions of Jesus were to continue into the rest of Christian history. The idea of a supernatural vision of Jesus is neither novel nor heterodox. From its earliest days, some of the holiest and wisest men and women of Christendom—ranging from St. Augustine to St. Francis of Assisi—have reported such visions, and these visions were accepted as genuine by the church as a whole. Despite the antisupernaturalism of some of the Reformers, Martin Luther stated that he did not "detract from the gifts of others, if God by chance reveals something to someone beyond Scripture through dreams, through visions, and through angels."[224]

Table 17.4 displays a chronology of the visions of Jesus given in E. C. Brewer's *Dictionary of Miracles* and cited in Phillip Wiebe's *Visions of Jesus*.[225]

TABLE 17.4

Witness	Period	Vision
Pope Alexander I	118	Jesus as an infant
Forty Christians in prison	320	Jesus commends them for courage in facing death
St. Philomena	320	Infant Jesus
St. Gregory the Great	540–604	Jesus as a beggar
St. Porphory	353–420	Jesus on the cross
St. Jerome	347–419	Instructed by Jesus to spend more time on Scripture
St. Hubert of Brittany	c. 714	Jesus as a beggar
St. Wulsin of Sherbourne	10th century	Jesus reigning in heaven
Emperor St. Henry	1014	Jesus celebrating Mass in St. Mary Major
Hildegard of Bingen	1098–1179	Wrote of heavenly vision shown by Jesus
St. Antony of Padua	1195–1231	Seen with the infant Jesus
Mechtild of Magdeburg	1207–1282	Jesus' messages about God's love
St. Francis of Assisi	1221	Jesus gives him roses to commend his actions
St. Rosa of Viterbo	1235–1252	Jesus on the cross
St. Lutgard	1246	Jesus appears to bring her to faith, shows his heart
St. Gertrude the Great	1256–1302	Infant Jesus; Jesus in glory; stigmata
St. Hyacinth of Kiev	1257	Jesus crowning the Virgin Mary
St. Mechtilde of Heldelf	1293	Vision of Jesus during Mass
Blessed Angela of Foligno	1309	Visions of Jesus and messages
St. Bridget of Sweden	c. 1312	Jesus crucified
St. Clara	1346	Jesus on the throne
St. Catherine of Siena	1347–1380	Jesus as king; Jesus crucified
St. Vincent Ferrier	1396	Healed by Jesus
Julian of Norwich	1450	Suffering of Jesus
St. Columba	1477–1501	Jesus crucified
St. Teresa of Avila	1515–1582	Various visions of Jesus
St. Catherine dei Ricci	1522–1590	Suffering of Jesus; stigmata
St. Angela of Brescia	1535	Set up Ursuline Order after vision of Jesus
St. Ignatius of Loyola	c. 1537	Jesus crucified
St. Rose of Lima	1586–1617	Jesus as a child; stigmata
St. Margaret Mary Alacoque	1648–1690	Sacred Heart of Jesus, the most influential of the visions of Jesus
Sr. Mary of St. Peter	1816–1848	Messages from Jesus on the Holy Face
Sr. Conchita of Mexico	1862–1937	Messages from Jesus; victim-soul
Sr. Mary of the Divine Heart	1863–1948	Visions of the Sacred Heart
Sr. Josefa Menendez	1890–1920	Messages from Jesus; victim-soul
Sr. Mary of the Trinity	1901–1942	Messages from Jesus; victim-soul
St. Consolata Betrone	1903–1946	Messages from Jesus; victim-soul
St. Faustina Kowalska	1905–1938	Divine Mercy

WHY ALL OF THIS MATTERS

A definite portrait of Jesus emerges from the councils and creeds, the ancient liturgies and writings of the church fathers, the witness of the martyrs and the mystics. Theirs is a portrait of Jesus echoed time after time. This is the portrait that should serve as the touchstone of truth for any Christian understanding of Jesus. And this is the understanding of Jesus that is conveyed to us: Jesus is fully God; Jesus is fully man. He has a divine nature and a human nature. What is proper to human nature is a soul and body, that is, intellect and will, flesh and blood. Jesus has a human soul and body. What is proper to divine nature is an infinite mind and will and the fullness of all perfection. Jesus, in his divine nature, has all of this.

But if you ask who he is, we say that he is only one person, one "center" of consciousness, intellect, and will—and this one person is a divine person— the second person of the Trinity as we shall see soon.

The ancient church proclaimed him to be God and man because he is a divine person who united himself with a human nature. Only a person who is fully human and fully divine could save humanity from the consequence of its sin against the divine because the offense was both infinite—since it was committed against an infinite being—and finite, or human, since it was committed by the "first family" and all subsequent generations. The redemptive death of Jesus was simultaneously a human act and the act of an infinite person, and hence it served as a reparation that was sufficient and final.

From the dawn of recorded history, evil seems embedded in humanity. We have seen in part 1 of this book how religious history is marked by an awareness of shame and guilt and the need for reparation and expiation. Moreover, the most ancient human societies have believed that the origin of evil lay in some primordial catastrophe. This insight has been formalized in the Christian doctrine of original sin. The teaching of original sin simply tells us that evil had its beginning in the abuse of human freedom and that evil once unleashed leaves its mark on every human psyche. Our evil streak is obviously a matter of experience.

The fact that evil of any kind erects an insurmountable gulf between us and God is a discovery shared by all religions. In parallel, there has been the human effort to overcome this gulf through reparation and sacrifice. It is here that we recognize the significance of Christ as Savior. For it is he, as God incarnate, who bridges the gulf, he who makes atonement and redeems us, he who divinizes us. In short, we know that we have a problem: we do not know every detail of its origin, but we know what it does to us here and now. Most important, we know that we have a solution to the problem.

Of course, those who do not recognize that they have a problem, have a real problem.

DISCOVERY AND ENCOUNTER

There is a great urgency to this question in each of our lives: who was Jesus? We know what his followers and his church have said. We know what the New Testament texts proclaim. But how do we ourselves make a decision on this question? Was he indeed God and man and Savior?

To repeat, ultimately the answer to this question can only come from our own personal journeys of discovery and encounter. Discovery and encounter do not mean, of course, a simple leap in the darkness. As has often been said, faith is a leap to the light—although it can just as easily and legitimately be done in the midst of darkness.

The "light" that could lead one to personally believe and proclaim that Jesus is God and man and Savior may be categorized in terms of grounds and dimensions. By grounds we mean the rational grounds on which such an affirmation may seem justified. By dimensions we refer to the dimensions of the phenomenon of Jesus that could lead to such an insight. Here are fifteen grounds and dimensions that may serve as launching pads for your flight of faith.

1. Man on a mission

Let us look past the historians. The immediate impression left by reading any one of the Gospels is the image of a man on a mission. We see for ourselves someone who was "sent": "For this I was born and for this I came into the world, to testify to the truth. Everyone who belongs to the truth listens to my voice" (Jn. 18:37).

He calls disciples and sends them out in his name. He has come not only to announce the kingdom of God but also to offer up "my blood of the covenant, which will be shed on behalf of many for the forgiveness of sins" (Matt.

26:28). It is this mysterious sense of a mission not of this world but for this world that drives all those whose lives he touches. There is no time to lose and nothing that is not important. These are the thoughts that one expects of the source and goal of being, the Alpha and the Omega.

2. God's representative and God

He acted as God's representative on earth and as God. He forgives sins. He demands total allegiance. To be persecuted for him is to secure blessings. "Blessed are you when they insult you and persecute you and utter every kind of evil against you (falsely) because of me" (Matt. 5:11). His words are valid forever and have greater authority than the Old Testament. He determines your eternal destiny, and to accept or reject him is to accept or reject God.

Understanding Jesus' Jewishness has led to a greater awareness of the coded significance of what he said. When he spoke of himself as a Bridegroom, as the Son of Man, as judge, as the person to whom you should dedicate your life, as the forgiver of sins, he was explicitly claiming for himself the attributes that belonged in the Jewish mind only to Yahweh. If a man came to us and said he is the chief resident of the White House, that his personal transportation vehicle is Air Force One, and that he is the commander in chief of the U.S. military, then he would explicitly be stating that he is the president of the United States. This is indeed what Jesus did by describing himself in the very terms that his contemporaries understood as those of divinity.

After reviewing the evidence concerning Jesus, Richard Swinburne concludes,

> It is not merely the case that Jesus is the only serious candidate in human history about whom we have evidence that he lived the right kind of life which ended with a divine signature. Jesus was both the only prophet in · human history about whose life there is good historical evidence of the first kind (evidence that he or she lived a perfect life with much suffering, claimed to be divine, claimed to be making atonement, gave plausible moral and theological teaching, and founded a church to continue his work), and also the only prophet about whose life there is good historical evidence of the second kind (evidence that his or her life ended with a miracle recognizable as a divine signature).[226]

3. The purpose of life

If death is the end, then none of our actions on earth have any ultimate meaning or point. This is the problem that the philosophers and the sages could not resolve since they themselves were destined for oblivion. If Jesus was truly God incarnate, then we would expect him not only to acknowledge the problem but also to give us a solution. He did both, going right to the heart of the problem: "What profit is there for one to gain the whole world and forfeit his life? What could one give in exchange for his life?" (Mk. 8:36–37). "For whoever wishes to save his life will lose it, but whoever loses his life for my sake and that of the gospel will save it" (Mk. 8:35). "Then the king will say to those on his right, 'Come, you who are blessed by my Father. Inherit the kingdom prepared for you from the foundation of the world. . . . And these [the wicked] will go off to eternal punishment, but the righteous to eternal life" (Matt. 25:34, 46). His answer was the only viable one, the one that only God could give: we are called to live forever, and our choices in this life determine our everlasting destiny. To make the wrong choices is to lose it all. Everything matters. Everything is meaningful.

4. The incarnation of the holy

"Blessed are the clean of heart, for they will see God" (Matt. 5:8).

"If your right eye causes you to sin, tear it out and throw it away. It is better for you to lose one of your members than to have your whole body thrown into Gehenna" (Matt. 5:29).

"It would be better for him if a millstone were put around his neck and he be thrown into the sea than for him to cause one of these little ones to sin" (Lk. 17:2).

"When Simon Peter saw this, he fell at the knees of Jesus and said, 'Depart from me, Lord, for I am a sinful man'" (Lk. 5:8).

At the center of the human experience of God is the awareness of the sacred. The revelation of God in the Old Testament is the All-Holy, before whom nothing defiled can stand. And the coming of the Christ is nothing less than the incarnation of the Old Testament's Holy of Holies.

5. The exorciser of the world

"The Son of God was revealed to destroy the works of the devil" (1 Jn. 3:8). "Now is the time of judgment on this world; now the ruler of this world will be driven out" (Jn. 12:31). "The ruler of this world has been condemned" (Jn. 16:11). "Then he summoned his twelve disciples and gave them authority over unclean spirits to drive them out" (Matt. 10:1). "These signs will accompany those who believe: in my name they will drive out demons" (Mk. 16:17). "The whole world is under the power of the evil one" (1 Jn. 5:19). "Our struggle is not with flesh and blood but with the principalities, with the powers, with the world rulers of this present darkness, with the evil spirits in the heavens" (Eph. 6:12).

Any honest reading of the Gospels and the New Testament as a whole tells us that both Jesus and his followers proclaimed the existence of an infernal adversary and his minions. The world as a whole was "possessed" until the coming of Jesus the great exorcist, who "casts out" the devil through the Cross. But we are warned that, until the end of the world, our "opponent the devil is prowling around like a roaring lion looking for (someone) to devour" (1 Pet. 5:8).

6. Savior

The problem is that we are sinful—and we need to be saved from our sins. The problem is that our sin is against God—it is a sin that has led to the current human condition: evil, suffering, death. To make atonement for this sin, to pay the price for this sin, the person who does so must be capable of doing so in terms of making an infinite reparation while also being human. And this reparation must be such as to make heaven possible for us, must cure the evil that is within us, must decisively allow us to go beyond death, must make happiness possible here and now. And all of this must take place in the course of human history because that is the matrix that determines human destiny.

And it is all of this that the New Testament writers claimed about Jesus: "You are to name him Jesus, because he will save his people from their sins" (Matt. 1:21). From the very beginning there was no doubt as to the meaning of the mission of Jesus. "Just as through one transgression condemnation came upon all, so through one righteous act acquittal and life came to all" (Rom. 5:18).

The suffering for the sins of humanity that Jesus took on himself was for sins past, present, and future—"Through his suffering, my servant shall justify many, and their guilt he shall bear. . . . He shall take away the sins of many, and win pardon for their offenses" (Isa. 53:11–12). When Jesus asks Saul, "why are you persecuting me?" we are given to understand that this persecution of Christians personally afflicts him.

In fact, those who reject the faith they had once accepted, apostate Christians, "are recrucifying the Son of God for themselves" (Heb. 6:6). If he was divine and human, then his death was the reparation required: his divine nature sufficed to make the infinite reparation; his human nature made it a truly human act. To understand the possibility of one man taking on the consequences of the actions of other humans, we have only to reflect on the "solidarity" of all humanity in the consequences of sin.

The choices of a father shape and affect his children just as the acts of a head of state affect and involve the nation as a whole. But the same cause-and-effect web that connects negative choices with their consequences also links positive choices with their consequences. And that is why it was possible for Jesus—the new Adam—to be the redeemer of humanity.

The liberation from sin offered by Jesus is unprecedented. Stanley Jaki notes that the writers of the Old Testament "agonized over their sins, over their offenses to God's holiness," but they do not show the same "certainty about having gained forgiveness" as Paul, Peter, and John do in their epistles. These epistles go far beyond "what is found in Psalm 50 (51), the Miserere, and in Psalm 129 (130), the De profundis. In both there is hope but no certainty that one's sins have been forgiven." The forgiveness and purification Jesus offers is illustrated in the assurance given to Peter "by Jesus that he and the other apostles were all clean after He had washed their feet. There was enough pagan lore in Judaea for the apostles to perceive that in Jesus the divine appeared in a sense infinitely superior to the best which the pagan gods evoked. . . . The Incarnate God in whom the Church wanted to keep faith was wholly different from those gods because Jesus himself noted, and most emphatically, that no one could accuse him of any sin."[227]

There are three universal desires: to be absolved of guilt and shame; to love and be loved; to make sense of and cope with suffering. He absolved, he loved, and his suffering gave meaning to all suffering.

7. Divinizer

God "humanized" himself so humans could be divinized. All humans are invited "to share in the divine nature" (2 Pet. 1:4). This, in brief, is the Christian message. This is the central truth that makes sense of all the natural and supernatural phenomena of history. "We are the offspring of God," said St. Paul (Acts 17:39). "For the Son of God became man so that we might become God," said St. Athanasius. "He gave us divinity, we gave him humanity," wrote the famous St. Ephrem of Syria. The Eucharist—which is the offering to us of the flesh and blood of Jesus and thereby the very life of God—divinizes the rightly inclined recipient.

"He gives a sharing in the divine life by making himself food for those whom he knows and who have received from him the same sensibility and intelligence," writes Maximus the Confessor. "Thus in tasting the food they know with a true knowledge the Lord is good, he who mixes in a divine quality to deify those who eat, since he is and is clearly called bread of life and of strength."[228] He saves us by divinizing us.

8. Miracles

The miracles attributed to Jesus were not performed to amaze or impress. They were acts of compassion in response to tearful requests. He was no wonder-worker. He was a healer and provider. He gave sight and speech. He cured the lame, the paralyzed, and the leprous. He brought the dead to life. He gave food to the hungry. He did what an infinite lover would do.

9. Resurrection

He was the only religious leader of whom it is claimed: he rose from the dead and still lives among those who give themselves to him. The testimony of the transformed apostles and the entire church from its earliest days to the present is singular in its unanimity and consistency: the crucified Jesus physically rose from the dead. Earlier we assembled the evidence offered for the Resurrection because of its centrality to the Christian claim.

For if Jesus rose from the dead, then everything is possible, everything makes sense. In all of our lives, all of history, nothing is lost. Fulfillment awaits all who want it enough to say yes. The bits and pieces of goodness and love and joy we experience here and now can be enjoyed in all their fullness forever if we so desire. That is the promise of the Resurrection.

10. The rendezvous of the religions

All the great pre-Christian religious movements and ideas and rituals—from India to Persia, China to Israel, Greece to Babylon—point to sacrifice and expiation, incarnation and salvation. These themes come to a climax in the life and teaching, the death and resurrection of Jesus. If Jesus was part of the divine plan of incarnation and salvation, then it would seem that the minds and hearts of the human race would be prepared for his coming. All the evidence available indicates that the psyche and intellect of humanity in the first century AD was attuned to the coming of Jesus.

11. The world-historical process

On a natural level, Jesus' coming could not have been better "timed." The spread of Christianity was made possible because of numerous factors: the laws instituted by the Romans (*Pax Romana*) and the roads they built across their far-flung empire; the philosophical treasury bequeathed by the Greeks (deployed in the doctrinal definitions of Christianity) along with the emergence of Greek as a universal language and culture thanks to Alexander the Great (hence the rapid distribution of Greek versions of the New Testament); the theological "purification" of the Jews in terms of monotheism and temple worship; and the ideas of incarnation, sacrifice, and atonement in the major world religions and mythologies.

Moreover, the conceptual matrix of monotheism, incarnation, and divine law made possible the birth of modern science (which, in its turn, played a major role in the spread of Christianity). Each one of these developments was essential to the dissemination and assimilation of the Christian message. If God were to become a man, it would have to be at some point in history, and it can certainly be argued that if God was incarnate in Jesus the timing was optimal. It should be noted also that 98 percent of all the humans who ever lived have lived after the era of Jesus.

12. How Jesus' apostles and followers understood him

Jesus' apostles understood him to claim that he was divine and human. This is what they proclaimed, how they baptized, and why they traveled to every corner of the world dying with his name on their lips. It might be asked why Jesus did not come right out and say "I am God." There are two reasons why this was not possible: first, to say that he was God would have seemed like saying he is a god, namely a pagan god. This is the deadly idea that had been finally expunged from the Israelite mind—and it was obviously not an idea that Jesus would have wished to reintroduce. Second, as his followers understood it, he was a divine person united to a human nature—and understanding and explaining this required some further elaboration of the Trinitarian nature of God (already found in embryo in the Jews). Clearly he was not God acting solely in his divine nature, and to say "I am God" could have led to this misconception among those who did not know the distinction between person and nature. Despite these obstacles, by his acts and words, Jesus proclaimed his identity with the God of Israel. That is why he was crucified, and that is also why his followers could not become just another sect in Judaism. All future doctrines of Christology, in some fashion or other, were organically linked to this core witness of Jesus and his apostles.

13. What his followers experienced

Look at the behavior of the first followers of Jesus. As we have said, we see proclamation, martyrdom, liturgies, baptisms, popes, synods, councils, and a going forth to all the world. Their actions spoke for what they believed. But it is not just a matter of studying the behavior of the first Christians.

Hundreds of millions of people over the centuries have claimed to experience him either mystically or spiritually but always personally: whether they be Pentecostals or contemplative nuns or missionaries or social workers who see Jesus in the poorest of the poor. There is no comparable phenomenon where a historical person is believed to be encountered and experienced across history; there are, of course, mass movements of various kinds, but what is unique here is the centering of the movement on the lived experience of a person active and present across centuries and continents.

14. The supranatural

Then there are the numerous saints and mystics, the apparitions and visions. The spread of Christianity was always accompanied by claims of the miraculous. The miracle stories of the Gospels are paralleled by miracle traditions associated with the ministries of all the apostles. And this has been followed by a tidal wave of claims of miracles of every kind—from the appearances of Christ that we have reviewed to stigmata to multiplication of food to healings to multiple other phenomena. Scholars face the temptation of living entirely in the world of the text. They tend not to realize that the events reported in the text pertain to the real world—let alone to the supernatural realm.

Theirs is a different mind-set from that of either the primordial Christians or the believers of today: the devout are in touch with the world of the supernatural, and many report a response from the other side. Unfortunately, the gulf between the scholars' world of the text and the world of the supernatural is virtually unbridgeable. But if there is indeed a supernatural impetus behind the worldwide dissemination of the message of Jesus, this would comport well with the claims made about him by his followers. One would almost expect such an impetus.

15. A new understanding of God

The greatest teaching of Jesus was his revelation of the inner being of God. If Jesus was who he said he was, then our entire understanding of God has to change. Jesus at one level of nature is the human face of God, but at the level of person he is the second of three "centers" in the one God. God is to be perceived and worshiped as Trinity, a beginningless endless act of love. There is no room for polytheism or idolatry, monolatry or pantheism. There is no going back. Henceforth, our entire understanding of God is shaped by what we have seen and touched and felt.

When we consider these fifteen dimensions of the life, mission and person of Jesus, we might think of them as pieces of a puzzle that need to be matched to give a picture. If we have no knowledge of the most important of these dimensions, it is quite possible that we will never (short of a miracle) be able to match the pieces—and thereby never be able to see the picture. In this context, we note that each person's perspective on Jesus is formed by what they know of the facts about him. They are limited by the information available to them (in addition to the limitations of the human condition). Hence the importance of considering all dimensions of the life of Jesus when making a judgment on his identity. Nevertheless, even those who have studied all key dimensions of the life, mission, and person of Jesus have to do the matching of the pieces of the puzzle for themselves. We are invited to match the pieces but it is an invitation that we can accept or reject.

For we either end up seeing the pieces as meaningless or—when matched—as a picture that makes sense of everything. And once we have seen the picture, we cannot seriously think of ever seeing the pieces as separate again. Curiously, when we begin the processes of discovery and encounter we might think of ourselves as sitting in judgment on the evidence. But, if we do see a picture forming, we soon become aware that it is we who are being judged. For it is we who need to be saved from our sins, who need meaning, who need to be healed, who need the Eucharist. It is we who need to be resurrected.

CHAPTER 18

Godhead: The Greatest Secret of All

If we accept the affirmation that Jesus is God and man, an immediate and ancillary question arises. How can we possibly affirm this while simultaneously holding that Jesus' Father is God, as is the Spirit he sends us after his ascension? And all of this while declaring that there is only one God! This, of course, leads to the larger mystery of the Godhead. For, as never before or after in human history, what emerges is a glimpse of the inner being of God.

As the follower of Jesus sees it, the answer to the question of what God is like in himself is the climactic revelation that God is Trinity, three persons in one God. And yet, there is a widespread failure to grasp the true meaning of this unthinkably exciting revelation. The greatest secret about the revelation itself is that it makes sense of everything in our experience.

Sadly, most popular ideas of the Trinity, of foe and friend alike, tend to be caricatures or outright misconceptions. Even such luminaries of the past as Thomas Jefferson, Voltaire, and Immanuel Kant had primitive if not juvenile ideas of this greatest of truths. At the popular level, even among Christians, the Trinity is generally thought of as a hopelessly obscure piece of doctrine at best and a self-contradiction at worst.

In response to this common way of thinking, let me say that nothing could be further from the truth. Far from being obscure, the doctrine of the Trinity is the breathtaking truth that makes sense of all other truths, the luminous mystery that illuminates all other mysteries, the dazzling sun that allows us to see all things except itself (and this not because of darkness but its excess of light). All of human thought and experience point in one way or another to the summit of knowing and loving that we call the Trinity. It is the revelation that makes sense of everything in our experience, *everything*.

THE REVELATION AND DISCOVERY OF THE TRINITY

Why is the revelation of the Godhead so important, and how does it relate to the phenomenon of Jesus the Christ? The answer is simple: we act as we believe, and we become what we act. In this respect our understanding of the ultimate reality can have a dramatic effect on the kind of persons we become. Those who believe that God is cruel or monstrous will not necessarily become cruel or monstrous, but certainly they are less likely to have qualms about barbaric behavior. Those who believe that God is impersonal or unapproachable or unknowable are unlikely to place a high premium on personal relationships. Those who believe that the universe is ruled by two equally powerful beings, one good and the other evil, will be unable to recognize the primacy of goodness and love. The kind of God we believe in, then, is fundamental to human fulfillment and the creation of a rightly ordered community.

But how can we find out what God is like, and how can we know that what we believe about God is true? Ultimately we can only know if we believe that this truth about God has been revealed to us by God.

We have seen how the New Testament account of Jesus leads inevitably to the affirmation that he is divine and human. But the Gospel narratives show that Jesus, the man who was God, also spoke of the Father and the Spirit as divine—"God" and "Father" are used synonymously, and the sin against the Holy Spirit is called blasphemy. It is surely significant as well that both Father and Spirit are shown in a "joint appearance" with Jesus on at least two key occasions: his conception and baptism:

> The holy Spirit will come upon you, and the power of the Most High will overshadow you. Therefore the child to be born will be called holy, the Son of God. (Lk. 1:35)

> After Jesus was baptized, he came up from the water and behold, the heavens were opened (for him), and he saw the Spirit of God descending like a dove (and) coming upon him. And a voice came from the heavens, saying, "This is my beloved Son, with whom I am well pleased." (Matt. 3:16–17)

The Spirit is sometimes called the Spirit of the Father and at others the Spirit of Christ (Rom. 8:9; 2 Cor. 3:17), signifying his relationship to both.

By far the most important Trinitarian formula in Scripture is Jesus' final command to his apostles in the Gospel of Matthew: "Go, therefore, and make disciples of all nations, baptizing them in the name of the Father, and of the Son, and of the holy Spirit" (Matt. 28:19). Critics have said that this was not an actual utterance of Jesus but an addition reflecting late first-century church teaching. But this contention actually concedes a major point, namely, that from its earliest days the Christian church considered the Trinity as the foundation of its proclamation and act.

The biblical revelation of the Trinity had to be followed by the discovery of the Trinity: what was revealed had to be described and explained at least to the extent of showing that it was neither incoherent nor inconsistent with the evidence. Almost immediately, Christians protected the truth of the revelation by incorporating it in the earliest baptismal formulas, creeds, and teachings of the church. The work of articulation and systematic formulation fell to the councils and the great Christian thinkers called the fathers of the church.

Their process of "discovery" went through three distinct stages. In the first stage, the church fathers who lived and taught before and during the Council of Nicaea forcefully articulated the divinity of the Son and focused their attention primarily on Father and Son. In stage two, the post-Nicene fathers upheld the divinity of the Holy Spirit and explored the implications of this doctrine for the Godhead in the so-called Greek and Latin theologies of Son and Spirit. In the third and final stage, Trinitarians from East and West mined the classical corpus that emerged from the crucible of the councils and gave us the great synthesis—the idea that the love of God is the life of God. It is this great synthesis, embodied in the works of Richard of St. Victor, St. Bonaventure, St. John of the Cross, and St. Maximilian Kolbe from the West and St. Gregory Palamas, Sergei Bulgakov, and Paul Evdokimov from the East, that helps us to make sense of the Trinity as a doctrine of God.

The major point made by Richard of St. Victor (d. 1173), for instance, is that the infinite perfection of God demands that the Godhead be a Trinity of persons. He starts off with the affirmation that true love is not possible if it is not love directed to another, if it is not self-transcending and self-donating—and this is especially true of infinite love. God being the supreme and absolutely perfect good must have true and supreme love. For his love to be perfect it must be directed to another of equal dignity, a divine person.

Moreover, the fullness of happiness that God as God necessarily enjoys must come from a mutual love, a love that arises from giving and receiving. Thus the total self-donation that is fundamental to true love calls for at least two divine persons in one God who are eternal and equal. Taking this train of thought one step further, Richard points out that two perfect lovers would want to have a common object of their love, a communication of their love for each other that is itself a person.

The great synthesis remains faithful to our pre-revelation intuitions and insights about God. So much so, Richard of St. Victor has even been accused of trying to "prove" the Trinity from reason—without recourse to revelation. Unquestionably the Trinity is not a doctrine we can "deduce" from our natural knowledge. But once we've been supernaturally shown the big picture, there is no reason why we can't recognize how the natural pieces of the jigsaw fit together. The Trinity *is* "the big picture"!

The clearest formulation of the doctrine of the Trinity came at the Second Council of Constantinople, in AD 553:

> If anyone does not confess that (there is) one nature or substance of the Father and of the Son and of the Holy Spirit, and one power and one might, and that the Trinity is consubstantial, one godhead being worshipped in three subsistences or persons, let such a one be anathema. For there is one God and Father, from whom are all things, and one Lord Jesus Christ, through whom are all things, and one Holy Spirit, in whom are all things.

The Athanasian Creed had already declared that "so the Father is God, the Son is God and the Holy Ghost is God. And yet there are not three Gods, but only one God."

THREE AND ONE

I grant that the language of one substance and three "hypostases" and traditional formulations in terms of "nature," "person," and "subsistent beings" are not meaningful to many moderns. These formulations are coherent and binding, but they do not communicate the truth in all its power to those not already steeped in the subtleties and nuances of the underlying intellectual framework. A more fruitful approach for today is one in which we employ terms that are easily understood. So here is one way to restate the traditional doctrine, which is faithful to the underlying truth.

Knowing and willing are the two fundamental acts of human beings and God. A human being has a mind and a will, and God has an infinite mind and an infinite will. Each human mind and will is, so to speak, "operated" by one agent that we call the self. The doctrine of the Trinity tells us that there is one God—that is, one infinite mind and will—but that this one and the same mind and will is equally and without confusion "operated" by three agents, three selfs, three *I*'s.

The idea of the persons of the Trinity as *I*'s is eminently biblical. The Father declares: "You are *my* beloved Son, with you *I* am well pleased" (Mk. 1:11, with parallels in the other three Gospels). The Son proclaims: "The Father and *I* are one" (Jn. 10:30). The Spirit commands: "Set apart for *me* Barnabas and Saul for the work to which *I* have called them" (Acts 13:2). The three selfs are inextricably related to each other (and not self-enclosed), and their mutual relationships are usually described by reference to their "origin": the Father is unbegotten, the Son is begotten from the Father, and the Holy Spirit is neither unbegotten nor begotten but proceeds from the Father through the Son.

These relations of origin have no bearing either on priority in time or equality. All three entirely, equally, and eternally possess the divine being. But the Father gives all that he is to the Son, the Son receives all that he is from the Father, and their love for each other "breathes" forth the Spirit. Thomas Weinandy observes that "a proper understanding of the Trinity can be obtained only if all three Persons, logically and ontologically, spring forth in one simultaneous, nonsequential, eternal act in which each person of the Trinity subsistently defines, and equally is subsistently defined by, the other Persons. The Trinity is one simultaneous and harmonious act by which the Persons are who they are, and they are who they are only in the one act of being interrelated."[229] Laurence Cantwell suggests another way of looking at the mystery:

> The divine nature is possessed in three distinct ways. The same infinite
> power, knowledge and love, all the things we have to attribute to God when

we think about him, are possessed equally and indivisibly from three distinct centers of freedom. They are possessed by the Father as sourceless source of self-giving and ultimate goal to which everything proceeds, by the Son as totally responsive recipient and counterpart of the Father, by the Holy Spirit as love given and received. The Father is personal because he is God in all his inviolability, hiddenness and spontaneity. . . . The Son is personal because he is God in all his radiance, manifestation and presence. . . . The Holy Spirit is personal because he is God in all his mutual possession, communication and gift.[230]

When you ask this question of any spiritual being: are you one being? the question really is: is there one mind and will here? There is only one mind and will in the God of the Christian Bible, and therefore there is only one God. This one mind and will are exercised by three selves, subjects, centers. We can say that each one of these "centers" or persons is God because each has the mind and will that is God. So it is equally true to say that the Father is God or the Son is God or the Holy Spirit is God as to say there is a God. By God we mean the one infinite mind and will that is indwelt by three persons. And, as Weinandy puts it, "The three persons *are* the one nature of God. One does not have a 'nature' or 'substance' apart from or even distinct from the three persons, and thus there is neither a priority of person nor of substance because what the one God is, is a trinity of persons."[231]

THE TRINITY AND EVERYDAY EXPERIENCE

All of this brings us to the second point. While the doctrine of the Trinity could only have been known from the direct revelation of God, it nevertheless "fits in" with all of our experience and makes sense especially of the greatest mysteries.

- How is it that there is such a phenomenon as knowing, the capacity for understanding, pondering, seeing, meaning?
- How did willing, the power of intending, choosing, loving, and giving of oneself, arise?

- How is it that there is such a thing as the self, the *I* that knows and loves and finds fulfillment in communion with other *I*'s?
- How is it that a new *I* comes to be from the loving union of two other *I*'s (a kind of loving that is also called "knowing" in the Bible)?
- How is it that we have life, the dynamism that powers all other activities?

These five mysteries are simply inexplicable in themselves but make sense in the light of the doctrine of the Trinity. It is only through the Trinity that we can find coherent answers to these fundamental questions.

At the origin of all things, all phenomena, is God, the eternally existent plenitude of all perfections. All human knowledge of God is analogical, which means that when talking of God we extrapolate from our experience of the world. We see likenesses between things in the world and God but also unlikenesses: there is resemblance but not identity. On the natural level, we learn of God's attributes by the process of negation and affirmation: God is good but not good simply in the way we are (or can be) good; his goodness infinitely surpasses human goodness.

However, the created world does not tell us anything about the inner being of God. Only the direct revelation of God can do this. When we have received such a revelation, we consequently come to see that the world of our experience reflects God's inner being. In other words, the Trinity is neither alien to human experience nor discontinuous with our natural knowledge of God. It is, in fact, embedded in everything we know, implicit in being as a whole, all-pervasive.

The doctrine of the Trinity tells us that the most fundamental mysteries in our experience originate from and embody the most basic truth about things. We know because God is knowing. We love because loving is the life of God. We are selves with minds and wills who commune and reproduce because the infinite mind and will is a communion of interacting selves who eternally beget and receive and proceed.

Essentially, the doctrine of the Trinity tells us that the mysteries of knowing and loving and reproducing that constitute human experience spring forth from and participate in the infinite-eternal knowing and loving of the divine being. Every time we think and love, every time we bring a new person into being, we manifest, however imperfectly, the beginningless-endless act of knowing and loving, generating and spirating that is the Trinity.

How mysterious it is that we can understand and see meaning, feel compassion and "fall" in love, unite ourselves with another to "create" a conjoint "copy" of our selfs. Nothing in physics or biology, cosmology or neurology can describe, let alone explain, understanding and willing, concept-generation and idealistic self-sacrifice. How humans are able to generate concepts (a universal idea without a concrete object, e.g., the concept of intelligence) is a mystery for philosophers. Also, scientists have no idea how the phenomenon of reproduction that we take for granted in living beings originated. Even more puzzling in this context is the reproduction of persons found in human beings. The fruit of the love of man and woman is a person, a child that is a living embodiment of their love. Neither science nor philosophy can tell us how this is possible and why reality is structured this way. (Genetics simply tells us what codes and processes are involved in the system of transmitting traits but not how the system originated let alone how "persons" can come to be.)

Now it should be obvious to us that the basic goods and values we recognize in this world could not originate in anything less than themselves. Thus, consciousness, intellect, beauty could not possibly have arisen purely and simply from particles and energy fields. Only a consciousness and an intelligence free of any limitation whatsoever could serve as an explanation for the existence of any consciousness and intelligence in this world. When it comes to love and the communion of persons that we experience in the world, it is just as clear that these exist only because there is loving and giving and receiving and communing at the very heart of reality.

The Trinity, then, is not a mystery that dropped out of nowhere. It is, rather, the picture that connects for us all the disjointed dots, the great theory of everything that integrates all the mystifying data of our experience of the world and ourselves. It's not as if everything about us was normal and clear until we were asked to believe the paradox of the Holy Trinity. On the contrary, nothing seemed normal and clear until we received, accepted, and grasped this revelation of the true nature of reality. At the center of being, we now know, there is meaning and communion, knowing and loving, agenthood and activity. And the entire dynamic of the universe is driven by the endless creativity, rationality, and energy of the Triune life.

Coming Full Circle

Now, if the Trinity is the truth about the Godhead—the ultimate truth about reality—it must "fit in" with our everyday experience. We have seen that this indeed is the case. But if true, neither can it be foreign to the religious experience of humanity. And so we return to our starting point, *Homo religiosus*.

In part 1 we spoke of the primordial themes of incarnation, atonement, sacrifice, and salvation that culminate in the coming of Jesus. We saw that Hinduism, Judaism, and the Taoist religion of China intuitively reached out to the idea of three centers in the one God. In Hinduism it was *saccidananda*: being, intelligence, bliss. In Judaism you had the world-creating Wisdom, the eternally existing law (Torah), and the divine presence in the temple (Shekinah). In the *Dao De Jin*, Chapter 42, we read, "Tao gives birth to One, One to Two, and Two to Three; and Three gives birth to all things." Hsing Tsung Huang tells us that "the belief in a trinity of three supreme beings was already a part of Chinese popular religion in the second century B.C."[232]

This mystery of the Godhead lies at the root of the human search for meaning. To be sure, whether or not God exists makes all the difference to the question of the purpose of life. But we are concerned not simply with the question of whether there is a God but with what kind of God there is. Likewise it is not just a matter of knowing *that* God exists but how this makes a difference to our everyday life. And this is where the revelation of the tripersonal God is particularly relevant to religious history.

Consider for a moment the thought that reality at its most fundamental level is a relationship, an interpersonal, self-giving relationship of infinite love. If such were the case, then our lives, our priorities, our values, our goals should be reshaped to fit this template of reality, for those who refuse to live by the "rules" of reality will have to live "outside" it. In the long run, there is no room for savagery and exploitation, hatred and self-worship in the sphere of love that is ultimate reality. In the larger scheme of things, persons and loving relationships are infinitely more important than empires, states, revolutions, causes, ideologies, and institutions. And by the nature of the case, we who were loved into being will not find fulfillment except in endless love. This is the script that writes itself in the intuitions and insights that constitute the religious history of humankind.

This is also the vision that emerges in our encounter with the Jesus of history, theology, and experience. Consider one final time the astounding idea that a person named Jesus actually walked this earth teaching what he did. Astounding but incontrovertible if we believe the ordering of our calendar or wish to explain the origin of the movement that speaks in his name. But take it one step further and imagine the possibilities if what he said was indeed true—for just as astounding are the ideas that he was actually God, that the transcendent intervenes decisively in history, that human life continues without end, that we can receive the divine life here and now. This is precisely what is claimed, and this is precisely why the claim of the Resurrection, the transformation of the apostles, and the two-thousand-year witness of the church are so intriguing.

We have reached a stage where each of us has to continue on our own this journey we have thus far jointly taken through religious history. For some, the final phase is a voyage of discovery and encounter, of conversion or *metanoia*, the radical transformation of heart and mind and soul that is both divinely gifted and humanly chosen. They have only to surrender themselves to the infinite lover, who has pursued us at every moment of our lives.

It is the human face of this lover that we meet in the Gospels, reaching out to our hearts and urging us to speak to him. For Jesus as phenomenon is not a matter of history or biography or even theology. No—it is Jesus here and now, doing what his name proclaims: "saving his people." And his "saving" is a story of love—total, unconditional love—which he offers every one of us and asks that we show to "the least" among us. No one else ever came with a message of such overwhelming, overpowering, all-embracing, all-pervasive love: asking total surrender, total trust, offering nothing but total love. Exceptionally holy men had spoken of detachment from the world, of showing compassion to all living beings, and of leading a pure life. But none had spoken of actively loving your enemies, of selflessly serving your fellow beings and thereby serving God, of giving up your very life to save your neighbor. The very idea of loving and forgiving your murderers while they are driving nails into your flesh is so unthinkable, so unnatural, that it could not have been invented. This is love itself. This is the phenomenon. This is *God*.

In recognizing the divine personhood of Jesus we are drawn into the Triune life of God. "But when the fullness of time had come, God sent his Son, born of a woman, born under the law, to ransom those under the law, so that we might receive adoption. As proof that you are children, God sent the spirit of his Son into our hearts, crying out, 'Abba, Father!' So you are no longer a slave but a child, and if a child then also an heir, through God" (Gal. 4:4–7). Through the indwelling of the Spirit, the Father and the Son become present in our life.

The more we reflect on the Triune God, the deeper we are drawn into a new way of life.

"If we do not fully understand how it is possible for there nevertheless to be only one divine power, knowledge and love it is because as creatures we cannot conceive total giving," writes Laurence Cantwell:

> When we give, we give what we have. When the Father gives, he gives what he is and keeps no residue to himself. When we receive, we take something and make it our own. When the Son receives, he receives everything that he is. The Holy Spirit is the completely shared life of the Father and the Son, and since there is no failure in communication, he is everything they are. Such love is beyond the scope of the human heart, but it is nevertheless the infinite horizon towards which we are being called, and we shall never be satisfied with anything less.[233]

All humans are invited—but not compelled—"to share in the divine nature" (2 Pet. 1:4). God took on a human nature so that humans may take on the divine nature. God "humanized" himself so humans could be divinized. This, in brief, is the Christian message proclaimed unanimously by the New Testament writings, the Fathers, and the liturgies. Here indeed lies the movement of the mystical that opens all doors. Here indeed we touch the Other. Here indeed is the true and the real in the midst of the transient and the temporal.

TO BE IS TO BE LOVED

All this talk about being divinized or being indwelt by the divine might seem to imply that God is some kind of an impersonal force that powers you up once you're plugged in. But this is not the case at all. The life of God is love, and love by its very nature is love between persons. To be divinized is to enter into the "love life" of the Triune God.

"Before" anything finite existed, there was infinite-eternal love, the beginningless-endless state of in-love-ness that is the life of God. "Then" came three unsurpassable acts of unconditional love: creation, redemption, sanctification. (Time-conditioned words like *before* and *after* apply to finite beings like us but not to God, who is "outside" space and time.) First, creation—in an act of infinite and entirely gratuitous generosity the Godhead brought forth the world of spirit and matter. Second, redemption—when humankind rose in rebellion and rejected its divine destiny, the infinite-eternal love would not leave it in darkness and death. Instead, divinity bore the consequence of humanity's insanity and malice by suffering as a human being the vilest and most agonizing of deaths. Third, sanctification/divinization—in order to bring humanity into fullest union with the Godhead, divinity indwelled those who accepted the invitation to love. Appropriately enough, the three persons became known through this threefold act of the one Godhead: the Father in Creation, the Son in redemption, the Spirit in sanctification.

Above and beyond all else, the outpouring of the Holy Spirit, divinization, is a baptism into a state of being "in love." It is an opening of the eyes of the heart, a complete and permanent catharsis that rips aside structures and rules, masks and superstitions, prejudices and resentments. It is a tidal wave that tears through all thoughts and attitudes, emotions and habits. It is perceiving and proclaiming the magnificence and munificence of God in all things; it is seeing every person, every being and thing, as God sees them and loving them as he loves them. Everything is mystery and magic, everything is gift, everything is God speaking his infinite love to us. To be is to be loved.

ACKNOWLEDGMENTS

This work was made possible by the generous assistance of numerous individuals, most especially:

Anne Seggerman

Tom Moore

Christina Granville

Aravindaksha Menon

Chan Kei Thong

Mark Drogin

Monsignor George Manikarott

Fr. Paul Felix

My typists Rachel and Michael Varghese

Mary Varghese

Above all, I want to thank my editors: Jon Sweeney for the exceptional job he did in separating the wheat from the chaff, and Bob Edmonson for his labor of love in making this book come to life.

PART ONE
THE CHRIST CONNECTION

1. POPULAR MODELS OF THE GROWTH OF RELIGION

1 Jonathan Z. Smith, "Dying and Rising Gods," in *The Encyclopedia of Religion*, ed. Mircea Eliade (New York: Macmillan, 1987), 4:521.

2 T.N.D. Mettinger, *The Riddle of Resurrection: "Dying and Rising Gods" in the Ancient Near East* (Stockholm: Almqvist & Wiksell, 2001), 7, 40–41.

3 Paul Vitz, *Sigmund Freud's Christian Unconscious* (Grand Rapids, MI: Eerdmans, 1988), 218–20.

4 Karl Jaspers, *Way to Wisdom: An Introduction to Philosophy* (New Haven: Yale University Press, 1951), 135.

5 Steve Farmer, John B. Henderson, and Michael Witzel, "Neurobiology, Layered Texts and Correlative Cosmologies: A Cross-Cultural Framework for Premodern History," *Bulletin of the Museum of Far Eastern Antiquities* 72, no. 2000 (2002): 61.

6 See the following: David Braine, *The Human Person—Animal and Spirit* (South Bend, IN: University of Notre Dame Press, 1994); Peter Geach, *God and the Soul* (London: Routledge & Kegan Paul, 1969); James F. Ross, "Immaterial Thought," *Journal of Philosophy* 89 (1992): 136–50.

7 Farmer, Henderson, and Witzel, "Neurobiology," 81, 77.

8 Rudolf Otto, *The Idea of the Holy* (Oxford: Oxford University Press, 1923), 48.

9 Farmer, Henderson, and Witzel, "Neurobiology," 77.

10 Wilhelm Schmidt, *The Origin and Growth of Religion,* 1st ed. (New York: Cooper Square, 1912), 257.

11 David Rooney, "The First Religion of Mankind," *Faith and Reason* (Summer 1993). Quoted at http://www.ewtn.com/library/HUMANITY/FR93206.TXT, accessed March 1, 2011.

12 Mircea Eliade, *Patterns in Comparative Religion*, trans. R. Sheed (London: Sheed & Ward, 1958), 38.

13 Ninian Smart, *The Religious Experience of Mankind* (London: Collins, 1969), 53–55. See also Ninian Smart, *The World's Religions* (Upper Saddle River, NJ: Prentice Hall, 1989), 35, 40.

3. THE PRIMEVALS

14 Wilhelm Schmidt, *The Origin and Growth of Religion* (London: Methuen, 1935), 255, 257–62, 264–68, 275.

15 Walter Burkert, *Homo Necans: The Anthropology of Ancient Greek Sacrificial Ritual and Myth*, trans. Peter Bing (Berkeley: University of California Press, 1983), 17.

16 Walter Burkert, *Structure and History in Greek Mythology and Ritual* (Berkeley: University of California Press, 1979), 56.

17 Ibid.

18 Burkert, *Homo Necans*, 296.

4. AFRICA

19 John S. Mbiti, *African Religions and Philosophy* (New York: Praeger, 1969), 29.

20 Aloysius M. Lugira, *African Traditional Religion* (New York: Chelsea House, 2009), 36.

21 Ibid., 10.

22 Ibid., 15.

23 Ibid., 16.

24 Ibid., 43.

25 Ibid., 47.

26 Ibid., 123.

27 Ibid., 38.

28 Henryk Zimo, "African Spiritual and Religious Values as the Basis for Interreligious Dialogue," http://ufar.ff.cuni.cz/info/prilohy/05v3_Zimon .pdf, accessed December 11, 2010.

29 John S. Mbiti, *Introduction to African Religion* (New York: Praeger, 1975), 44–46, 47, 55, 57–60, 63–64, 81, 123.

5. INDIA

30 Michael Witzel, "Autochthonous Aryans? The Evidence from Old Indian and Iranian Texts," *Electronic Journal of Vedic Studies* 7, no. 3 (2001): 1–93.

31 Ibid., 4.

32 P. T. Raju, *The Philosophical Traditions of India* (Delhi: Motilal Banarsidass, 1992), 31, 40.

33 *Rig-Veda* 1:164:46. http://www.eng.vedanta.ru/library/prabuddha_ bharata/June2005_the_concept_of_god_in_the_vedas.php. This is an online repository of information on the Hindu scriptures. Accessed March 1, 2011.

34 *Rig-Veda*, Book 10. http://1stholistic.com/prayer/Hindu/hol_Hindu -vedas-and-vedic-concepts.htm.

35 *The Holy Vedas*, trans. Bibek Debroy and Dipavali Debroy (New Delhi: B. R. Publishing, 2002), 190.

36 M. P. Christanand, *One God Worship* (Delhi: Macmillan, 1979), 57.

37 "Arya Samaj in Hindu-Dharma," Vedic Cultural Centre, http://www .vedicculturalcentre.com/hindu.htm, accessed March 1, 2011.

38 *Yajur-Veda* 40:9.

39 *Yajur-Veda* 32:3.

40 Quoted in B.N.K. Sharma, *A History of the Dvaita School of Vedanta and Its Literature* (New Delhi: Motilal Banarsidass, 2000), 159.

41 *Rig-Veda* 10:133:6.

42 T. V. Philip, *Krishna Mohan Banerjea* (Bangalore: CISRS, 1982), 195.

43 Krishna Mohan Banerjea, *The Aryan Witness* (Calcutta: Thacker, Spink, 1875), 10.

44 Koshy Abraham, *Prajapathi—The Cosmic Christ* (Delhi: ISPCK, 1997), 13, 19.

45 Aravindaksha Menon, *Divine Harmony* (Muringoor, India: Divine, 1997), 32.

46 See http://www.mailerindia.com/slokas/mantras/index.p?purushasuktham. This is a research website on the Vedas. Accessed March 1, 2011.

47 Swamy Desikan, *Devanayaka Pancasat*, Sanskrit text with English commentary by Sri Nrusimha Seva Rasikan, http://www.scribd.com /doc/2525482/devanayaka-panchasat, accessed March 1, 2011.

48 Menon, *Divine Harmony*, 95, 32.

49 Standard translation from Ralph T. H. Griffith, http://www.astrojyoti .com/purushasuktam.htm, accessed November 18, 2010.

50 Griffith, http://www.astrojyoti.com/purushasuktam.htm, accessed November 18, 2010.

51 Menon, *Divine Harmony*, 96. The same idea is also found in *Yajur-Veda* 31:18.

52 Griffith, http://www.astrojyoti.com/purushasuktam.htm, accessed December 11, 2010.

53 See http://www.gurjari.net/ico/Mystica/html/brahamana.htm and http:// www.indohistory.com/brahmanas.html, accessed December 11, 2010. See also J. M. Nallasvami Pillai's book *Studies in Saiva-Siddhanta* (Madras: Madras Meykandan Press, 1911).

54 See http://worshipspot.blogspot.com/2005/04/sacrifice-by-renowned-hindu -scholar.html, accessed December 11, 2010. See also Koshy Abraham's *Prajapathiyagam* (Cochin, Kerala: Mantra, 2009).

55 Abraham, *Prajapathi*, 62–63.

56 B. F. Showrayya, "The Rigveda's Revelation," *Hindu*, April 7, 2007, http://www.hindu.com/mp/2007/04/07/stories/2007040701390100.htm, accessed March 1, 2011.

57 G. A. Mankar, *Life and Works of the Late Mr. Justice M. G. Ranade* (Bombay: Canton Printing, 1992), 1:195.

58 P. C. Mozoomdar, *The Spirit of God* (Boston: Geo. H. Ellis, 1894), 49–50.

59 Dom Bede Griffiths, *The Marriage of East and West* (London: Collins, 1982), 98–100.

60 Jose Pereira, "Christian Theosophists," *Dilip* 16, no. 6 (November/December 1990): 17.

61 Ibid., 18.

6. PERSIA

62 Michael Witzel, "Autochthonous Aryans? The Evidence from Old Indian and Iranian Texts," *Electronic Journal of Vedic Studies* 7, no. 3 (2001): 5.

63 See http://indiaculture.net/talk/messages/128/9523.html?1040718556, accessed December 11, 2010. Originally at http://www.conncoll.edu /academics/departments/relstudies/290/iranian/zoroastrianism/roots.html.

64 Witzel, "Autochthonous Aryans"?, 64.

65 Avesta, xvii, 4–6, cited in F. Max Muller, *Theosophy or Psychological Religion, The Gifford Lectures 1888–1892* (London: Longman, Greens, 1899), 39–41. See also Ernest Busenbark, *Symbols, Sex and the Stars in Popular Beliefs* (San Diego: Book Tree, 1949), 372.

66 Mary Boyce, *Zoroastrianism: Its Antiquity and Constant Vigour* (Costa Mesa, CA: Mazda, 1992), 109.

67 See http://www.britannica.com/eb/article-8138/Zoroaster, accessed March 1, 2011.

68 Geoffrey Parrinder, *World Religions: From Ancient History to the Present* (New York: Facts on File, 1983), 181.

69 Ibid., 178.

70 Peter Clark, *Zoroastrianism: An Introduction to Ancient Faith* (Brighton, UK: Sussex Academic Press, 1999), 15.

71 Parrinder, *World Religions*, 178.

72 Avesta, Farvardin Yast 13:129 (from Andrew Wilson, ed., *World Scripture: A Comparative Anthology* [St. Paul: Paragon, 1995], 785).

73 See http://www.crystalinks.com/zsaoshyant.html, accessed December 11, 2010. This is a New Age website with accurate information on saoshyant.

7. CHINA

74 Chan Kei Thong, *Faith of Our Fathers: God in Ancient China* (Shanghai: Orient Publishing Center, 2006), 89–90.

75 Geoffrey Parrinder, *World Religions: From Ancient History to the Present* (New York: Facts on File, 1983), 314.

76 Ibid., 305.

77 Ibid.

78 Thong, *Faith of Our Fathers*, 275.

79 Ibid.

80 Ibid., 156.

81 Ibid., 162–64, 167, 175.

82 Ibid., 89.

83 Guy Sorman, "Earthquakes and the Mandate of Heaven," *Wall Street Journal*, May 17, 2008.

84 Thong, *Faith of Our Fathers*, 115–16.

85 Ibid., 312–13.

86 Ibid., 314.

87 Ibid., 317–18.

88 Ibid.

89 Ibid., 319.

90 Ibid., 318–19.

8. GREECE AND THE NEAR EASTERN SOCIETIES

91 Jonathan Z. Smith, *Drudgery Divine: On the Comparison of Early Christianities and the Religions of Late Antiquity* (Chicago: University of Chicago Press, 1990), 101.

92 Walter Burkert, *Structure and History in Greek Mythology and Ritual* (Berkeley: University of California Press, 1979), 9–10.

93 Ibid., 52.

94 Ibid., 64.

95 Walter Burkert, *Homo Necans: The Anthropology of Ancient Greek Sacrificial Ritual and Myth*, trans. Peter Bing (Berkeley: University of California Press, 1983), 3.

96 Odo Casel, *The Mystery of Christian Worship* (New York: Crossroad, 1999), 32.

9. THE ISRAELITES

97 Stanley L. Jaki, *Why Believe in Jesus?* (Pinckney, MI: Real View, 2002), 9.

98 Ibid., 75.

99 Richard Bauckham, "Biblical Theology and the Problems of Monotheism," in *Out of Egypt: Biblical Theology and Biblical Interpretation*, ed. Craig Bartholomew et al. (Milton Keynes, UK: Paternoster, 2004), 210.

100 Shmuley Boteach, *The Wolf Shall Lie with the Lamb: The Messiah in Hasidic Thought* (Northvale, NJ: Aronson, 1993), 7.

PART TWO
THE JESUS PHENOMENON

INTRODUCTION

101 Daniel N. Schowalter, "Churches in Context: The Jesus Movement in the Roman World," in *The Oxford History of the Biblical World*, ed. Michael Coogan (New York: Oxford University Press, 1998), 396.

11. FROM EXPLANATION TO ENCOUNTER

102 David F. Strauss, *Life of Jesus, Critically Examined*, trans. Marian Evans (New York: Calvin Blanchard, 1860).

103 Friedrich Waismann in *Contemporary British Philosophy*, 3rd Ser., ed. H. D. Lewis (London: Allen & Unwin, 1956), 489.

104 Peter Stuhlmacher, "Jesus of Nazareth: The Christ of Our Faith," in *Crisis in Christology*, ed. William R. Farmer, Great Modern Debates 3 (Livonia, MI: Dove, 1995), 273.

12. A HISTORY OF THE HISTORICAL JESUS QUEST

105 A fuller study of the more significant theories, movements, and personalities cited below can be found in N. T. Wright, *Jesus and the Victory of God* (Minneapolis, MN: Fortress, 1996), and Charlotte Allen, *The Human Christ: The Search for the Historical Jesus* (New York: Free Press, 1998).

106 Quoted in http://www.religioustolerance.org/chr_jcse_his.htm, accessed December 17, 2010.

107 Rudolph Bultmann, *Jesus and the Word* (New York: Charles Scribner's Sons, 1934), 9. Gerd Lüdemann is a contemporary expositor of Bultmann's methodology.

108 Günther Bornkamm, *Jesus of Nazareth* (Minneapolis, MN: Fortress, 1995).

109 Hugh J. Schonfield, *The Passover Plot* (London: Thorsons Element, 1965).

110 G. A. Wells, *The Jesus of the Early Christians* (Wilton, CT: Pemberton, 1971).

111 G. A. Wells, *Did Jesus Exist?* (Amherst, NY: Prometheus Books, 1975).

112 Elaine Pagels, *The Gnostic Gospels* (New York: Random House, 1989).

113 Elaine Pagels, *Beyond Belief: The Secret Gospel of Thomas* (New York: Random House, 2003).

114 Jacob Neusner, foreword to *Memory and Manuscript: Oral Tradition and Written Transmission in Rabbinic Judaism and Early Christianity* with *Tradition and Transmission in Early Christianity* (combined volume), by Birger Gerhardsson (Grand Rapids, MI: Eerdmans, 1998), xxvi–xxvii.

115 John Hick, ed., *The Myth of God Incarnate* (London: SCM Press, 1977).

116 Robert W. Funk et al., *The Five Gospels: The Search for the Authentic Words of Jesus. New Translation and Commentary by Robert W. Funk, Roy W. Hoover, and the Jesus Seminar* (New York: Macmillan, 1993).

117 Barbara Thiering, *Jesus the Man* (New York: Atria Books, 1992).

118 N. T. Wright, *Who Was Jesus?* (Grand Rapids, MI: Eerdmans, 1992).

119 Timothy Freke and Peter Gandy, *The Jesus Mysteries: Was the "Original Jesus" a Pagan God?* (London: Thorsons, 1999).

120 E. P. Sanders, *Jesus and Judaism* (Minneapolis, MN: Fortress, 1985).

121 N. T. Wright, *The New Testament and the People of God*, vol. 1 of *Christian Origins and the Question of God* (Minneapolis, MN: Fortress, 1992).

122 N. T. Wright, *Jesus and the Victory of God*, vol. 2 of *Christian Origins and the Question of God* (Minneapolis, MN: Fortress, 1996).

123 N. T. Wright, *The Resurrection of the Son of God*, vol. 3 of *Christian Origins and the Question of God* (Minneapolis, MN: Fortress, 2003).

124 Bart Ehrman, *Misquoting Jesus: The Story Behind Who Changed the Bible and Why* (San Francisco: HarperSanFrancisco, 2005).

125 Bart Ehrman, *Orthodox Corruption of Scripture* (San Francisco: HarperSanFrancisco, 2005).

126 Ben Witherington, "Misanalyzing Text Criticism—Bart Ehrman's 'Misquoting Jesus,'" *Ben Witherington Blog*, March 15, 2006, http://benwitherington.blogspot.com/2006/03/misanalyzing-text-criticism-bart.html, accessed March 1, 2011.

127 Christopher Hitchens, *God Is Not Great* (New York: Twelve Books, 2007).

128 Deepak Chopra, *The Third Jesus* (New York: Random House, 2008).

129 Deepak Chopra, *Jesus: A Story of Enlightenment* (New York: HarperCollins, 2008).

130 Jon Levenson, "Chosenness and Its Enemies," *Commentary*, December 2008, 29.

131 Albert Schweitzer, *The Quest for the Historical Jesus*, trans. W. Montgomery (London: A & C Black, 1910), http://www.earlychristianwritings.com/schweitzer/chapter1.html, accessed December 11, 2010.

132 Ibid., http://www.earlychristianwritings.com/schweitzer/chapter20.html, accessed December 11, 2010.

133 Allen, *Human Christ*, 284.

13. THE THREE AMIGOS—SPECIES OF SKEPTICS WE WILL ALWAYS HAVE WITH US

134 G. A. Wells, *The Jesus Myth* (LaSalle, IL: Open Court, 1999).

135 Jeffery Jay Lowder, "Josh McDowell's 'Evidence' for Jesus: Is It Reliable?" Internet Infidels, May 15, 2000, http://www.infidels.org/library/modern/jeff_lowder/jury/chap5.html.

136 Much of the material cited below and in this section as a whole is described in more detail in Robert Van Voorst, *Jesus Outside the New Testament* (Grand Rapids, MI: Eerdmans, 2000), 6, 14, 16; and James Hannam's splendid website, Bede's Library, www.bede.org.uk/contents.htm.

137 J. M. Robertson, *The Jesus Problem* (London: Watts, 1917), 3.

138 Joseph McCabe, "Hotch-Potch of Amateur Historians," *Truth Seeker*, July 1944.

139 Archibald Robertson, "A Humanist Theory of Christian Origins," *Monthly Record*, March 1945, 10.

140 Maurice Goguel, *Jesus the Nazarene: Myth or History* (London: T. Fisher Unwin, 1926), 157–58.

141 Tacitus, *Annals*, trans. J. Jackson (Cambridge, MA: Harvard University Press, 1925).

142 Daniel N. Schowalter, "Churches in Context: The Jesus Movement in the Roman World," in *The Oxford History of the Biblical World*, ed. Michael Coogan (New York: Oxford University Press, 1998), 402.

143 James Charlesworth, *Jesus Within Judaism* (New York: Doubleday, 1988), 96.

144 Michael Grant, *Jesus: An Historian's Review of the Gospels* (New York: Charles Scribner's Sons, 1977), 200.

145 Goguel, *Jesus the Nazarene*, 156, 157–58.

146 From the introduction to *The Four Gospels: According to the Eastern Version*, trans. George M. Lamsa (Philadelphia: A. J. Holman, 1933), x.

147 Eusebius, *Ecclesiastical History* 6.14.5–7.

148 "What Life Means to Einstein: An Interview by George Sylvester Viereck," *Saturday Evening Post*, October 26, 1929, 117, http://www.saturdayeveningpost.com/wp-content/uploads/satevepost/what_life_means_to_einstein.pdf, accessed December 11, 2010.

149 Charlotte Allen, *The Human Christ: The Search for the Historical Jesus* (New York: Free Press, 1998), 5.

150 Rudolf Bultmann, *History of the Synoptic Tradition* (San Francisco: HarperSanFrancisco, 1976), 6.

151 Rudolf Bultmann, *New Testament and Mythology and Other Basic Writings*, ed. and trans. Schubert Ogden (Philadelphia: Fortress, 1984), 23.

152 Ibid.

153 Ibid., 17.

154 *Rudolf Bultmann: Interpreting Faith for the Modern Era*, ed. Roger Johnson (Minneapolis, MN: Fortress, 1991), 185.

155 Burton Mack, "Gilgamesh and the Wizard of Oz: The Scholar as Hero," *Foundations and Facets Forum* 1, no. 2 (1985): 24.

156 N. T. Wright, *Jesus and the Victory of God* (Minneapolis, MN: Fortress, 1996), 40, 43.

157 Quoted in Halvor Moxnes, "The Construction of Galilee as a Place for the Historical Jesus—Part II," *Biblical Theology Bulletin* 31 (2001). See http://findarticles.com/p/articles/mi_m0LAL/is_2_31/ai_94332333/, accessed December 11, 2010.

158 *Biblical Archaeology Review* 26, no. 4 (July/August 2000). This issue of the journal was titled "Spotlight on Sepphoris" and included three articles on Sepphoris.

159 Wright, *Jesus and the Victory of God*, 33.

160 Jacob Neusner, "The Rabbi Who Defends the Gospels," *30 DAYS*, January 1994, 45–49.

161 John Dominic Crossan, *The Historical Jesus: The Life of a Mediterranean Jewish Peasant* (San Francisco: HarperSanFrancisco, 1991). Other books include *Jesus: A Revolutionary Biography* (San Francisco: HarperSanFrancisco, 1994); *Who Killed Jesus? Exposing the Roots of Anti-Semitism in the Gospel Story of the Death of Jesus* (San Francisco: HarperSanFrancisco, 1995); with Richard G. Watts, *Who Is Jesus? Answers to Your Questions about the Historical Jesus* (Louisville: Westminster John Knox, 1996); *The Birth of Christianity: Discovering What Happened in the Years Immediately After the Execution of Jesus*

(New York: HarperCollins, 1998); with Jonathan L. Reed, *Excavating Jesus: Beneath the Stones, Behind the Texts* (New York: HarperCollins, 2001).

162 John Dominic Crossan, "Exile, Stealth and Cunning," *Foundations and Facets Forum* 1, no. 1 (1985): 61.

163 Paul Copan, ed., *Will the Real Jesus Stand Up? A Debate Between William Lane Craig and John Dominic Crossan* (Grand Rapids, MI: Baker, 1998), 152.

164 Friedrich Nietzsche, *The Will to Power*, trans. Walter Kaufmann and R. J. Hollingdale (New York: Vintage, 1968), 14.

165 Illtyd Trethowan, *Absolute Value: A Study in Christian Theism* (London: George Allen & Unwin, 1970), 5.

166 Excerpt from *The Quest for the Historical Jesus*, in *Albert Schweitzer: An Anthology*, ed. Charles R. Joy (Boston: Beacon, 1962), 310.

14. A RETURN TO THE ROOTS OF THE JESUS STORY

167 Richard Burridge, *What Are the Gospels? A Comparison with Greco-Roman Biography*, 2nd ed. (Grand Rapids, MI: Eerdmans, 2004), viii–ix.

168 Quoted in ibid., 254.

169 The following list is highlighted in James V. Morrison, review of Richard Burridge, *What Are the Gospels? A Comparison with Greco-Roman Biography*, 2nd ed. (Grand Rapids, MI: Eerdmans, 2004), *Bryn Mawr Classical Review*, May 31, 2005. Morrison cites pp. 188 and 193 specifically.

170 Burridge, *What Are the Gospels?*, 304.

171 David Aune, "Greco-Roman Biography," in *Greco-Roman Literature and the New Testament*, ed. D. E. Aune (Atlanta: Scholars Press, 1988), 125.

172 E. P. Sanders, *Jesus and Judaism* (Philadelphia: Fortress, 1985), 2.

173 Quoted in *Time*, August 15, 1988, 41.

174 Marcus J. Borg and N. T. Wright, *The Meaning of Jesus: Two Visions* (San Francisco: HarperSanFrancisco, 1999), 66.

175 Craig A. Evans, "Life-of-Jesus Research and the Eclipse of Mythology," *Theological Studies* 54 (1993): 19.

176 Paula Fredriksen, *Jesus of Nazareth, King of the Jews: A Jewish Life and the Emergence of Christianity* (New York: Vintage, 2000), 8.

177 Albert Schweitzer, *The Quest for the Historical Jesus*, in *Albert Schweitzer: An Anthology*, ed. Charles R. Joy (Boston: Beacon, 1962), 310.

178 Charlotte Allen, *The Human Christ: The Search for the Historical Jesus* (New York: Free Press, 1998), 328.

179 N. T. Wright, *Jesus and the Victory of God* (Minneapolis, MN: Fortress, 1996), 89.

180 Allen, *Human Christ*, 322.

181 Ibid., 319.

182 Ibid., 315.

183 Joseph Klausner, *Jesus of Nazareth*, trans. Herbert Danby (London: Macmillan, 1925), 363, 368, 374, 413.

184 Schalom Ben-Chorin, *Brother Jesus: A Jewish Point of View on Nazareth* (Brescia, Italy: Morcelliana, 1985), 27, citing Martin Buber, *Zwei Glaubensweisen*, Werke, vol. 1 (Zürich: Manesse, 1950), 657.

185 Ben-Chorin, *Brother Jesus*, 41.

186 Stephen S. Wise, "The Life and Teaching of Jesus the Jew," *Outlook*, June 7, 1913, 295.

187 David Flusser, *Dawickristentum—eine jüdische Religion* (Christianity—a Jewish Religion) (Munich: Kösel, 1990), quoted in http://www.jcrelations. net/en/?item=738, accessed March 1, 2011.

188 Sholem Asch, *One Destiny* (New York: G. P. Putnam's Sons, 1945), 5–8, 83–84.

15. THE AIMS AND CLAIMS OF JESUS

189 Martin Hengel, "Jesus, the Messiah of Israel," in *Crisis in Christology*, ed. William R. Farmer, Great Modern Debates 3 (Livonia, MI: Dove, 1995), 237–38.

190 Jacob Neusner, *A Rabbi Talks with Jesus* (New York: Doubleday, 1993), 8.

191 Ibid., 85.

192 Joseph Ratzinger, Pope Benedict XVI, *Jesus of Nazareth* (New York: Doubleday, 2007), 114.

193 Ibid., 116–17.

194 N. T. Wright, "Merely Christian? Reflections on C. S. Lewis's Apologetic after 60 Years" (paper delivered at the annual meeting of the Society of Biblical Literature, Washington, DC, November 2006).

195 N. T. Wright, *The Challenge of Jesus* (Downers Grove, IL: InterVarsity Press, 1999), 105.

196 Peter Stuhlmacher, "Jesus of Nazareth: The Christ of Our Faith," in *Crisis in Christology*, 288.

197 Jean Galot, *Who Is Christ? A Theology of Incarnation* (Chicago: Franciscan Herald Press, 1981), 114.

198 Ibid., 115–16.

199 Paula Fredriksen, *From Jesus to Christ: The Origins of the New Testament Images of Christ*, 2nd ed. (New Haven: Yale University Press, 2000), xx.

200 Brant Pitre, *Jesus, the Tribulation, and the End of the Exile* (Grand Rapids, MI: Baker Academic, 2005), 505–6.

201 N. T. Wright, *Jesus and the Victory of God* (Minneapolis, MN: Fortress, 1996), 562.

202 Pitre, *Jesus, the Tribulation, and the End of the Exile*, 442–43.

203 Ibid., 443.

204 Joachim Jeremias, *The Eucharistic Words of Jesus* (Minneapolis, MN: Fortress, 1977), 170–71.

205 Otto Betz, *Das Mahl de herrn bei Paulus* (Tübingen: Mohr Siebeck, 1990), 217–51.

206 The following is drawn from Brant Pitre, "Jesus and the End Times," http://www.brantpitre.com/documents/printable_outlines/J_E_T_ Outline.pdf, accessed March 1, 2011.

16. COMEBACK—"ON THE THIRD DAY"

207 Marcus J. Borg and N. T. Wright, *The Meaning of Jesus: Two Visions* (San Francisco: HarperSanFrancisco, 1999), 130, 135.

208 N. T. Wright, *The Resurrection of the Son of God* (Minneapolis, MN: Fortress, 2003), 710.

209 John Dominic Crossan, "Wounds Not Bones," *On Faith Blog*, http://newsweek.washingtonpost.com/onfaith/john_dominic_crossan/2007/04/wounds_not_bones.html, accessed March 1, 2011.

210 Marcus Borg and John Dominic Crossan, *The Last Week: A Day-by-Day Account of Jesus's Final Week in Jerusalem* (San Francisco: HarperSanFrancisco, 2006).

211 See http://www.sbcbaptistpress.org/bpnews.asp?id=20376, accessed December 11, 2010.

212 Paul Copan, ed., *Will the Real Jesus Stand Up? A Debate Between William Lane Craig and John Dominic Crossan* (Grand Rapids, MI: Baker, 1998), 161.

213 Mordechai Aviam et al., "The Talpiot Tomb Controversy Revisited," *SBL Forum*, January 2008, http://www.sbl-site.org/publications/article.aspx?articleId=748, accessed December 11, 2010.

214 Ludwig Wittgenstein, *Culture and Value*, trans. Peter Winch (Oxford: Blackwell, 1980), 33.

215 Richard Swinburne, *The Resurrection of God Incarnate* (New York: Oxford University Press, 2003), 27–28.

216 N. T. Wright, "Can a Scientist Believe in the Resurrection" (James Gregory Lecture, St. Andrews, December 20, 2007), www.philosophy-religion.org/world/pdfs/Tom_Wright_Lecture.pdf, accessed December 11, 2010.

217 Interview with the author, 1983.

218 Pinchas Lapide, *The Resurrection of Jesus: A Jewish Perspective* (Minneapolis, MN: Augsburg, 1983), 125–26.

219 Ibid., 129–30.

220 Ibid., 130.

17. WHO DO I SAY THAT YOU ARE?

221 From "The First Epistle of Clement to the Corinthians," Chapter XVI, quoted at http://www.ccel.org/ccel/schaff/anf01.ii.ii.xvi.html, accessed December 20, 2010.

222 From http://www.fordham.edu/halsall/basis/const3.html, accessed December 11, 2010.

223 Eusebius, *The History of the Church from Christ to Constantine*, trans. G. A. Williamson (London: Penguin, 1965), 140, 143, 147, 139, 140.

224 Martin Luther, *Luther's Works*, ed. Jaroslav Pelikan (St. Louis: Concordia, 1958–67), 6:329.

225 Phillip Wiebe, *Visions of Jesus* (New York: Oxford University Press, 1997), 15–21. E. Cobham Brewer, *A Dictionary of Miracles* (Philadelphia: J. B. Lippincott Company, 1894).

226 Richard Swinburne, *Was Jesus God?* (New York: Oxford University Press, 2008), 132.

227 Stanley Jaki, *Why Believe in Jesus?* (Pinckney, MI: Real View, 2002), 46–49.

228 Maximus the Confessor, *Selected Writings*, trans. George Berthold, Classics in Western Spirituality (Mahwah, NJ: Paulist, 1985), 83–84.

18. GODHEAD: THE GREATEST SECRET OF ALL

229 Thomas Weinandy, "Clarifying the Filioque: The Catholic Orthodox Dialogue," *Communio* 23 (Summer 1996): 364.

230 Laurence Cantwell, *The Theology of the Trinity* (Notre Dame, IN: Fides, 1969), 86.

231 Thomas Weinandy, "Zizioulas: The Trinity and Ecumenism," *New Blackfriars* 83 (September 2002): 411.

CONCLUSION

232 Both of these citations are taken from Hsing Tsung Huang, "Tao, Modern Science and Destiny," in *Cosmic Beginnings and Human Ends*, ed. Clifford N. Matthews and Roy Abraham Varghese (Chicago: Open Court, 1995), 182.

233 Laurence Cantwell, *The Theology of the Trinity* (Notre Dame, IN: Fides, 1969), 86.

INDEX

ABOUT PARACLETE PRESS

WHO WE ARE

Paraclete Press is a publisher of books, recordings, and DVDs on Christian spirituality. Our publishing represents a full expression of Christian belief and practice—from Catholic to Evangelical, from Protestant to Orthodox.

We are the publishing arm of the Community of Jesus, an ecumenical monastic community in the Benedictine tradition. As such, we are uniquely positioned in the marketplace without connection to a large corporation and with informal relationships to many branches and denominations of faith.

WHAT WE ARE DOING

Books

Paraclete publishes books that show the richness and depth of what it means to be Christian. Although Benedictine spirituality is at the heart of all that we do, we publish books that reflect the Christian experience across many cultures, time periods, and houses of worship. We publish books that nourish the vibrant life of the church and its people—books about spiritual practice, formation, history, ideas, and customs.

We have several different series, including the best-selling Paraclete Essentials and Paraclete Giants series of classic texts in contemporary English; A Voice from the Monastery—men and women monastics writing about living a spiritual life today; award-winning literary faith fiction and poetry; and the Active Prayer Series that brings creativity and liveliness to any life of prayer.

Recordings

From Gregorian chant to contemporary American choral works, our music recordings celebrate sacred choral music through the centuries. Paraclete distributes the recordings of the internationally acclaimed choir Gloriæ Dei Cantores, praised for their "rapt and fathomless spiritual intensity" by *American Record Guide*, and the Gloriæ Dei Cantores Schola, which specializes in the study and performance of Gregorian chant. Paraclete is also the exclusive North American distributor of the recordings of the Monastic Choir of St. Peter's Abbey in Solesmes, France, long considered to be a leading authority on Gregorian chant.

DVDs

Our DVDs offer spiritual help, healing, and biblical guidance for life issues: grief and loss, marriage, forgiveness, anger management, facing death, and spiritual formation.

Learn more about us at our website:
www.paracletepress.com, or call us toll-free at 1-800-451-5006.

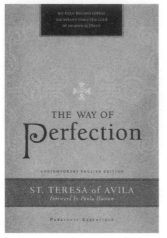
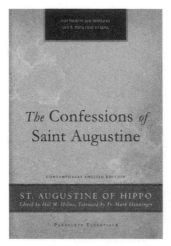